Practising Existential Psychotherapy

Practising Existential Psychotherapy

The Relational World

Ernesto Spinelli

Los Angeles • London • New Delhi • Singapore

'seeker of truth' is reprinted from Complete Poems 1904–1962, by
e.e. cummings, edited by George J. Firmage, by permission of
W.W. Norton & Company. Copyright © 1991 by Trustees for the
e.e. cummings Trust and George James Firmage.

First published 2007
Reprinted 2007, 2008

SAGE Publications Ltd
1 Oliver's Yard
55 City Road
London EC1Y 1SP

SAGE Publications Inc.
2455 Teller Road
Thousand Oaks, California 91320

SAGE Publications India Pvt Ltd
B 1/11 Mohan Cooperative Industrial Area
Mathura Road,
New Delhi 110 044

SAGE Publications Asia-Pacific Pte Ltd
33 Pekin Street #02-01
Far East Square
Singapore 048763

Library of Congress Control Number: 2007923293

British Library Cataloguing in Publication data

A catalogue record for this book is available from the British Library

ISBN 978-1-4129-0774-3
ISBN 978-1-4129-0775-0 (pbk)

Typeset by C&M Digitals (P) Ltd., Chennai, India
Printed in Great Britain by The Cromwell Press Ltd, Trowbridge, Wiltshire
Printed on paper from sustainable resources

This book is dedicated to my dear friends and colleagues
Freddie Strasser,
Bo Jacobsen
and
Al Mahrer.
Thank you for unlimited optimism and encouragement . . . and your wisdom.
And to the memory of
Hans Cohn
who, I suspect, would have both appreciated and disapproved of this book.

Contents

Acknowledgements

The origins of this book can be traced back to a series of seminars that I facilitated on the Advanced Diploma in Existential Psychotherapy programme offered at the School of Psychotherapy and Counselling, Regent's College, London. I am grateful to all of the trainees who participated in these seminars for the wealth of critical insight that they brought to our discussions. I am grateful, as well, to my colleague and Director of the Programme, Ms Lucia Moja-Strasser, for having permitted me to present my views and ideas even though she was well aware of some of the confusion and controversy that they might provoke for the trainees.

I would also like to acknowledge the very generous and equally patient staff at SAGE Publications and, in particular, Alison Poyner, Senior Commissioning Editor. Alison's faith in this book at times surpassed my own. I hope that she will find her efforts to have been worthwhile.

I am very grateful to have been given the opportunity to travel to many parts of the world in order to meet with all manner of colleagues and trainees who share this odd passion for, and fascination with, existential psychotherapy. The informal discussions we have had have influenced and shaped this book in a multitude of ways. Thank you all and in particular to my friends from The Society for Existential Analysis, UK; the I-Coach Academy, UK and South Africa; The Forum for Existential Psychotherapy, 'The London Group', 'The Copenhagen Group' and The New School of Psychology in Denmark; the Portuguese Society for Existential Psychotherapy; the East European Association for Existential Therapy in Lithuania; the Australian Existential Society and Psychotherapy in Australia; the International Society for Existential Psychology and Psychotherapy in Canada; the Psychology Department at Duquesne University, Pittsburgh, Pennsylvania, USA; the International Human Science Research Group; and, of course, my comrades – past and present, staff and students – at the School of Psychotherapy and Counselling, Regent's College.

I am also remarkably lucky to have known the late Hans W. Cohn. While he was alive, Hans and I held regular 'irregular' lunch-time discussions in Regent's College's Faculty Dining Room. These were occasions that we both used to discuss our shared and divergent views regarding existential psychotherapy, engage in peer supervision and, just occasionally, catch up on the latest gossip from the existential world. I have no way of pinpointing just how or in what ways something of these discussions has seeped its way into this book. But I am certain it has.

Finally, let me simply state that this has been by far the most difficult book I have yet written. In my naivety, before I began it I was happily telling one and all how easy it would be. Unfortunately, the gods must have heard me. Fortunately for me, however, I have been blessed with friends whose good humour, encouragement and just plain insistence that I get on with it and stop moaning kept me at it. So . . . Thank you to Peter and Stuart and Barbara and Charles and Laurence and Susanna and James and Helen and Abbey. And, as always, to my 'best friend', Maggi.

Ernesto Spinelli
London, 2006

Introduction

This – is now my way – where is yours? Thus did I answer those who asked me 'the way'. For the way – it doth not exist. Friedrich Nietzsche

In common with all other contemporary systems of psychotherapy, *existential psychotherapy* arose out of the attempt to formulate a sound and effective approach with which to deal with the dilemmas of mental unease and disturbance. However, unlike other systems, whose primary indebtedness is to clinically derived and oriented suppositions allied to medicine and natural science, the pivotal focus for existential psychotherapy rests upon a number of seminal ideas and conclusions drawn from a philosophical system which has become most generally known as *existential phenomenology* (Cohn, 1997; Cooper, 2003; Spinelli, 2005; Valle and King, 1978; van Deurzen and Arnold-Baker, 2005).

Existential phenomenology is a relatively recent twentieth-century philosophical movement that has been, and continues to be, deeply influential within Continental European philosophy but which has had far less impact upon dominant trends within British and North American philosophy. It is mainly due to this particular and somewhat alien grounding that existential psychotherapy emerges as an approach that is distinctively different from that of the other models and systems within contemporary Western psychotherapy. Further, it is through these self-same assumptions and principles that existential psychotherapy provides a set of significant challenges to, and critiques of, contemporary Western psychotherapy both at the level of theory and of practice.

There already exists a substantial amount of writing that seeks to describe and delineate the *theoretical* underpinnings of existential psychotherapy (Boss, 1963, 1979; Cohn, 1997, 2002; May, 1969, 1983; Spinelli, 1994, 1997, 2005; van Deurzen-Smith, 1988, 1997; Yalom, 1980, 1989). As the authors of such texts have sought to explain, existential psychotherapy cannot be properly understood without reference to its philosophical underpinnings. While this is undoubtedly so, these arguments are often presented and subsequently misunderstood to suggest that existential psychotherapy's singularity lies in the fact that, unlike other psychotherapeutic systems, it is uniquely philosophically grounded. This is, of course, utter nonsense.

All psychotherapeutic theories are underpinned by philosophical assumptions and postulates, even if, in many cases, these remain implicit and covert for the majority of their adherents and practitioners. It could be reasonably argued that existential psychotherapy initially stands out from other approaches precisely because it acknowledges explicitly and utilises overtly its foundational philosophical assumptions. But this should not lead anyone to conclude that its openly admitted philosophical grounding *in itself* distinguishes existential psychotherapy from other systems and approaches.

Rather, the distinctiveness of existential psychotherapy lies in the particular set of philosophical suppositions which it espouses. It is this difference in philosophical orientation that serves to set it apart from the various current competing alternative models of psychotherapy. Equally, while the great majority of contemporary models of Western psychotherapy can be distinguished from, and contrasted with, one another, it is nonetheless the case that, regardless of such divergences, they typically share the very same, or highly similar, foundational philosophical underpinnings. As such, their differences, while no means minimal and often rancorous, are of a different *kind* to those arising from a comparison with, and contrast to, existential psychotherapy.

It is, I believe, because of this critical difference in its philosophical grounding that authors have, rightly, placed so much emphasis on the elucidation of the theoretical principles that define existential psychotherapy. Without wishing to repeat their efforts, it remains necessary to address a number of key principles and assumptions since it is through these that the practice of existential psychotherapy is derived. My attempt to distil what I consider to be the key philosophical principles and theoretical assumptions underpinning existential psychotherapy make up Part One of this book.

In contrast to the ever-growing number of texts dealing with various forms and expressions of existential theory, the paucity of literature focusing directly and methodically upon the application of existential-phenomenological theory to psychotherapeutic practice seems somewhat surprising. Although some recent literature exists on the topic (for example: Cohn, 1997; van Deurzen-Smith, 1997; Yalom, 2001), it tends to be scattered and, where available, often serves to clarify or make more concrete a particular theoretical point being addressed by the author. While the writings of Irvin Yalom (1980) and Emmy van Deurzen-Smith (1988, 1997) in particular go some way towards redressing this imbalance, it is my view that these authors place the practice of existential psychotherapy too closely within the structural assumptions and applied framework of other existing approaches, most obviously psycho-analytic approaches. While such attempts are valuable and deserving of close consideration and analysis, in my opinion they fail to illuminate sufficiently the unique qualities and possibilities of an existential approach. More tellingly, I suggest, a critical weakness of such attempts at a partial rapprochement is that it leads to conclusions regarding the practice of existential psychotherapy that do not fit well, and at times can be seen to contradict, several of its key philosophical underpinnings.

While I can readily attest that it is no easy task to describe and discuss existential practice, there remains the obvious question as to why it should be that so few practitioners have attempted to do so. I believe that this somewhat unusual reticence highlights the concern of many existential practitioners that such attempts might only succeed in 'technologising' or 'operationalising' practice, thereby limiting it to a rigid set of techniques which would severely contradict the intangible and 'uncapturable' emergent possibilities of any immediate and open encounter between therapist and client as might arise in a unique and specific set of circumstances and conditions. In brief, the argument runs: to discuss existential psychotherapeutic practice encases it in such a way that it contradicts and misrepresents precisely that which is being attempted – a classic case of 'whatever is said about what it is, it isn't' (Korzybski, 1995). This concern is both important and valid; I would certainly be in agreement as to the undesirability of such an unwelcome outcome. Is there no alternative? Clearly, there must be, since what existing attempts there have been to discuss practice have not provoked that which has been so feared.

The reluctance to discuss the practice of existential psychotherapy, while arising in part from the concerns summarised above, also contains another, less appealing and rarely acknowledged, contributing factor. This is, as I see it, the tendency on the part of existential psychotherapists to somewhat over-mystify the numinous practice-based qualities and skills which they claim to bring to any given encounter. This latter stance has a whiff of dubious superiority that evokes a self-aggrandising sense of arcane 'specialness'. Far too many times, when questioning colleagues as to their unwillingness to attempt some delineation of practice, I have received replies that are all too reminiscent of Wittgenstein's celebrated injunction: 'Whereof we cannot speak, thereof we must pass over in silence' (Wittgenstein, 2001: 90). Personally, I have found myself over the years becoming increasingly irritated by my colleagues' near-adoration of this quote. Were it the case that the practice of existential psychotherapy *was* something which, of necessity, must remain unspoken, then so be it. Personally, I remain unconvinced.

Part Two of this text sets out my counter-argument. It provides a structural model for the practice of existential psychotherapy that remains alert to the theoretical grounding from which its practical applications arise.

Notwithstanding the above, having stated that I retain a fair measure of sympathy with colleagues who have voiced their concerns surrounding the potentially undesirable consequences of such an enterprise, I want to reduce the likelihood of the fulfilment of their, and my own, worst fears as far as possible by making plain two critical points:

First, let me state from the outset that there exists *no* exclusive or singular form of existential practice as applied to psychotherapy. In the same fashion, it is evident that there exists no single means by which to practise psycho-analysis. Or cognitive-behavioural psychotherapy. Or person-centred psychotherapy. Or any other sort of contemporary psychotherapy. Acknowledging this in no way makes it impossible to set out an explicable and describable structural framework for practice that can be critically considered, compared to and contrasted with other frameworks, whether they be within the same psychotherapeutic approach or, perhaps as importantly, between differing approaches.

Second, the exposition of existential practice as discussed in this text seeks to reflect *my own* attempts to understand, describe and apply existential theory to the practice of existential psychotherapy. While I would not be writing this book if I presumed that such an idiosyncratic account would be of little, if any, value to anyone else, at the same time it is not my purpose to convince readers that what is discussed herein should be treated as a 'tool-kit' for, much less anything approaching 'the final word' on, the practice of existential psychotherapy.

In summary, acknowledging that the specific focus being presented is expressive of my own particular and current understanding of, and relation to, existential psychotherapy – and hence, *a* way rather than *the* way to address and explicate its practice – nonetheless, my aim throughout this text is fourfold:

First, that what is proposed provides a coherent and consistent structure for psychotherapeutic practice that remains grounded in the existential-phenomenological principles being espoused.

Second, that the ideas discussed will inform and clarify for readers what it is that may be said to be distinctive about practising existential psychotherapy.

Third, that the views and arguments being presented may serve to provoke readers, regardless of the model or approach they adopt, to reconsider critically and re-appraise their own understanding and application of psychotherapeutic practice.

And finally, that, via the challenges contained in the above points, readers will be able to express more clearly, and to own with deeper understanding and commitment, that which is *their* way of psychotherapeutic practice.

PART ONE

Practising Existential Psychotherapy: Theoretical Underpinnings

1

The Philosophical Foundations of Existential Psychotherapy

INHERENT DEFINING PRINCIPLES

Clarity arises in the spaces in between. Henning Mankell

In the Introduction to this text, I stated that the practice of existential psychotherapy cannot be reduced to a single and particular structure and methodology. Nor, indeed, can *any* form of psychotherapy truly be restricted and expressed in such a way.

Nevertheless, it is of pivotal importance to understand that for every contemporary approach to psychotherapy there exist certain *inherent defining principles*, what phenomenologists might refer to as 'universal structures', that permit a form of therapy to be identified and labelled. Psycho-analysis, or cognitive-behavioural psychotherapy (CBT), for example, are each made identifiable and distinctive through such inherent defining principles.

For instance, the assumption of a separate and discrete mental processing system – the *unconscious* – in contrast to that of conscious processing – would be an inherent defining principle for psycho-analytic thought and practice even if the interpretation and use of the principle might vary both subtly and significantly between differing sub-systems or models within psycho-analysis (Ellenberger, 1970; Smith, 1991). Similarly, within CBT, which consists of a huge diversity of views and, at times, quite starkly contrasting emphases, there also exist certain underlying defining principles that run across, and to this extent unify, its various strands. Critical among these, for instance, would be the shared assumption 'that cognitive content, processes and structures directly influence or mediate behavior and emotion' (Clark, 1995: 157). Equally, a central characteristic of all forms of CBT is their allegiance to, and reliance upon, formal experimental design as the critical means to both verify and amend clinical hypotheses (Salkovskis, 2002).

As important as they are in providing the means by which both to identify approaches and models and to allow contrasts and comparisons within and between them, these inherent defining principles are rarely made explicit by the majority of practising psychotherapists. This seems somewhat odd since it is through such principles that the practice particular to any specific model emerges – or, at least, is claimed to emerge. Whatever this might say about the state of contemporary psychotherapy, what is important to the present discussion is the acknowledgement that if an agreed-upon set of inherent defining principles for existential psychotherapy can be discerned and described, then it becomes more possible to highlight the various practice-based expressions and extensions of such principles as applied in the therapeutic process. The attempt to respond to such a challenge immediately illuminates two central questions.

First, and most basic, we are bound to ask: *What would an application of existential psychotherapy that remained true to its inherent defining principles begin to look like?*

Implicit in this question lies a critique of the current state of affairs regarding discourse on the practice of existential psychotherapy both in general and at the formal training level. As was discussed in the Introduction to this text, perhaps because of their reluctance to operationalise and explicate various qualities and skills of practice, existential psychotherapists have tended to take on board attitudes, assumptions, behavioural stances and 'ways of doing' psychotherapy that originate from other models and approaches without sufficiently considering how well, if at all, these 'fit' with the defining principles of their chosen approach. For example, existential psychotherapists' stances and attitudes towards issues such as those surrounding therapist disclosure and anonymity and the establishment and maintenance of a specific therapeutic 'frame', to name but two, reveal that they tend to adopt numerous structural positions that are indistinguishable from those assumed by psychotherapists from other approaches, and, most typically, from psycho-analytic approaches. Perhaps, with reflection and analysis, this stance might well reveal itself to be both sensible and appropriate. But little consideration has been given to such matters by contemporary existential psychotherapists. Rather, much like Medard Boss's *daseinsanalysis* which maintains the basic operational structure of psycho-analysis but 'situates' this within a distinctly different, even contradictory, theoretical system (Boss, 1963, 1979), existential psychotherapists have *assumed* attitudes, stances and structures borrowed from other traditions and considered them as required for the practice of psychotherapy without sufficient – if any – questioning of, and challenge to, these assumptions.

Might it not be possible, for instance, that at least some of the operational structures being adopted might blunt, impede or contradict the underlying principles of existential psychotherapy? Alternatively, if such structures are truly coherent with the enterprise of existential psychotherapy, then might it not be appropriate to clarify just what that coherence is and how it may or may not differ from whatever coherence the same set of structural principles might have for any other approach?

Such questions reveal a second set of concerns: *What would an existential psychotherapy that was not unnecessarily burdened by the structural attitudes, assumptions and practices that have been derived from other approaches in psychotherapy begin to look like? How would it 'work'?*

When considered together, these questions alert us that we have embarked upon an enterprise that attempts to reconfigure existential psychotherapy as a novel enterprise which does not seek to imitate, assimilate or rely upon the assumptions and practices of either historically pre-existing or concurrent contemporary models or approaches within psychotherapy, and which instead formulates its own stance regarding what it is to be an existential psychotherapist and what it might mean to practise existential psychotherapy.

Obviously, no such enterprise can, or should, either dismiss or deny current standards and ethics of practice as delineated by governing bodies for the profession of psychotherapy. If it wishes to be acknowledged and approved by these bodies, it must remain situated within the facticity of their professional rules and regulations. As such, there is nothing considered or discussed in this text regarding the practice of existential psychotherapy that does not seek to adhere to currently existing standards of practice as presented by the major UK and international Professional Bodies. Nonetheless, as I hope to demonstrate, what remains possible within that body of appropriate professional practice permits the expression of an overarching 'existential attitude' towards psychotherapy that may serve both to clarify the overall enterprise of existential psychotherapy as distinct from that of other approaches, and to provide a challenge to the dominant set of structural assumptions regarding the practice of psychotherapy in general.

At its broadest level, this 'existential attitude' seeks to bring back to contemporary notions of psychotherapy a stance that re-emphasises a crucial aspect that is contained within the original meaning of *therapeia* – namely, the enterprise of 'attending to' another via the attempt to be beside, or with, that other as he or she is being and acts in or upon the world (Evans, 1981). It is this attempt that, I believe, underpins the broadly shared enterprise of all existential psychotherapists.

It has to be acknowledged that when considering what has been, and continues to be, written about the practice of existential psychotherapy (however limited this may be) a reader is likely to be confronted with diverse, perhaps innumerable, forms of its description and expression. This variety has led existential psychotherapists to conclude (perhaps even 'celebrate') that there is no one single way of practising existential therapy. Further, their conclusions acknowledge a conviction, undoubtedly derived from existential phenomenology, that cultural, historical, professional and individual views, variations and emphases are inevitable and that there exist as many unique expressions of existential psychotherapy as there are unique beings who engage in and practise it.

Considered from this perspective of uniqueness and diversity, it would appear to be difficult to claim, much less provide evidence for, the existence of shared underlying principles in the practice of existential psychotherapy – unless, I suppose, one were to argue that the one governing principle was that of *avoiding* shared principles.

However, if an alternative to the above conclusion does exist, as this text argues it does, how might one begin to 'tease it out' of the presenting instances of distinctive divergence and variation? It is my view that the starting point to a solution is made possible via existential-phenomenological theory itself.

Existential practitioners are correct in asserting that a key philosophical principle of existential phenomenology emphasises the uniqueness of each being's experience of relating with, and construing meaning from, the world. However, just as importantly (though often minimised or missed by those drawn to this philosophy), existential phenomenology also stresses that the very possibility of unique expressions and experiences of being and reflections upon being arise from an over-arching set of universal 'givens', be they 'structural invariants' as suggested by Edmund Husserl (Ihde, 1986a, 1986b) or ontological 'existentials' as presented by Martin Heidegger (Cohn, 1997; Condrau, 1998).

A useful analogy here might be that of 'the snowflake'. Each snowflake, it would appear, is entirely unique. No one snowflake's shape or appearance is exactly the same as any other. At the same time, however, all snowflakes come into being through the same specific set of programmed structural invariants. Each unique snowflake is also a universal snowflake in that it contains and exhibits all the necessary invariants required in order 'to be' a snowflake.

If we keep this analogy in mind, we can ask whether existential psychotherapy shares something that is akin to this principle. That is to say, within the (potentially) infinite unique expressions of existential psychotherapy, do there also exist invariant underlying shared principles that permit a particular unique expression to be identified as 'being' existential psychotherapy?

I believe that there are, and I would argue that this belief is shared, however tacitly, by those who claim to practise existential psychotherapy, on the simple grounds that in the very act of naming what we do as 'existential psychotherapy' we are at the very least acknowledging an assumption of the existence of underlying shared principles which underpin all of the unique expressions or forms of existential psychotherapy.

So . . . The obvious question arises. If it is being claimed that these principles exist, just what *are* they? I propose to suggest that there exist three pivotal hypotheses and assumptions that together provide the key underlying principles of existential phenomenology and, hence, of existential psychotherapy.

THE THREE KEY UNDERLYING PRINCIPLES
OF EXISTENTIAL PHENOMENOLOGY

Purely objective truth is nowhere to be found . . . . The trail of the human serpent is thus over everything. William James

Phenomenology, as a unique philosophical system, arose in the early years of the twentieth century. Its initiator, Edmund Husserl, sought to establish phenomenology as the fundamental philosophy for all scientific investigation (Husserl, 1965). In attempting such, both Husserl and, subsequently, his principal assistant, Martin Heidegger, came to challenge a foundational assumption that ran throughout scientific enquiry: the 'dualistic split' between subject and object upon which modern-day natural science is based. Instead, existential phenomenology proposed that all reflections, analyses and interpretations regarding every aspect of human existence are inter-relationally derived.

This view stands in stark opposition to the assertions of natural science regarding the investigator's ability to consider, describe and manipulate the focus of investigation from an impersonal and detached standpoint so that, through research and investigation, the true, factual and objective nature of reality can be discerned. In contrast, existential phenomenology proposes that no investigator, no matter how seemingly objective, can truly exclude him or her self from that which is being investigated – be it the study of essences or objects, or of being and existence. Indeed, we are all enmeshed in an inevitable and influential matrix of inter-relations. Just as the investigator influences the focus of investigation in any number of ways both subtle and obvious, so, too, does the act of investigation impact upon the investigator in ways and means that cannot be foreseen. And, further, any particular act of investigation influences not only that particular investigator and that specific focus of investigation, but also 'ripples' on to *all* investigators and foci of investigation.

Such conclusions, while by no means alien to numerous non-Western cultures and philosophies, remain incompatible with contemporary Western culture's abiding embrace of dualism. Indeed, this view is so embedded within every aspect of Western culture that any alternative explanation is limited by its dominating influence. The English language, for example, would seem to be structured in such a way that attempts to articulate the existential-phenomenological counter-argument to assumptions of objectivity derived from natural science must resort to statements that are inevitably imbued with an inherent dualism. For instance, the term most commonly employed to address existential phenomenology's basic stance of indivisible relatedness, *being-in-the-world*, still suggests, in spite of the hyphenation between the words, a conjunction of two separate and distinct entities, namely 'the being' and 'the world'. On further consideration, even novel terms designed to express indivisibility cannot be defined without recourse to a language imbued with dualistic dividedness. And as if such obstacles were not sufficient, it is evident that the 'alien language' of existential phenomenology adds substantially to the (in my opinion, erroneous) view held by many that the ideas and concepts propounded by this philosophy are difficult to comprehend, rather too abstract and deeply limited with regard to any useful applications.

Even so, in spite of such difficulties, the philosophical arguments and concerns of existential phenomenology continue to tantalise many of those who come upon them and, by so doing, provoke an examination of their implications not only for philosophy itself, but for the related arenas of psychology and, more recently, psychotherapy. Therefore, while acknowledging the many difficulties, be they cultural, linguistic or conceptual, that arise immediately in any attempt to address and clarify existential phenomenology's key arguments and assumptions, let us nonetheless attempt to engage with them.

The First Principle: Relatedness (Inter-relation)

The world and I are within one another. Maurice Merleau-Ponty

The principle of *relatedness or inter-relation* is so pivotal to the whole rationale of existential phenomenology that its presence resonates through every point and argument presented by the approach. Because it is so foundational, and at the same time so counter-intuitive to Western thought, it requires extended consideration.

At its simplest, this principle argues that all of our reflections upon and knowledge, awareness and experienced understanding of the world, of others and of our selves emerge out of, and through, an irreducible *grounding of relatedness*. We cannot, therefore, understand or make sense of human beings – our selves included – on their own or in isolation, but always and *only* in and through their inter-relational context. As will be discussed later and in Part Two of this book, this principle has enormous implications for the practice of existential psychotherapy, not least because it no longer permits existential psychotherapists to focus their attention on their client in isolation. Indeed, via this principle, it can be argued that existential psychotherapy's focus is not even primarily upon the client *per se*, but rather on the particular ways through which *relatedness* expresses itself: first, through the narratives of the experience of being that are provided by the client and, second and no less importantly, through the psychotherapist's and client's currently lived experience of relatedness as it unfolds, and enfolds them both during the therapeutic encounter.

The significance of, and implications arising from, this critical first principle are often minimised or missed entirely by commentators on existential psychotherapy as well as, I suspect, by a substantial number of those who claim to practise it. For, if we consider the immediate consequences of this first principle we are confronted with a major challenge to the related notions of *subjectivity* and *the individual*.

Subjectivity

Why should the healthy hand attend to the wounded foot? The Buddha

A recent issue of the *Journal of Consciousness Studies* was dedicated to the work of the physicist and Fellow of the Royal Society, John Ziman, and to his writings on intersubjectivity (Ziman's preferred term for relatedness) in particular.

One of Ziman's papers, 'No man is an island' challenges 'the axiom of subjectivity' (Ziman, 2006:18) that runs through scientific enquiry.

Specifically, Ziman asks his readers to 'suppose that the mutual recognition and understanding required for interpersonal communication and sociability is treated as a basic life-world characteristic' (Ziman, 2006: 22). Making his argument more explicit, Ziman adds: 'I have not come across any evidence that the subjective mode of consciousness is prior – in the species or in the phenotypical modern individual – to its intersubjective copartner' (ibid.: 23). This view, while still a radical challenge to contemporary scientific investigation, is easily embraced within the first principle of existential phenomenology.

Of relevance to these points are the comments provided by the anthropologist Alan Macfarlane in his response to Ziman's paper (Macfarlane, 2006: 43–52). He writes:

> With the growth of comparative anthropology it became clear that our individualistic, capitalistic, self-consciousness, rather than being the normal state of things, is indeed a western peculiarity, something produced by the strange form of individualistic, monotheistic religion and western law and economy. When anthropologists reported back on what they had found in South American or South East Asian jungles, or in New Guinea or among Australian aborigines, they described relational, inter-subjective, world views not wholly different from that which Ziman is suggesting. (Macfarlane, 2006: 46)

Macfarlane acknowledges that 'these societies could be ignored as to a certain extent peripheral vestiges of a disappearing world' (ibid.: 47). Such conclusions would be erroneous.

> [A]s anthropologists and historians turned their attention increasingly to large, literate, market-based, peasant civilizations outside western Europe they found that they also were based on the premise of inter-subjectivity . . . . One example was Chinese civilization . . . . A second was India . . . . A third comes from the attempts to understand Japanese civilization . . . . (ibid.: 47)

Paralleling these arguments, the psychologist and philosopher Riccardo Manzotti has recently argued for a process-oriented framework of human perception in which 'the classic separation between subject and object must be reconceived so that the two, while maintaining their identities as different perspectives on a process, actually occur as unity during perception' (Manzotti, 2006: 7).

Manzotti argues that the assumption of separateness between subject and object creates explanatory problems for both the representational and phenomenal aspects of the neural processes involved. As a counter-example that serves as an entry point to his developing theory of perceptual processing, Manzotti considers the rainbow as 'a condition where the distinction between observed object/event and the observing object/event is not evident' (Manzotti, 2006: 12).

> When the sun is sufficiently low on the horizon and projects its rays at an appropriate angle against a cloud with a large enough volume of drops of water suspended in the atmosphere, an observer sees an arch with all the spectrum of colours . . . . The position of the rainbow depends on the position of the observer . . . . It makes no sense to speak of a rainbow as something that is physically out there . . . . The notion of a rainbow as an autonomous object/event/state of affairs is thus discarded in favour of a process version of the rainbow. (ibid.: 12)

Manzotti argues that the rainbow does not exist independently of the act of observation. Rather than a 'thing', it is a process of relation between perceived and perceiver. Considered in this process-like way, all acts of perception and all that is perceived reveal their inherent relatedness. Perceiver and perceived, subject and object, self and others 'do not enjoy a separate autonomous existence' (ibid.: 14).

The various arguments briefly summarised above resonate with existential phenomenology's assertion that subjectivity is just one variant form or expression of the more foundational state of relatedness or inter-relational being. In this sense, subjectivity can be understood as an expression of relatedness that seeks to minimise or dismiss its very grounding in relatedness and which, instead, seeks to impose a relational divide upon one's experience of being through the distinction and separation of 'self' from 'other' (or 'world'), as if each were independent in terms of its existence, identity and meaning.

From the standpoint of existential phenomenology, 'subjectivity' does not arise or exist in contrast to, or distinct from, relatedness, nor can it be placed alongside relatedness as a separate and alternative mode of being and experiencing. Rather, subjectivity is seen as a particular, perhaps culturally specific, emergent consequence and expression of relatedness.

The individual

> It is not that there is experience because there is an individual, but that there is an individual because there is experience. Kitaro Nishida

As with contemporary Western thought in general, the dominant ethos of psychotherapy assumes the primacy of the individual subject. Is is common for theories to suggest that it is only once the individual has 'found', 'accepted', or 'authenticated' him or her self, and by so doing begun to deal with the issues and obstacles impeding or imposing upon the experience and expression of one's 'true', 'authentic' and/or 'self-actualising' potential for being, that he or she is capable of focusing upon and addressing the possibilities of relationship with others and the world in general. Existential phenomenology (and, as a consequence, existential psychotherapy) takes a distinctively different stance in that it argues that no self can be 'found', nor individual 'emerge', other than via the a priori inter-relational grounding from which our unique sense of being arises.

Following on from the previous discussion on subjectivity, it becomes apparent that in contrast to the dominant tendency to view the individual as the a priori source, or pre-relational constituent, through which relations become possible, existential phenomenology proposes the reverse of this argument. While this reversal might initially seem at best odd and at worst absurd by readers and commentators, it may begin to be considered less so in light of ongoing research on mirror neurons.

In a recent paper, Becchio and Bertone write that just over a decade ago, 'a particular class of motor neurons was discovered in a sector of the ventral premotor cortex of monkeys, called F5 . . . . [These neurons] fire when the recorded monkey observes another monkey – or even the experimenter – performing a similar action. These neurons were designated as "mirror neurons"' (Becchio & Bertone, 2005: 21). Mirror neurons have been located in both primates and humans and have generated a great deal of interest because they appear to 'map actions in a multisubjective neural format neutral with respect to the agent . . . . The action can be ascribed to both the executor and the observer . . . [and] the action representation is immediately shared between self and other' (ibid.: 23). In other words, the mirror neurons of a particular subject (for instance, an infant human being) 'mirror' or reflect the behaviour of another (for instance, the infant's mother) as though it were the subject (the infant) who had performed the action (Gallese, 2003).

The significance of mirror neurons to this discussion is that they provide the means to consider an alternative explanation for the development of an individual's awareness of, and connection with, others. Indeed, the noted social scientist Helga Nowotny has gone so far as to state that 'there is now some good empirical evidence for the neural basis of intersubjectivity "as an irreducible natural phenomenon"' (Nowotny, 2006: 65).

A similar conclusion appears in a recent text by the developmental psychologist and psychotherapist, Daniel Stern (2004). Stern, too, addresses the findings regarding mirror neurons and considers these as neural correlates of, and implicit evidence for, an intersubjective matrix suggestive of the human capacity 'to imitate, understand, empathise with and synchronise with others' (Mearns & Cooper, 2005: 12). Indeed, Stern posits that all human beings share a motivational system whose aim is that of intersubjective knowing (Stern, 2004).

The study of mirror neurons raises a significant dilemma for currently dominant Western assumptions. The irresolvable question arising from dualistic perspectives is how each individual subject is able to discern the existence of others, or, more generally, the existence of a separate and distinct external reality. With the discovery of mirror neurons, and their implications, the problem is reversed: the critical question now becomes how such a boundary or divide comes into being.

In line with this view, the philosopher David Midgley (commenting upon the work of John Ziman discussed above) proposes that as well as access one another's experiences, we also participate in them and, in participation 'become who we are' (Midgley, 2006). In taking this view, Midgley agrees with Ziman's contention that the 'bias towards atomic individualism not only bedevils the human and social sciences: it distorts the whole philosophy of nature' (Ziman, 2006: 21). By so doing he successfully summarises existential phenomenology's radical challenge 'that individual consciousness is actually a part or subsystem of a larger [interrelational] consciousness' (Midgley, 2006: 100).

Within the arena of psychotherapy, perhaps the most radical reconsideration of currently dominant views surrounding the individual can be found in the writings of a philosopher whose ideas have had a major impact upon existential phenomenology – Martin Buber.

Buber's now famous contrast between 'I–It' and 'I–Thou' relations can be most directly understood in the following way: one can approach 'the other' from the standpoint wherein the other is experienced as a separate *object* of one's experience and self-consciousness such that the other's meaning and relation to the scrutinising 'I' can be shaped and formulated via the imposition of the 'I''s preferred meaning stance. Alternatively, one can approach 'the other' as an inter-related co-subject with whom the 'I' is in a perpetual dialogical encounter through which mutually revealing inter-relational meaning possibilities unfold themselves (Buber, 1970, 2002).

The former is an 'I–It' attitude that is grounded in separateness and control. The latter is an 'I–Thou' attitude that is grounded in inseparable relatedness and whose focus lies upon the meanings emergent *between* persons. If the former demands that the 'I' must 'fix' him or her self in an attitude of authority, the latter equally demands that the 'I' remains open to the reconstituting and redefining of its own meaning base via the attitude taken toward the other. The former attitude equally objectifies both the 'I' and the other ('It'); the latter reveals that both the 'I' and the other ('Thou') co-exist as an inseparable inter-relation whose truthful meanings are not 'handed down', directed toward, imposed or predetermined via a process of objectification (Buber, 1970).

Buber was also careful to distinguish 'persons' from 'individuals'. His view of the person served as an expression of what it is to be human – a being who inhabits an inseparable relation with the world, and is an expression of that relation. He was deeply critical of Western culture's (and psychotherapy's) elevation of the individual *per se*. He railed against the sort of 'fascism of self-autonomy' that runs rampant through Western thought and is so alien in its views from those of so many other philosophies and systems in the world (Kirschenbaum and Henderson, 1990).

For Buber, being a person is far more than simply individuating. Being a person means being 'in real reciprocity with the world in all the points in which the world can meet man' (Kirschenbaum and Henderson, 1990: 63). As Buber stated: 'I'm *against* individuals and *for* persons'. And, in a similar vein, argued that one may make him or her self 'more and more an individual without making him [or her] more and more human' (ibid.). Indeed, Buber continually endeavoured to remind us that we become our selves *through* relation. For Buber, 'In the beginning is relation' (Buber, 1970: 32).

From his own early experiences in the world of theatre, Buber distinguished the actor who can merely *imitate* a role with the actor who *lives within* the role and, thereby experiences the polarity between him or her self and the role he or she plays (Friedman, 1982). This distinction provided Buber with the basis for what he would eventually term *inclusion*. While he never provided a precise definition for this term, in part because of his conviction that it could not ever be fully captured by definition, Buber sought to express via inclusion the experience of relatedness: the experiencing of the other in the relationship without either overwhelming and shaping the other's 'otherness' so that it becomes a mere extension of 'I', while at the same time neither neglecting, minimising nor abdicating one's own presence in the relationship (Buber, 2002).

Thus, the great paradox presented by Buber is that the individual truly emerges and experiences the uniqueness of his or her being not prior to, or through the relinquishing of, relatedness but rather by the embracing of an inclusionary relatedness. In this, I suggest, Buber was uncommonly prescient. Today, the constant blathering of marketeers and politicians about the sanctity and protection of 'the individual', and the wants or pursuits associated with it, has permitted an unprecedented and highly manipulable allegiance to blandness, mediocrity and predictability in people's goals, aspirations and experience of their existence. In minimising, if not removing, the foundational constituent of relatedness from our understanding of individuality, our relations – be they with self or others – have become all too commonly enmeshed in the objectifying strictures of 'I–It' encounters.

Relatedness as 'worlding'

> The objective world simply is, it does not happen. Only to the gaze of my consciousness, crawling upward along the line of my body, does a section of this world come to life as a fleeting image in space which continuously changes in time. Hermann Weyl

Earlier, I considered the difficulty of conveying the notion of relatedness. I suggested that this difficulty lies not only in the novelty or complexity of this view but also in the difficulties arising from language itself. I argued that the English language immediately imposes a 'split' upon all discourse that seeks to express relatedness in a direct way. If I were to state, for instance, that both you and I are both always responsible for whatever happens between us, I would be attempting to communicate a key inter-relational axiom via the 'split' language of 'I', 'you' and 'us'. Such an attempt blunts and diminishes the intended inter-relational meaning of the statement; in effect it seeks to express relatedness via a language that, at best, obscures the inseparability that lies between or, perhaps more appropriately, encompasses, 'I' and 'you'.

Acknowledging this, I might be more accurate in stating that the principle of relatedness leads us to the conclusion that 'I–you' always affects 'I–you.' Or, that 'I–you' chooses and is always responsible for what happens to 'I–you' through the inter-relational stance that 'I–you' takes. Assuming that 'I–you' even remotely understood what has just been communicated (which is itself an enormous assumption) at some point or other 'I–you' might well ask: 'Who or what or where or when or how or even why is the constituent "I" or the constituent "you" that is contained in this notion of "I–you"?' And, at that point, any response would once again be at a level wherein a 'split' or isolationist focus was imposed upon the attempted explanation.

Indeed, on reflection, the very terms 'relatedness' and 'inter-relation' impose an implicit split. If we state that there is a foundational and inevitable inter-relational unity between what we call 'subject"and 'object', the language we employ works against our enterprise and imposes a division at the heart of our inter-relational statement. A major part of the problem is that what is being attempted is a description and communication of some *thing* – be it 'I' or 'you'. Instead, what relatedness posits is a description or communication that is more akin to a *process*. Or, to put it another way, what is being pointed to is more *verb-like* than it is *noun-like*. In considering relatedness from a noun-like perspective, tensions and problems come into being that complicate an already confusing enterprise.

In some ways, this confusion can be seen to have its parallel in the attempts to communicate concepts and ideas from quantum physics. For instance, the oft-noted quantum conclusion that light is both 'wave-like' and 'particle-like' expresses a similar dilemma in communication and, as well, provokes (for some at least) the added confusion of attempting to 'hold' what appears to be a contradictory statement as 'true'. If we consider the many conceptual conundrums to do with time, space, locality and materiality thrown up by quantum physics it is both evident and somewhat startling to note how closely such conundrums resonate with the inter-relational principle that underpins existential phenomenology (Bohm and Hiley, 1995).

The terms we employ to grasp and express relatedness encase and restrain, and impose a passivity and/or closure upon a notion that yearns to communicate movement, openness and a sort of perpetual 'becoming', rather than point towards a captured entity or structure. In like fashion, the terms that existential phenomenologists have tended to apply, such as 'being-in-the-world' or 'figure/ground', remove all sense of movement and indeterminacy, and remain too static for that which they seek to embrace.

In light of this, and as a partial attempt to counter such tendencies, I have elected to employ the term 'worlding' as a means of expressing relatedness from an experiential perspective. Although the term can be found in the English translation of Martin Heidegger's *Being and Time* (1962), the use I make of it should not be confused with Heidegger's, even though some points of similarity do exist. As inadequate and clumsy as it still is, 'worlding', as I employ the term, at least alerts us to an *active and continuing process-like foundational principle* that underpins existential phenomenology. Worlding refers to the ongoing, ever-shifting, process-like, linguistically elusive living of being.

In contrast, when, as human beings, we reflect upon and attempt to explicate worlding, we can only do so through the imposing of structural limitations that encase the process-like activity so that it is essentialised and appears as 'thing-like'. This structural containment of worlding is expressed via the term 'the world-view'. The worldview expresses the structural consequence of all human reflections upon worlding which, necessarily, must always be viewed from a specific point of focus (such as 'self', 'other', 'subject', 'object'). In doing so, the attempted expression of process-like worlding through the essentialising structure of the worldview imposes an inevitable 'split' perspective in a structural sense (what it is) and as well in how that point of focus both experiences being and is experienced as being.

The distinction between worlding and the worldview will be discussed further below. However, for now it is essential to understand that even this 'split', structural point of focus remains an expression of worlding. *Worlding is* – regardless of the essence-like appearance imposed upon it. Indeed, it is only through worlding that appearance and structure can emerge. Thus, the questions regarding worlding can never be about 'how do I "world" more or better?' or 'what is lacking in my "worlding"?' Rather, our questions (and experiences of unease or dissatisfaction) can only be concerned with the structural *point of focus* being adopted with regard to the experience of worlding – that is to say, the worldview. As will be discussed in Part Two, it is this latter set of questions, centred on the degree to which the worldview adequately reflects the process-like experience of worlding, that forms the focus of investigation for existential psychotherapy.

As a simple analogy that might express concretely what is being discussed, consider the following: Construct a mental picture of the world. If you now single out any aspect of it, say, 'Italy', or 'the Pacific Ocean' or 'Fremantle, Western Australia', it will stand out as a structural *focus point*. This structural focus point permits a view of the world from its particular and unique perspective. Equally, it permits a view of that structural focus point *itself* either from its own perspective or from the perspective of any other particular structural focus point, or from the perspective of the whole world structural focus point.

It is never the case, however, that the singling out of any structural focus point *removes* it from the world. It may 'stand out' temporarily as a structural focus point, but it cannot be said that it is no longer part of the world. The structural focus point is always *in and of* the world, just as the world would not be 'the world' if that particular structural focus point were removed from it.

At the same time, it is evident that the structural focus point that has been highlighted is in many ways an *artifice*, a *construct*. It is not fixed and static, but only appears to be so. Instead, it is continually changing not only though the impact of various 'forces of nature' that erode and re-shape it, both slowly over time or in sudden cataclysmic upheaval – but also via human-imposed variables. A country called Moravia, for instance, might once have been a potential structural focus point but, for the present at least, is no longer.

Equally, and more challenging, as any aspect of the structural focus point alters, be it by the influences of nature or humankind, so, too, does this change the world, both in terms of each potential structural focus point and as a whole. Thus, both the world and any highlighted structural focus points *are constantly becoming*.

In addition, it can be seen that this 'constant becoming' is not truly divisible or separable in terms of the structural focus point or the world. The 'constant becoming' of the structural focus point *is* the 'constant becoming' of the world, just as the 'constant becoming' of the world *is* the 'constant becoming' of any and every particular structural focus point.

When the structurally imposed restrictions upon 'constant becoming' are removed, the ever-shifting flux of being can be expressed in terms such as 'process-like' and 'action-based'. *Worlding*, I propose, is another, perhaps more adequate, term.

In spite of its limitations, I hope that something sufficient has been expressed regarding the notion of worlding as an ongoing, indivisible process and of the worldview as its reflectively-construed structural counterpart. Equally, I hope that readers have understood that, however it is considered, worlding reveals a foundational relatedness in all human reflections upon and experiences of existence.

I will return to the discussion of these terms when considering their specific implications for the practice of existential psychotherapy. For the moment, let me end this necessary, if still somewhat lengthy account of the first principle of existential phenomenology, with a brief summary.

Relatedness: a summary

What is spoken is never, and in no language, what is said. Martin Heidegger

The first general principle that defines and identifies existential phenomenology is that of relatedness or inter-relation. This principle asserts that all human reflections and investigations of and upon any aspect of existence, as well as all conclusions derived from them, originate from a foundational inter-relational grounding.

This assumption of a foundational relatedness challenges the dominant Western tendency to divide and isolate and thereby generate a 'split' between what are, as a consequence, viewed as distinct and separate 'subject' and 'object' which may or may not relate to one another or whose way of relating may impact on both, or or one or the other alone. Existential phenomenology rejects this split between 'subject' and 'object' as an originating source-point and instead argues that this seeming 'split-ness' is but one particular expression of relatedness. It denies the possibility of 'non-relatedness' and instead suggests that the avoidance or denial of relatedness is itself, again, one form or expression of relatedness. It denies that the impact, direction and consequence of any form of relatedness can be isolated, and instead proposes that *any* aspect of relatedness inevitably impacts upon *every* aspect or expression of relatedness.

Although Western thought is not predisposed to the central ideas surrounding this first principle, nonetheless they lend themselves to various types of investigation and, while complex, are reasonably open to comprehension. Much of their immediate difficulty arises from the attempt to describe and communicate this principle both as process and as a structure. Attempts to do so have generated, and continue to generate, all manner of confusion and have given rise to difficult, if highly rewarding descriptive narratives as well as to any number of half-baked 'deep and meaningless' guru-like statements and descriptors. Whether my preferred term of worlding (and its relation to the worldview) will turn out to be an instance of the former or the latter remains to be seen.

The Second Principle: Existential Uncertainty

> That which is in opposition is in concert and from things that differ comes the most beautiful harmony. Heraclitus

The second principle that runs through all existential phenomenology states that if all of one's reflective experience, knowledge and awareness of self, others and the world in general arises through and within relatedness then what is revealed is an inevitable and inescapable *uncertainty or lack of completeness in any and all of our reflections*.

Why should this be so? Because in placing all reflective experience within an inter-relational matrix, those reflections upon existence, be it in general or having to do with 'my own' existence, can no longer be held *solely* by me or exist in some way 'within' me. Rather, meaning-reflections emerging through inter-relation expose me to the many uncertainties of relatedness – uncertainties having to do with meaning, control, responsibility and so forth. From an inter-relational perspective, no one structural focus-point (such as 'I') can ever fully determine with complete and final certainty what and how other sructural focus-points (such as 'the world' or 'others') will be, nor can it fully determine what and how it, itself, will be since, as a structural focus-point, it can never remove or separate itself from its counterparts.

Does this suggest that existential phenomenology recognises absolutely no certainties whatsoever? Not at all. There exist any number of certainties that are requirement conditions for the maintenance and continuity of life. For instance, it is certain that all human beings must be able to breathe, take in nourishment and excrete waste products if they are to continue to exist. Similarly, death is a certainty for all human beings. Acknowledging this, existential phenomenology nonetheless argues that each human being's *lived experience* of such certainties is open to multiple possibilities – and hence remains uncertain. For example, even with the certainty that my life is moving towards its inevitable end, I remain uncertain in that not only do I not know when that ending will be or how it will occur, but also my very stance toward this ending, my way of relating to the certainty of death, is always open to differing stances and attitudes that may arise and change unpredictably throughout my life.

Although he could never be said to have been an existential philosopher, and would almost certainly have been displeased to be so labelled, it is my view that, in his theory of *value pluralism*, Isaiah Berlin provides the most insightful analysis of several key implications arising from this second principle. Berlin's principal argument criticised the general Western assumption that

> the answers to all the great questions must of necessity agree with one another; for they must correspond with reality, and reality is a harmonious whole. If this were not so, there is chaos at the heart of things: which is unthinkable. Liberty, equality, property, knowledge, security, practical wisdom, purity of character, sincerity, kindness, rational self-love, all these ideals . . . cannot conflict with one another; if they appear to do so it must be due to some misunderstanding of their properties. No truly good thing can ever be finally

incompatible with any other; indeed they virtually entail one another; men cannot be wise unless they are free or free unless they are just, happy, and so forth.

Here, we conspicuously abandon the voice of experience – which records very obvious conflicts of ultimate ideals – and encounter a doctrine that stems from older theological roots – from the belief that unless all the positive virtues are harmonious with one another, or at least not incompatible, the notion of the Perfect Entity – whether it be called nature or God or Ultimate Reality – is not conceivable. (Berlin, 2006, quoted in Gray, 2006: 20)

In a recent article on Berlin's theory of value pluralism as expounded in his posthumous book, *Political Ideas in the Romantic Age: Their Rise and Influence on Modern Thought* (Berlin, 2006), John Gray emphasises Berlin's

consistent rejection of the idea – which Berlin rightly viewed as being fundamental in the Western intellectual tradition – that all genuine human values must be combinable in a harmonious whole. In this view conflicts of values are symptoms of error that in principle can always be resolved: if human values seem to come into conflict that is only because our understanding of them is imperfect, or some of the contending values are spurious; and where such conflicts appear there is a single right answer that – if only they can find it – all reasonable people are bound to accept. (Gray, 2006: 20)

Berlin's counter-argument to this view asserts that, on the contrary, 'conflicts of values are real and inescapable, with some of them having no satisfactory solution. He advanced this view not as a form of skepticism but as a universal truth: conflicts of value go with being human' (Gray, 2006: 20).

From a political standpoint, Berlin contended, this Enlightenment idea of an ideal and monistic harmony and perfection in human values generated the novel expressions of tyranny that dominated the century just past. For at the heart of this idea lay 'the intellectual roots of some of the major political disasters of the twentieth century' (Gray, 2006: 20). When considering the excesses of political intolerance and curtailment of freedom of expression associated with twentieth-century Communist regimes, for example, Berlin's view was that these could not 'be adequately explained as a product of backwardness, or of errors in the application of Marxian theory. It was the result of a resolute attempt to realize an Enlightenment utopia – a condition of society in which no serious conflict any longer exists' (ibid.: 21).

The point being made by Berlin addresses the key concerns and assumptions to be found in the second principle of existential phenomenology. Together, they ask us to embrace existence's lack of completeness, and the inevitable failure of any attempt to complete it by realising all our possibilities (Cohn, 2002).

The primary consequence of an inter-relational grounding exposes the inevitable uncertainty and openness of existence. At any moment, all prior knowledge, values, assumptions and beliefs regarding self, others and the world in general may be 'opened' to challenge, reconsideration or dissolution. In addition, the embodied attitudinal and affective experience of being that accompanies this shift might also challenge and surprise or disturb. Relatively common statements such as 'I never thought I would act like that', or 'She seemed to turn into someone I didn't know', or 'Recent world events convince me that I just can't make sense of things any longer' point us to positions that at least temporarily acknowledge the uncertainties of being.

What this second principle argues is that existential uncertainty remains a constant given of human experience rather than revealing itself to be just an occasional and temporary consequence of unusual circumstances. It suggests that the structural point of view we make of self, others and the world in general is always incomplete, unfixed in any final shape or form – and, hence, uncertain. Every moment of worlding is novel and unique, never to be repeated, never identical to any other. In contrast, the worldview provides structurally focused reflections regarding any aspect of worlding that suggest, at least in part, an essentialising stasis or constancy over time. In this sense, the worldview provides *the* basic structural means through which the full impact of the inherent uncertainty accompanying the experience of *worlding* can be partially withstood and allayed. This limiting of uncertainty should not be understood solely in terms of 'neurotic defence patterns' and the like. Simply because it is a *structure*, and hence, of necessity, requiring some degree of fixedness and coherence over time, the worldview cannot embrace the total impact of uncertainty. To do so would set about its own structural existence.

The principle of uncertainty is both shattering in its implications and initially counter-intuitive. For example, I might say to myself: 'I know that since the age of seven I have loathed the taste of eggs. I know, therefore, that just as yesterday I rejected the possibility of eating eggs, I will do so again today, and will continue to do so tomorrow and almost certainly all the remaining tomorrows in my life. And even if it should come to pass that for some reason or other I am placed in a position at some point in the future where the eating of eggs becomes a necessity, I might do so but I will certainly continue to loathe their taste and feel a physical revulsion at the thought of eating one.' What the second principle insists upon is the acknowledgement of a basic uncertainty regarding this certain stance I currently adopt. That 'I' have adopted it, places this stance within the reflective arena of the worldview. From the worldview's structural perspective, its reflections upon worlding must, at least in part, remain fixed. In this way, I can state categorically that my stance toward eggs (or anything – or anyone – else, for that matter) will remain the same over time – even though, from a worlding standpoint no such assumption can be made.

If we look at this from a seemingly opposite perspective, all of us are likely to have had the experience of changing our view regarding something or someone. A trusted friend acts in a way that betrays my trust and brings the friendship to an end. I discover a new-found ability that alters the direction of my professional life. I watch a film that I initially thought to be a work of genius but which now seems superficial and pedestrian. If such obvious possibilities of uncertainty were all that this second principle sought to highlight, then it is hardly deserving of overmuch attention. Surprising and unexpected events come upon us all at some time or other during our lives. What must be recognised is that these experiences of uncertainty are expressed *within* the structural conditions of the worldview. These instances of uncertainty are as necessary to the maintenance of the worldview as are its points of invariance and fixedness over time.

The uncertainty being addressed in the second principle is at the level of worlding. It proposes that uncertainty remains a constant given in our experience of being. Paradoxically, uncertainty is a certainty of existence. In this sense, the uncertainty of worlding expresses its presence at the worldview level not only in the surprising events in our lives, but just as equally and forcefully in the expected and (seemingly) fixed meanings and circumstances of everyday existence. Uncertainty, therefore, as expressed by this second principle *includes* rather than stands in opposition to the certainties construed and demanded by the worldview. This existential uncertainty points us not only to questions that address the 'uncertain certainties' and the 'certain uncertainties' that may befall being at any time, but, far more significantly, toward concerns regarding what and how it is to be an uncertain being within the open-endedness of inter-relational existence.

From an obvious standpoint, the principle of uncertainty alerts us to the constant possibility of the unexpected. Less obviously, it urges us to treat 'the expected' as novel, full of previously unforeseen qualities and possibilities. This second perspective of uncertainty is rarely discussed or considered by existential psychotherapists, or psychotherapists in general, for that matter. In not doing so, they miss potentially critical insights.

For example, the principle of uncertainty suggests that the experience of boredom or of 'being in rut' is not directly due to the rigidity of habitual behaviour, but rather to the degree of uncertainty that is permitted to exist within that repeated behaviour. Television 'lifestyle' experts or newspaper agony aunts, for instance, forever suggest novel positions or activities as ways of 'spicing up' a couple's moribund sexual life. In taking this stance, they fail to consider how it is that any number of other couples may be happily satisfied with, and require no 'spicing up' of, their sexual relations, even though what they do and when they do it might be characterised as being habitual and predictable. Equally, such pundits avoid alerting their audience to the awareness that even the novel position or activity may all too rapidly come to be experienced as boring and bland. What such examples make plain is that the experience of pleasurable excitement in one's sexual relations, or the lack of it, has little to do with matters of novelty or habit, but rather reveals the consequences of an openness toward, or an avoidance of, uncertainty. *In sum, worlding, in its uncertainty, is always surprising.*

Perhaps most tellingly (at least for Western societies and culture), at the worldview level, 'being an uncertain being' challenges that most basic and central assumption concerning the self and its subjective know-ability. Uncertainty extends not just toward others or the world but also to each 'I' who both inhabits and questions the world. Just as I might be shaken and surprised by the unexpectedness and challenge of novel events, circumstances and behaviours that might contradict or require me to reshape my assumptions about how an other or others in general are and behave, so too might those self-same challenges arise from the appearance and behaviour of an 'I' who, in some ways, is not recognisable as 'I' and yet is. If I return to my earlier example of my dislike of eggs, I can see that changing my view of eggs ('Uhmm! I love eggs!') alters not merely my relation to eggs, but also my relation to 'me'. If I once defined my self as 'I am Ernesto who hates eggs', who am I now if 'I am Ernesto who loves eggs'? And moreover, the impact this re-definition of 'Ernesto' will have on 'Ernesto', and whether this impact will be limited or dramatically life-changing, cannot be known until it has occurred. This aspect of uncertainty brings a somewhat quixotic quality to the quest 'to know my self'. While the *attempt* in such a quest may retain some, even substantial, value, the assumption of uncertainty makes it clear that it can never be more than incomplete.

Considered in a slightly different fashion, uncertainty opens our experience of being to a multitude of 'points of departure'. That we may elect to go down or be forced to follow any number of such points is inevitable. At the same time, whatever the number or duration or quality of such departures, none of us will ever truly 'arrive' in any final and complete sense. Our life journeying may provoke a felt sense of a mistaken direction, or of having missed or been denied a critical junction. It may seem at times as though our directed point of arrival recedes ever further into the distance or appears so tantalisingly close that we can almost believe we are there. From an uncertain standpoint, we are always in some relation to the potential of arrival and yet never arrive.

In summarising Isaiah Berlin's analysis of value pluralism as discussed earlier in this section, John Gray cites a particularly revealing and relevant passage from Joshua Cherniss's 'Introduction' to Berlin's text. Cherniss writes: 'Man is incapable of self-completion, and therefore never wholly predictable; fallible, a complex combination of opposites, some reconcilable, others incapable of being resolved or harmonised; unable to cease from his search for truth, happiness, novelty, freedom, but with no guarantee . . . of being able to attain them' (Cherniss, 2006, quoted in Gray, 2006: 21). This quote serves as a reasonable summary of the second principle of existential phenomenology.

And yet, if certainty is to be viewed only as a necessary fixture for the maintenance of the worldview, it remains to be asked: if the worldview is the structural attempt to reflect worlding, what leads it to deviate so far from, and discredit, the evidence of uncertainty? How does existential theory respond to this all too evident point? To provide at least an initial answer, we must turn to its third key underlying principle.

The Third Principle: Existential Anxiety

Freedom's possibility announces itself in anxiety. Søren Kierkegaard

The third principle that I believe to be a necessary constituent of all existential psychotherapies follows on from the implications of the first two. It asks us to consider the human reflective reaction to inter-relationally derived uncertainty and proposes that our response is inevitably one of unease, discomfort or, most broadly, *anxiety*. But why should this, and *only* this, be the response? To begin to answer this question, we must first address a seemingly unrelated aspect of 'being human' – our ability to generate *meaning* out of our lived experiences of, and relations to and with, the world.

Meaning

> The way of life means continuing. Continuing means going far. Going far means returning.
> Tao Te Ching

As far as we can know at present, our unique form of evolutionarily derived consciousness has as its primary function the construction of a meaningful reality, or, as I have suggested as the title to an earlier book, an *interpreted world* (Spinelli, 2005). Existential phenomenology argues that one of the essential distinguishing characteristics of being human is that we require meaning of, and impose meaning on to, the world. It is through our relatedness to the world that we experience our selves as meaning-making beings. We interpret the world via the human process of construing meaning from those 'things' or events which impinge upon our experience and with which we are in relation. Consequently, we are disturbed by the lack or loss of meaning; we can go to great lengths to avoid or deny those instances and experiences that challenge our most deeply fixed, or sedimented, existing meanings – even to the extent of disowning, or dissociating from, those experiences that challenge that currently maintained meaning (Cohn, 2002; Spinelli, 2005; Strasser and Strasser, 1997).

All of the above points accompany the overall structuring of lived experience via the worldview. From a worlding perspective, however, whatever worldview-related meaning constructions emerge – be they concerned with my notions of self, others or the world in general – remain necessarily incomplete and partially distorted expressions of worlding. In this way, it can be seen that meaning is the worldview's attempt to structure worlding.

As inadequate as these attempts may ultimately be, as several key existential theorists have highlighted, they continue to reveal that worlding-derived inter-relational foundation through which, at a worldview level, both 'subject' and 'object', or 'self' and 'other', are mutually and simultaneously made meaningful. Every instance of meaning does not *only* construct, or re-construct, the object of our focus. Just as significantly, the focusing 'subject' is also simultaneously constructed or re-constructed in and through the act (Ihde, 1986a; Merleau-Ponty, 1962; Spinelli, 2005).

The third principle argues that although meaning emerges through the worldview in that it is the primary means with which to structure the experiential openness of worlding, it, nonetheless, remains rooted in relatedness and, hence, is subject to the constant possibility of being de-structured. That is to say, all meanings are open to the threat of becoming meaningless.

This emphasis upon the inevitable openness of meaning can be expressed in terms of the ultimate *meaninglessness of meaning*. If the qualities, features and conditions of meaning cannot be fully 'captured', and instead remain inevitably open to novel interpretative possibilities then, in this sense of an ever-elusive finality, they are meaningless.

As an important instance of this conclusion, Heidegger made explicit the impossibility of deriving in any objective fashion that which modernist science has called 'truth'. This notion of truth depends upon both the possibility and actuality of 'capturing' meaning in such a way that it is no longer open to novel and alternative possibilities. If I have discerned *the* truth to my existence, or to any aspect of it, then its meaning is bound, its interpretation is final and fixed forever, and cannot be subject to alternative interpretative meanings. Instead, for Heidegger, the origin of our idea of truth reaches back to the notion of *aletheia* – the ever-disclosing, ever-revealing, openness to being. From this standpoint, my meaning may be 'truthful' in that it both reveals that which is there for me and, at the same time, *opens* that meaning which is there for me to further possibilities of meaning-extending (or disclosing) truthfulness. Truth, in this sense, is never complete or completed. The implications of this view, not least for psychotherapeutic practice, are extensive and significant. They imply, as the relational psychotherapist Leslie Farber proposed, that 'speaking truthfully is a more fitting ambition than speaking the truth' (Farber, 2000:10).

At the same time, engaging in the enterprise of truthfulness requires the perpetual 'holding' of complementary stances toward, on the one hand, the worldview's attempt to construct a certain and 'captured' reality whose meaning is fixed and final, and, on the other, the lived experience of worlding that points us to the uncertainty and openness of meaning. This ever-present tension, be it addressed in terms such as 'meaning/meaninglessness' or 'certainty/uncertainty', expresses itself experientially as *anxiety*.

Existential anxiety

Now is the age of anxiety. W.H. Auden

Existential anxiety is perhaps best understood if considered from two distinct, if inter-related, perspectives.

From an initial perspective, existential anxiety refers to the inevitable unease and insecurity that accompanies the worldview's partial and limiting attempts to reflect inter-relational uncertainty from a meaning-based perspective. In this sense, existential anxiety necessarily permeates *all* reflective experiences of relatedness. As such, it is neither avoidable, nor is it an aspect of pathology, but rather a basic 'given' of human existence as reflected from the structural standpoint of the worldview. Considered in this way, the dilemma of existential anxiety is not so much *that* it is, but rather *how* each of us 'lives with' it.

This shift in focus draws out the second understanding to be derived from existential anxiety. In this second sense, existential anxiety can be seen to be the source point or instigator of all attempts to embrace, to deny, or claims to have resolved, the uncertainties of an existence grounded in relatedness. Viewed in this way, existential anxiety encompasses *all* responses to the conditions of existence. Thus, it need not be the case that anxiety is experienced as solely or necessarily a debilitating, disruptive or problematic presence that must be reduced or removed. While anxiety may, and often does, provoke feelings of despair, confusion and bewilderment, it is equally the case that the experience of anxiety can also be stimulating, can re-awaken or enhance our connectedness to being alive, and arouses creativity – *but only so long as such experiences permit the reshaping and reconstructing of a novel meaning that can be accepted and 'owned'.* When no novel meaning arises, or alternatively, when the only possible meaning to present itself seems too perilous and destabilising to accept, then anxiety is experienced as destructive and as a threat to one's very existence. While it might make sense to seek to avoid such expressions of anxiety, the third principle forces us to recognise that a life that was anxiety-free would also be bereft of wonder, enthusiasm and excitement.

On further consideration, this second perspective also alerts us to the disturbing realisation that whatever the stance adopted, anxiety cannot be removed from our reflections upon our experience of existence. If I embrace anxiety, anxiety remains. Equally, my attempts to deny it provoke further expressions of anxiety. In this way, it can be seen that just as existential anxiety is the 'cause' of our attempts to respond at a reflective level to the uncertainties of an existence grounded in relatedness, it is also the 'effect' that emerges from those attempts.

As was discussed above, at the worldview level the 'given' of uncertainty provokes the experience of anxiety. As was the case with uncertainty, for the worldview to accept the full anxiety of worlding is to threaten the very maintenance of the worldview structure. The worldview's elevation of fixed meanings, truths, and certainties would seem to permit some escape from existential anxiety. At the same time, because the worldview remains an attempt to reflect worlding, existential anxiety continues to express itself as an agent or entity *within* the worldview structure. In this way, existential anxiety becomes 'essentialised' or structured in a 'thing-' or 'construct-like' manner and can be 'identified' as a symptom or a disorder in thought, affect and/or behaviour.

As will be discussed in Part Two, it is of particular concern to existential psychotherapy to focus upon these latter, structural derivations of anxiety. These typically express themselves in rigid and restrictive patterns of thought and behaviour that serve as attempts to avoid that which is perceived to be unknown and novel. Conversely, they may appear as determined demands and quests for the unknown and novel. What both these rigid and inflexible stances reveal in general are symptoms of unease, commonly expressed in terms such as obsessive or compulsive behaviours, phobias and addictive disorders.

In our attempts to avoid or diminish the disturbing aspects of anxiety, we seek out and assert fixed truths, facts and statements, and deny or dissociate from those instances in our experience that cast doubt or challenge our assertions of certainty and fixed meaning. This denial has been referred to as *inauthenticity* (Heidegger, 1962) or *bad faith* (Sartre, 1991) and its frequency and appeal lies precisely in that it serves to allay the unease and uncertainty of being-in-the-world (Cohn, 1997; Spinelli, 2005; Yalom, 1980). As Heidegger writes, 'Anxiety throws Dasein [i.e. the relational human being] back upon that which it is most anxious about – its authentic potentiality-for-Being-in-the-world' (Heidegger, 1962: 232).

The principle of existential anxiety points us toward the awareness that maintaining a truthful stance toward our existence is no simple or easy matter. At the same time, it is not only the sages and intellectuals who become aware of, and seek to grasp and communicate, our relationship with anxiety. The existential notion of *death anxiety*, for instance, requires no intermediary or meta-theoretical explanatory prompt for anyone to be aware of, and experience, his or her relatedness to it. All human beings become directly aware of the temporal nature of their life and its inevitable 'movement toward death'. At the same time, they also know that the conditions for death's occurrence (such as when and how it will occur, or what will kill us) remain uncertain and unpredictable. While culture and religious beliefs and broadly general or shared factors undoubtedly influence how each of us responds to the certainty of death, it is also evident that any specific response to the anxiety accompanying this awareness expresses itself through stances and attitudes that permeate all aspects of our worldview's structural attempts to reflect the experience of worlding. For example, the conviction that science is just one step away from discovering the secret of immortality or, equally, the certainty that I will continue to exist in some disembodied fashion can be seen as responses that seek to avoid the anxiety accompanying the 'realization that life is inevitably moving toward death' (Cohn, 1997: 70). But it is also evident that in order to maintain these convictions I am likely to be bound to the expression (or avoidance of expression) of certain behaviours or to the espousal (or repudiation) of particular views and attitudes that will, in turn, structure my overall stance toward existence. The consequences of these strategies were best summarised by the existential psychotherapist, Medard Boss, who wrote that 'people who are most afraid of *death* are those who have the greatest anxiety about *life*' (Boss, 1994: 112).

In brief, the third principle of existential phenomenology expresses the view that anxiety is an inevitable universal, or 'given', of human existence that pervades every expression of existence. At a worldview level, anxiety expresses itself through our ways of being with self, others and the world as a whole. At the same time, however, the third principle also acknowledges that those 'untruthful' responses to existential anxiety which seek to avoid or deny the experiential consequences of relatedness and uncertainty, will serve to 'fix' and focus existential anxiety so that it expresses itself through the 'structures' of symptoms and disorders.

The Three Principles: A Summary

Our life is the instrument we use to experiment with the truth. Eliot Pattison

It is my view that the three underlying principles discussed above – relatedness, uncertainty and existential anxiety – are *necessary* to any explication of existential-phenomenological theory. That they may be *sufficient* as well as necessary remains debatable. My own view is that these three conditions are sufficient in so far as they provide the most basic 'sketch' or 'ground-plan' of the terrain. At the same time, however, it is also my view that this sketch contains within it the necessary clues with which to tease out for further elaboration the specific 'points of departure' associated with the particular views and contributions of the various branches of existential phenomenology as represented by its foundational philosophical contributors – Edmund Husserl (1931a, 1931b, 1965), Martin Heidegger (1962, 1976, 2001) and Jean-Paul Sartre (1973, 1985, 1991). This is not to suggest that the contributions of these three philosophers, much less those of pivotal thinkers such as Martin Buber (1970, 2002), George Gadamer (2004), Karl Jaspers (1963), Immanuel Levinas (1987, 1999) and Maurice Merleau-Ponty (1962, 1964a, 1964b), among numerous others, can simply be *reduced* to these three principles. Nor is it being suggested that anyone claiming to espouse existential phenomenology is no longer required to grapple intellectually with many, if not all, of these philosophers (and any number of others left unmentioned).

What *is* being proposed is that any claim to the elucidation of, or affiliation to, *a* form of, or schema for, existential phenomenology *must* be able to address these three underlying principles as pivotal constituents of its approach and argument.

In particular, when considering these three principles from a predominantly psychotherapeutic, rather than philosophical, perspective, this text will seek to demonstrate how the principles of relatedness, uncertainty and existential anxiety not only provide the basis for the *practice* of existential psychotherapy, but, equally, emerge as the primary means for its definition, and contrast to, or comparison with, other systems of psychotherapy. Just as Part One of this text seeks to provide an overview of these principles considered from the standpoint of existential psychotherapy, Part Two will propose a specific structural possibility for the practice of existential psychotherapy that is both derived from the three principles and that expresses them.

Before moving to these areas, however, some further consideration of a number of corollaries arising from the three principles particularly pertinent to existential psychotherapy in practice is now required.

2

The Worldview

I had returned in particular to the question of whether the apparently continuous passage of time and movement given to us by our eyes was an illusion – whether in fact our visual experience consisted of a series of 'moments' which were then welded together by some higher mechanism in the brain. I found myself referring again to the 'cinematographic' sequences of stills, described to me by my migraine patients. Oliver Sacks

According to existential phenomenology, the three underlying principles of relatedness, uncertainty and existential anxiety highlight the *ontological* (or universal invariant) conditions of human existence. All human beings respond to, and enact, these conditions in every facet and expression of their lives. At the same time, these ontological conditions or 'givens' of human existence, when considered from the vantage point of a specific and particular human being are said to be *ontic* (or distinctive and unique) in that they reflect that actual embodied variation that has been given expression. Each human being's way of being reveals the ontological 'givens' of human existence through their particular and distinctive ontic expression. For example, as has been argued, relatedness is an ontological condition of human existence in that it reveals itself through every facet of every human being's existence. Equally, at an ontic level, relatedness reveals itself, or is expressed, through the distinctive way of relating that is adopted by any particular human being.

As was discussed above, *worlding* is the term I am employing to express the process-like experiencing of the ontological conditions of human existence both in general and in their specific and particular ontic expression. As was also discussed, however, every ontic attempt to reflect upon and respond to worlding's ongoing, ever-shifting process-like quality must adopt a specific point of focus, otherwise no reflection could be possible. This very attempt to reflect upon, identify and explicate worlding imposes a set of 'thing-like' or structurally binding constituents. As a further consequence, this shift from process to structure is necessarily selective. The structure cannot contain *all* that is the process, otherwise it would *be* the process and hence could not be the structure. When worlding is considered at this structurally selective level, it becomes the *worldview*.

The worldview expresses the selective focus or bias imposed upon the ontic experience of worlding. Further, simply *because* the worldview's structural focus upon the ontic experience of worlding is selective and biased, a dissonance between worlding-as-process and worlding-as-structural-worldview is inevitable. The latter can only partially reflect the former, and because the latter's reflection is partial, it *distorts* the former in myriad ways. As will be discussed below and in Part Two, existential psychotherapy is principally concerned with the investigation of the dissonances and distortions imposed upon the process-like experience of worlding by the structural worldview.

From the perspective of existential phenomenology, the worldview reveals *from a structural perspective* each person's ontic strategy (or, as Sartre (1991) suggested, *life project*) for existing within the ontological conditions of relatedness, uncertainty and existential anxiety. For instance, let us suppose that one means by which the ontological condition of uncertainty finds its ontic expression in my life is via the strategy I adopt toward my day-to-day experiences of insecurity. This strategy might be that for fifty weeks of every year my worldview is dominated by stances of regularity, habit and predictability all of which promote a felt sense of security which is experienced by me as both valued and necessary. In addition, however, it is equally the case that my worldview values and finds it necessary to be able to adopt a complementary stance of irregularity, unpredictability, risk-taking and an openness to the unknown during the remaining two weeks of the year, when I travel to a novel location.

As the above example highlights, the worldview can be, and often is, structurally complex in that it may hold competing, complementary or even contradictory stances depending upon the conditions or context within which it is placed. It becomes apparent, therefore, that the worldview also expresses that structural stance or strategy that makes the continuing possibility of being as opposed to non-being either desirable or at least sufficiently tolerable. In other words, *the worldview attempts to maintain a structure that places greater value upon the continuation of being rather than upon the cessation of being.*

Returning to the example above, how, for instance, would I respond to a life in which every single one of the fifty-two weeks each year was dominated by patterns of unrelenting ritual and habit? Or, alternatively, how might I respond to a life where every single day of the year was marked by the unpredictability, irregularity and moment-to-moment bombardment of multiple novel possibilities? In each case, I suspect, I would find either or both of these options to be intolerable ways to exist. I might experience living from a perpetual sense of unease or dissatisfaction or from a felt emptiness and pointlessness. In more extreme ways, I might express the intolerability of my existence through the damaging use of alcohol, or through abusive relations with others, or I might 'become psychotic' or exhibit various body disorders or turn suicidal.

Considering the above from the structural perspective of the worldview, these latter responses reveal that their impact destabilised its structure to such a degree that it could neither be maintained nor could it immediately re-constitute itself so that the conditions of existence could be made at least sufficiently tolerable. In such a circumstance, the worldview has become an obstacle to the maintenance of a greater value being placed upon the continuation of being. My 'destructive' acts might be seen as now being in the service of the cessation of being (or 'courting death' as van Deurzen-Smith has referred to it (1994)). However, I would suggest an alternative conclusion which is derived from the insights of Laing and his colleagues (Laing, 1960, 1967; Laing and Esterson, 1964). In my view, in many cases, these 'destructive' acts may not have so much to do with the desire to cease existing *per se*. Rather, they serve to break down or destabilise the currently maintained worldview in the hope that, by so doing, a new worldview may emerge which is better able to tolerate – however temporarily – the presenting conditions of existence and, in turn, ensure that greater value is placed upon the continuation of being. Even in the extreme example of the attempt at suicide, it would seem to me that it is the desire to bring an end to the particular worldview being currently maintained than it is to extinguish life itself, that propels the act. Of course, the risk is always there that my actions may not succeed in their aim or, alternatively, that they may increase the likelihood of the cessation of my existence. Nonetheless, the alternative view under consideration has the advantage of remaining consistent with the aim of the continuation of being rather than require the added explanation of how such an aim transforms itself into that which becomes focused upon the cessation of being in itself.

Whatever the case, as has been implied but can now be made explicit, the worldview expresses the way that each of us constructs all facets of our reflectively lived and embodied way of being. Equally, the worldview seeks to provide and maintain a groundedness in a time, location and narrative so as to make the continued experience of being at least a more tolerable option than that of non-being.

Included in the structure that is the worldview are various sub-structures that permit the worldview its complexity and at least some degree of flexibility in its ability to maintain its structure in the face of the challenges presented to it. Among these, I would propose that at least three primary sub-structures – the *self-construct,* the *other-construct* and the *world-construct* – can be identified.

Thus, the worldview structure contains and expresses:

1. The dispositional stances (which is to say, the sum total of all the beliefs, values, views, attitudes, meanings, assumptions and conclusions, together with their associated behaviours, feelings and emotions) being maintained regarding the construct labelled 'self' or 'I' (the self-construct).
2. The dispositional stances being maintained regarding the construct labelled 'others', be it any particular or specific 'other' or 'others' in general (the other-construct).

3. The dispositional stances being maintained regarding the construct labelled 'the world', be it in terms of its living and non-living components and/or its physical, environmental, biological, social, cultural, moral and spiritual dimensions (the world-construct).
4. The dispositional stances being maintained regarding each construct's relatedness to the remaining constructs.

This definition of the worldview serves to clarify existential phenomenology's avoidance of any subjective or intra-psychic statements that do not overtly acknowledge their inter-relational foundation. In addition, by extending the worldview's dimensions so that they express overtly the self-construct's inseparable relatedness to the other- and world-constructs, existential phenomenology raises an implicit critique of the vast majority of personality theories within contemporary Western psychology, viewing these as being too restrictive and limited in their definitions because of their isolationist focus upon the subjective 'self'.

In addition, the significance of considering issues regarding the 'self', 'others' and 'the world' as sub-structures of the worldview resolves many of the recurring problems concerning the question of 'self', in particular, within existential-phenomenological theory. I refer readers to more detailed discussions of this issue in two of my previous texts, *Demystifying Therapy* (1994) and *The Mirror and the Hammer* (2001). Nonetheless, in brief, it can be argued that, from an existential-phenomenological perspective, what is commonly termed 'the self' emerges only through worldview reflections upon worlding experience. Thus 'the self' is a pivotal means of expressing the process-like quality of existence from an essence-based, structural perspective. The self that arises at any given instance of reflection is a construct expressing a temporal narrative incorporating past experience, current mood and future expectations or goals. At the same time, as a construct, it is at best only a partial or selective focus point by which the ontic experience of worlding is expressed at a structural level. Hence, the term self-construct articulates with greater adequacy that which everyday notions of 'the self' attempt to communicate. The same argument can be seen to hold for both the other-construct and the world-construct.

I will refrain from more detailed discussion of the self-, other- and world-constructs until they can be considered within the framework of existential psychotherapy. However, for now I must simply state that the investigation of these three primary constructs within the worldview further reveals:

1. Those dispositional stances of the worldview structure that, in response to challenge, remain relatively flexible and open to redefinition. Such structures can be termed as *flexible dispositional stances*.
2. Those dispositional stances of the worldview structure that, in response to challenge, resist redefinition and remain relatively inflexible. Such structures can be termed *sedimented dispositional stances*.
3. Those dispositional stances of the worldview that are so deep-rooted in their fixedness and resistance to redefinition that only the most extreme challenges, or no amount of challenge, will alter them. Such structures can be termed as *deeply sedimented dispositional stances*.

Let us consider the first point. For example, from the worldview standpoint of the self-construct, I may hold the position that 'I am Ernesto who always system-atically plans and prepares his lectures.' Unexpectedly, this self-construct-focused view is challenged in that I am placed in a position where I must deliver a lecture that has not been systematically planned and prepared. If the position 'I am Ernesto who always systematically plans and prepares his lectures' reflects a flex-ible dispositional stance, I am not only able to deliver the lecture but, more impor-tantly, those dispositional qualities of the self-construct (such as its beliefs, values, and so forth) that are associated with the previously maintained stance of 'I am Ernesto who always systematically plans and prepares his lectures' are altered in various ways and, in turn, the self-construct is restructured so that now 'I am Ernesto who *usually* systematically plans and prepares his lectures and who also delivers unplanned and unprepared lectures.'

Flexible dispositional stances in the worldview make it plain that existential phenomenology rejects any entirely static definition of the worldview. Instead, it acknowledges the possibility of a continuing dynamic restructuring of the world-view via shifting dispositional stances throughout one's life. At the same time, however, existential phenomenology acknowledges not only the difficulty, but also possibly the impossibility, of restructuring *all* dispositional stances, and hence all structural aspects of the worldview. With regard to this latter conclusion, which is addressed in points 2 and 3 above, I have termed this resistance to structural alter-ation as *sedimentation*.

SEDIMENTATION AND THE WORLDVIEW

Nothing is more dangerous than a dogmatic worldview – nothing more constraining, more blinding to innovation, more destructive of openness to novelty. Stephen Jay Gould

Sedimentation refers to fixed patterns of rigid dispositional stances maintained by the worldview. For example: 'I can't tolerate making mistakes', 'No matter how honest you are, others will betray you', 'I'll take tea over coffee any time.' Nonetheless, sedimentation should not be viewed as being solely problematic or negative. On reflection, it becomes obvious that some degree of sedimentation is necessary in order to maintain an essence or structure-based focus upon the ontic experience of worlding. Without sedimentation the primary sub-structures that make up the worldview – the self-, other- and world-constructs – could not be con-strued or defined as (relatively) fixed and permanent essences. Although all sedi-mentations are resistant to challenges that seek to *de-sediment* the structural pattern, the degree of resistance may vary substantially – as is summarised in points 2 and 3 above. Point 2 alludes to those rigidly maintained sedimentations that are present in the worldview as a whole or in any of its primary sub-structures. Examples of these sedimentations might be: 'I must never, ever make mistakes', 'You're always going to end up being betrayed', 'I couldn't possibly drink coffee; it has to be tea for me.' Rigid sedimentations are expressed through typical dispositional patterns of relatedness that are adopted by a person. Shifts in and challenges to those patterns, as might well occur in the course of therapy, serve to initiate their de-sedimentation.

Point 3 alludes to the most rigidly maintained and deepest (or foundational) sedimentations that provide the worldview with its most basic structural bases. Examples of these deep sedimentations are not readily accessible, but I would suggest that they are likely to be expressed as brief, highly-charged and emotive relational statements such as 'Don't hurt me', 'I'm a good person', 'Love me', 'I must make you love me', and so forth. Though entirely speculative, my own research on these possible foundational sedimentations suggests that their dispositional influence permeates all other later sedimentations. In my opinion, these deep sedimentations cannot ever be fully de-sedimented, although their dispositional qualities may be open to taking on a greater complexity. For example, a deep sedimentation such as 'I'll show you' may initially be dispositionally focused upon stances of anger, aggression and the rejection of others. However, it might become dispositionally open to novel possibilities of relatedness that focus on demonstration, education, self-revelation and the like.

While it is evident that at least *some* sedimentations are capable of being fully or partially de-sedimented, it remains an open question as to whether *all* sedimentations can be. My personal view is that they cannot and that the insistent attempt to do so may be experienced as being so threatening to the worldview that it will destabilise to the extent that the felt experience of being becomes increasingly intolerable. For instance, consider the admittedly extreme example of a deeply sedimented dispositional stance of the worldview that maintains that 'I could never find pleasure in killing another human being.' Now imagine that such a sedimentation is, somehow, challenged enough so that the likelihood of de-sedimentation is high. In such circumstances, the destabilising of the maintained worldview might well be such that the embracing of some form of oblivion (whether focused on the destruction of the worldview or on the being's 'courting' of non-being) emerges as an option preferable to that of de-sedimentation. Any number of other, less extreme, examples, I am sure, should now readily spring to mind for readers.

How sedimentation occurs currently remains an open question, whether considered from the perspective of philosophical, psychological or neurobiological investigation. *That* sedimentation occurs, on the other hand, is both obvious and evident. Indeed, I would suggest that the whole profession of psychotherapy relies, to a large extent, upon its presence and impact.

In any case, what is being argued is that sedimentations both arise and are challenged as a result of their inter-relational meetings with the world. They arise when the need to maintain some specific dispositional stance in the worldview *as fixed, certain and secure* overrides any experientially derived challenge that is construed as threatening or destabilising of their certainty, security and fixedness. As an instance of this possibility, let us return to the previous example but this time consider it from the perspective of sedimentation. In this instance, 'I am Ernesto who always systematically plans and prepares his lectures' is a dispositional stance that is resistant to its being altered or amended in any way. Let us suppose, as before, that the circumstances of the challenge are such that the 'Ernesto who always systematically plans and prepares his lectures' actually does deliver an unplanned and unprepared lecture. If so, then the currently maintained sedimentation no longer holds and two primary options become available: *either* the challenge to the sedimented dispositional stance is permitted and thereby the stance is de-sedimented (as in the case of a flexible disposition) *or* the stance is maintained and is thereby retained as a sedimented dispositional stance. How can this second option be achieved? I would suggest: via the strategy of *dissociating* the experience either from the whole of the worldview or from that sub-structure in the worldview (in this case, the self-construct) whose sedimented dispositional stance is under threat.

Dissociation, in this sense, refers to the worldview's maintenance of a sedimentation by its distancing from, denial or dis-ownership of the impact and consequences of experientially derived challenges upon that sedimented dispositional stance.

Dissociation requires that the sedimentation is maintained either by the *suppression* of the experiential challenge via some form of denial of its presence or impact or, more commonly, by the *redirection* of the challenge away from that particular construct in the worldview wherein the sedimentation is being challenged to another construct in the worldview which can minimise or alter the significance of the challenge.

The apparent forgetting and denial of events as might occur in a traumatic reaction to overwhelmingly painful and dangerous circumstances serves as an example of the suppressive strategy of dissociation. Less dramatically, one might claim the 'forgetting' or 'lack of awareness' or dismissal of those events, or factors associated with the events, that challenge a particular sedimentation. To return to the previous example, Ernesto maintains the rigidly held belief that 'I am Ernesto who always systematically plans and prepares his lectures.' Faced with a contradictory set of circumstances such as those outlined above, Ernesto must now convince himself of any number of particular circumstances that might have led to his having been able to deliver the lecture without any previous planning or preparation. For example, Ernesto might insist that what he had delivered could not justifiably be labelled 'a lecture' but rather was more akin to a set of informal and somewhat spontaneous statements. Equally, Ernesto might claim to have 'forgotten' that he had, in fact, previously prepared a lecture on the self-same topic and that his ability to deliver this one had rested upon that earlier planning, so that the challenging event is defused of its de-sedimenting potential through the explanation of a time-keeping confusion or a prior forgetting of an earlier arrangement. In this way, the challenge to Ernesto's sedimented stance is suppressed and, as a consequence, the sedimentation can continue to be maintained.

As an example of the second strategy of redirection of the experiential challenge to the sedimented stance, consider the following scenario provided by one of my clients, Aretha. Aretha holds the sedimented perspective that she is exclusively heterosexually oriented. However, she awakens one morning to find her self in bed and in the embrace of another woman, Cynthia. As well as this, Aretha remembers a night of exciting and thoroughly satisfying sexual abandon with Cynthia. But how can this be? Aretha views her self, that is to say, constructs various disposi- tions of her self-construct, as being exclusively heterosexual. In order to maintain the sedimentation and reject the challenge of her de-sedimenting lived experience, Aretha 'explains' the events that had occurred as being due to the substantial amounts of alcohol and cocaine that she and Cynthia had taken. Further, she claims that she had been pushed or forced into such behaviour by Cynthia's power of persuasion and unrelenting demands. Dulled by alcohol and drugs, over- whelmed by Cynthia's manipulative behaviour, Aretha concludes that what has occurred is due to forces beyond her control and therefore it was not truly 'Aretha' who had participated in, or so enjoyed, the previous night's sexual encounter, but rather it had been a 'false' or 'possessed' or 'manipulated/non-free-will' Aretha who had done so. In brief, Aretha's strategy redirects the challenging events to the sedimentations in her self-construct so that they now seemingly belong to her other-construct (in the form of the other who is 'Cynthia' and to the other who is 'a false and possessed version of Aretha'). Further, Aretha redirects the challenging events to the world-construct (in the form of the stupefying effects of the alcohol and cocaine upon her mind and body which, in turn, give further cre- dence to her claim regarding 'a false and possessed version of Aretha'). By so doing, Aretha is able to maintain the sedimented dispositional stance of her self-construct that permits her to continue declaring her exclusive heterosexual orientation.

But why, in keeping with my two examples, would Ernesto wish to evoke dis- missal or forgetfulness and why would Aretha, or anyone else for that matter, wish to create such florid and deceitful dissociative strategies? What would be so terri- ble about de-sedimenting one's sedimentations?

SEDIMENTATION AND DISSOCIATION AS STRATEGIES FOR THE MAINTENANCE OF THE WORLDVIEW

> Life does not proceed by the association and addition of elements, but by dissociation and division. Henri Bergson

As has been discussed, the reliance upon sedimentations either in the structure of the worldview as whole or in any of its primary sub-structures permits not only some degree of fixedness, certainty and security in the structure itself, but also pro- vides the very 'structuredness' of the structure. Without sedimentations, the main- tenance of the worldview as a structure expressing a relatively fixed narrative and extending through time and space would be untenable. While a worldview with few, if any, sedimentations might initially appear as being desirable or 'healthy', it should be apparent that it would be decidedly limited in its defining qualities and characteristics and, in turn, would likely provoke levels of unease and uncertainty that might well be experienced as intolerable either by ourselves or by those others with whom we relate.

If the worldview provides persons with the basis with which to construe meaning in their experience of being, worlding constantly challenges and expands the limits of such meaning and by so doing directs the person toward the experience of meaninglessness. For each of us, it becomes necessary to navigate some tolerable path between meaning and meaninglessness. The worldview is that path. Although the worldview is the structural reflection of worlding, because it *is* a structure, its reflection can only be incomplete, compromised. Equally, because it is a structure, the maintenance of the worldview *requires* some necessary degree of sedimentation and dissociation so that it can withstand the full impact of perpetual deconstructive challenges of worlding. The differences between world-views, therefore, rest upon how and in what way each addresses the competing demands of a) attempting to reflect worlding in as adequate a structural fashion as possible and b) attempting to maintain its very structure.

That worldview which places greater emphasis upon the first demand runs a constant risk of destabilising. That is to say, the more open and fluid the worldview becomes, and hence the fewer its sedimentations and dissociations, the more con-sonant it is with the lived experiences of worlding. But as a consequence of this greater consonance, it becomes less possible to maintain the structural coherence, boundaries and identity that define the self-, other- and world- constructs as well as the worldview as a whole. The worldview retains fewer and fewer stable mean-ings and veers increasingly toward the meaninglessness of worlding.

On the other hand, the alternate tendency adopted by a worldview that attempts to maintain its very structure through necessary sedimentation and the consequent dissociation of those lived experiences that challenge the stability and coherence of the currently maintained worldview is also problematic. This option imposes ever-increasing restrictions upon the structural openness and flexibility of the worldview. The meanings being maintained by the worldview are secure but rigid. They are not sufficiently open to the possibilities of shifts or even loss of meaning (meaninglessness) and, instead, must respond to these experiences as though they arose from an 'alien' agency beyond its control or responsibility.

In sum, either strategy extracts its price.

Instances of the inability to maintain a sedimented stance might well be expressed as 'I don't know who I am any more', 'No one is trustworthy', or 'The world is just too frighteningly confusing and chaotic for me to feel able to relate to it.' Instances of particularly rigid and over-generalised sedimentations in the world-view, on the other hand, might be expressed in phrases like 'I feel so empty or dead inside', or 'Others are just robots going through the motions', or 'Cinemas have become such dens of depravity that they are to be avoided at all costs.'

While neither option emerges as entirely ideal or preferable, nevertheless it does appear to be the case that our more typical chosen stance relies upon the strategy of dissociation. Why should this be so? Recall that the first key principle of existential phenomenology posits an inevitable relatedness or inter-relational grounding to, and between, all lived experiences of worlding. If so, following this principle it can be surmised that the exposure of any particular sedimentation to a de-sedimenting challenge opens the *whole* of the structured worldview to that challenge. Further, in keeping with the conclusions of the second principle of uncertainty, we cannot know in advance just in what ways or to what extent the destabilising impact that the de-sedimentation of any particular stance will have upon the whole structured worldview. For instance, what might initially appear to be a relatively minor de-sedimentation in one construct may have vast and unpredictable consequences and repercussions upon any of the remaining constructs or upon the worldview as whole. Finally, the third principle of existential anxiety alerts us to the human tendency to experience as positive and life-affirming only those aspects of anxiety that suggest the possibility of a novel circumstance that can be accepted and 'owned' by the worldview. But if the effects of the de-sedimenting of any stance cannot be predicted before they occur, then what is required is a stance of acceptance and 'ownership' toward such effects *prior to*, and without secure knowledge of, their impact and consequences upon the structured worldview. This uncommon stance must therefore be one that is receptive to the anxiety being provoked. Considered from the perspective of the three principles, the more common, if seemingly less palatable, preference for dissociation becomes much more understandable.

In summary, whatever the worldview adopted, whatever the degree of its openness or rigidity, it imposes a necessary, structure-bound mode of experience upon worlding and, in doing so, essentialises existence. A necessary dissonance between the two therefore emerges simply through this act of construing process-like experiencing as a structure. Further, the worldview's ability to define and maintain its structure, as well as the sub-structures that are the primary constructs relating to self, others, the world and the relations adopted between them, must be selective in its determining of their definitional, meaning-based boundaries. This selectivity, of necessity, further limits and constricts the structurally 'owned' possibilities of the lived experience of worlding.

In this sense, the worldview can, in itself, be understood as being the most basic and profound attempted denial of the principles of relatedness, uncertainty and existential anxiety. The worldview reveals the *losses incurred* by the structuring of worlding which each of us finds necessary to make. Readers may now understand the insistence running throughout existential-phenomenological literature of the human tendency toward *inauthenticity* (Heidegger, 1962), or *bad faith* (Sartre, 1991) or *I–It* relations (Buber, 1970), and the like. What the discussion on the worldview reveals is that the various expressions of 'fallen-ness' (or existing in ways that are 'less than' that which is possible for us to be) occur simply through the act of construing structure upon that which is process-like. Those readers who are students of the teachings of The Buddha as interpreted by various schools of Buddhism may find interesting resonances with this conclusion (Siderits, 2003).

TIME

Each moment in time calls all the others to witness. Maurice Merleau-Ponty

How we relate to time, our dialogue with it, reveals our worldview from a temporal perspective. We are beings whose existence is 'captured' as essence *in* time and yet, just as significantly, it can also be said that time is *in* our being.

For Husserl, time was best expressed as *erlebnis*, which is to say 'the flowing process of lived experience' (Cohn, 2002). This view suggests that time, in terms of its divisions into hours, minutes, days, years and so forth, as well as its demarcations of past, present and future, does not exist independently and 'outside' of being. Rather, such distinctions as are made of time can be seen to be critical components emerging from, and definitionally necessary to, the maintenance of a worldview structure.

Following Heidegger, what is being proposed is that at the process-like lived experience of worlding the experience of time cannot be conceived of as linear and unidirectional (that is to say, following a sequence that can only be from past to present to future). Rather, as the existential psychotherapist, Susanna Rennie, has recently proposed, time-as-process calls forth images of 'unfolding and enfolding, changing, moving, flowing, constantly between past present and future. So time stops being an independent time line, a series of nows between birth and death, but is an unfolding process of logos, a within-time-ness' (Rennie, 2006: 337). These ideas suggest a temporal view being taken by existential phenomenology which acknowledges a continuous inter-weaving of past–present–future. It is only when worlding is essentialised as the worldview that time takes on those structural qualities through which it is most commonly expressed and understood.

Though it might at first appear – as so much else in existential phenomenology – to be a somewhat complex and alien concept, a consideration of the argument being proposed from the temporal standpoint of *the past* should both highlight and clarify this view on time.

The Past

On beginning to project a different future, I come to have a different past. Betty Cannon

As I have discussed elsewhere at greater length (Spinelli, 1994) many Western assumptions surrounding the past, particularly as understood and applied in psychotherapy, are deeply challenged by existential phenomenology. For instance, as well as psychotherapists themselves, many clients hold to a linearly causal, unidirectional view of the past and, through this view assume the task of the therapist to be that of uncovering the issues and influences of their past upon their current lives so that the conflicts and concerns that have arisen from, or which have been aggravated by, the past can be at least partially resolved.

While Sigmund Freud is perhaps most closely associated with the above view and, indeed, is assumed by many to be its originator within the arena of psychotherapy, it emerges that Freud actually maintained a far more complex view of the interaction between causality and the past. Irvin Yalom highlights this alternative perspective and proposes a vastly different reading of Freud's conclusions. According to Yalom, Freud suggests that an 'analyst who is not successful in helping the patient to recollect the past should … nonetheless give the patient a construction of the past as the analyst sees it. Freud believed that this construction would offer the same therapeutic benefit as would actual recollection of past material' (Yalom, 1980: 347).

Viewed from this perspective, what Freud is proposing is that whether the constructed past event is or is not historically 'real' or accurate matters far less than the process of constructing a reliable past. For, through construction the client is able to forge meaningful links with *a* hypothetical past. This revolutionary stance opens the way toward an understanding of the past-as-recalled as being essentially interpretative rather than historically fixed or real. The past, seen in this light, becomes a 'plastic' or flexible concept open to re-evaluation and re-creation dependent upon the current dispositional attitude and behaviour of the individual who experiences it. Viewed from the perspective of the worldview, Freud's strategy permits the appearance of a past that is either better able to maintain a previously weakened and fragmented worldview or which permits the re-construction of a more easily maintained or stronger worldview.

Further, just as the remembered past is 'plastic' in its meaning and significance, so, too, is it the case that the remembered past is always the product of a *selective* structure. Clearly, the remembered past makes up a minute percentage of the totality of sensory-derived events that our brain has perceived over the course of our lives. In addition, it is also evident that what we attend to or what stands out for us as being relevant, meaningful or significant within any memory of a past event is itself a highly limited selection of all the variables and constituents contained within that remembered event. Thus, taking all of the above into consideration, we are left with the conclusion that the remembered past – even at the level of its content alone – is a 'plastic', selective (and, hence, incomplete) interpretation of the totality of any lived past event.

What then does this alternative understanding of the remembered past propose? Partly in agreement with Freud's conclusion, existential phenomenology argues that *the past exists in the present.* Specifically, what is being suggested is that *the remembered past exposes, reflects and validates the current worldview.* If the worldview I hold contains the sedimented certainty that 'I am always honest' or that 'No one can cook gnocchi as well as my mother did' or that 'Geology does not interest me, but astronomy does', how do I 'know' that I *do* actually hold these views other than via some validating recourse to my remembered past? Considered in this way, it is apparent that the remembered past is so *relationally* tied to the present (via the worldview), that it is more accurate to speak of 'the-past-as-currently-lived' than of the past in itself.

On further consideration, this inter-relation of past and present must also take into account the role and impact of the *projected future.* Just as the present worldview is validated via the remembered past, so too is the present worldview shaped and defined by those assumptions, aspirations, goals, purposes and wishes that are its directed future. Thus, it is far more adequate to see the past as 'the-past-as-currently-lived-and-future-directed' than to conceive of the past as a fixed and unchanging event-laden moment in time.

As experiential 'evidence' for this contention consider what occurs when some component of the worldview is altered. For instance, my contention that 'I am always polite' is so challenged by the impact of actual lived experience that it de-sediments this assertion within the self-construct to the point where the worldview becomes 'I am usually, but not always, polite.' At this point, a surprising (if thera-peutically common) phenomenon occurs: I begin to remember seemingly forgot-ten or suppressed past instances of prior impoliteness. Why does this happen? While many explanations are available, existential phenomenology suggests that the new defining conditions within the worldview require validation so that its truthfulness will hold and buttress – or comply more adequately with – the chal-lenges of lived experience. Similarly, let us suppose that within the newly re-constructed worldview of 'I am usually, but not always, honest' is the additional component 'But I will try to be, even though I know how difficult that is.' Now, those events from my remembered past that both confirm this contention as well as serve to assist (or resist) its achievement will become more prominent in my current memories. New, previously seemingly forgotten examples will arise or existing examples will take on novel or more powerful meaning and significance and in this way serve, and validate the worth of, my future-directed aspirations.

In sum, the past, as it is remembered, has little to do with causal or determin-ing factors that have in some way made, or influenced, one's worldview as it is today. Rather, the remembered past provides the current worldview with the means to maintain or validate itself not simply in terms of what and how it defines itself today, but also with regard to what focused direction is required of it so that it may be that which it aspires to become at some future point in time. As Cohn summarised: 'the past is still present in a present that anticipates the future'(Cohn, 1997: 26).

SPACE

For the wise man looks into space and he knows there is no limited dimension. Lao Tsu

As with time, existential phenomenology emphasises an inter-relational grounding in the human experience of *space*. As Cohn has observed, severe disturbances such as agoraphobia and claustrophobia were considered by Medard Boss to be 'obstructive impairments in the spatiality of people' (Boss, 1979: 216, as quoted in Cohn, 1997: 80) in that they reflected the unease of relatedness as experienced from the perspective of 'too much' or 'too little' space.

Ludwig Binswanger, a contemporary of Boss as well as a significant early expo-
nent of existential analysis, argued that people's inter-relationship with physical
space and environment revealed their fundamental stance, or dialogue, towards
their being-in-the-world (Binswanger, 1963). Our own experience of varied, often
intense, moods and feelings depending on the space – be it a building, a particular
room, a busy city street, an empty beach, and so forth – in which we find ourselves
makes plain how space can affect us. Just as significantly, how we, in turn, shape
and re-shape space can reveal and define a great deal of both our personal and
cultural values, biases and aspirations.

In a previous text, I provided an account drawn from my work as an existential
psychotherapist which sought to explore issues surrounding the existential dimensions of space (Spinelli, 1997). In brief, my client, Russell, had constructed a
closed, restrictive space whose physical barriers prevented entry by others without
his assistance. In the course of our therapeutic sessions, Russell's relations with
others began to undergo significant change and, in parallel, so too did his relationship to his physical environment such that he began to feel a growing unease
and dissatisfaction with various aspects of his physical space (the colour of his
walls, for instance, the 'fit' of his work-chair, his inability to quite literally 'stretch
out' in the room). Russell's subsequent actions, which focused upon the 'opening-
up' of his physical space, resonated closely with movement toward greater openness to others. Though he valued such movements and judged them to be important,
valid and beneficial, nevertheless he recognised how they also provoked experiences of confusion and bewilderment. His shift away from the creation and maintenance of a 'world-space' that permitted him to 'shut out', and thereby control,
the impact and presence of others forced him to begin to inhabit a new space
within which some of that power had had to be relinquished. As well as regain-
ing human contact and relationship, Russell was also forced to embrace ever
greater degrees of uncertainty and risk. Indeed, over time, he came to dislike,
even loathe, his world-space. It provoked a queasiness that he expressed as an
insistent skin irritation. In the end, he declared that the space no longer suited
him, was not his any more and that he could not imagine who it might be who
would appreciate it.

Rather than view Russell's relationship to his 'world-space' as being either symbolic or some sort of displaced expression of his tensions with others, existential
phenomenology would view it *in its own right* as a particular focus point from
which his worldview revealed and expressed itself. Indeed, Russell's shift in his
relatedness to spatiality paralleled the wider shift in his worldview to the extent
that his rejection of that space, and re-shaping of a new one, reflected his aban-
donment and re-structuring of his worldview.

In general, our relation to space, viewed from an existential-phenomenological
perspective, argues that while existence must always be located and disclosed 'in
space', nonetheless that space is neither static nor separate; its dimensions and
shape are not merely physical but also, and always, existential.

CHOICE, FREEDOM AND RESPONSIBILITY

You are not the Do-er. The Buddha

The existential-phenomenological idea of *choice* has often been understood to suggest an open-ended or unlimited ability to choose how and what 'to be' or 'to do'. Similarly, with regard to *freedom* it is often assumed that existential phenomenology emphasises its subjective possibilities and champions all attempts at individual freedom. Likewise, when considering *responsibility*, the view with which existential phenomenology is commonly associated proposes that responsibility can be divided between, and separated by, boundaries which demarcate and segregate 'my' responsibilities from 'your' (or 'others'') responsibilities. As should hopefully be apparent to readers by now, each one of these conclusions both contradicts and is contradicted by existential phenomenology's key principles of relatedness, uncertainty and existential anxiety.

Viewed from the perspective of these three principles, choice, freedom and responsibility are always *situated within existential 'givens'* that express themselves both in their ontological and ontic modalities. From an ontological perspective, the 'given' of relatedness, for example, places any notions of freedom, choice and responsibility within an inter-relational matrix that precedes whatever subjective and isolationist 'I' might arise and express itself with regard to these concepts. From the ontic perspective of a specific worldview, the structural expression of these existential 'givens' (and, in particular, the 'given' of anxiety) will also locate the experience of choice, freedom and responsibility within an inevitable relational matrix, regardless of the degree to which the specific dispositional stances maintaining that particular worldview might hold a non-relational, subjectivist bias.

Choice

Life is the sum of all your choices. Albert Camus

Existential phenomenology, contrary to popular assumptions, insists that human beings are not *always* free to choose. There exist conditions of being where no choice presents itself. Primary among these is our *thrownness*. None of us had a choice in coming into existence. Rather, each of us was 'thrown into' being. Similarly, none of us will have any choice in the fact that we will be, at some certain, if indeterminate, point in time, 'thrown out' of existence, in that we will cease to be as a human being. Furthermore, we are all also 'thrown' into a particular body, a particular time, a particular culture, a particular set of prevailing attitudes and mores, stances and opinions. These, too, are beyond choice as are the infinity of stimuli or events 'thrown up' by the world to which we must all respond. Thus, such choices as may exist are always *situated* in a set of 'thrown' conditions, whose presence can neither be chosen nor truly controlled. As Cohn expresses it:

'Our thrownness is the unchosen basis on which our freedom to make choices rests' (Cohn, 2002: 96).

In proposing that choice arises only within a situated inter-relational context, what is being asserted is that our choices cannot be at the stimulus or *event-level* (that is to say, choices about *what* occurs or *when* it will occur), but rather at the *interpretative* level (how we respond to events, what meanings we bestow upon them). Our choices reflect how we engage with the contextual situation in which we find ourselves (Cohn, 1997; May, 1981). I do not choose an event in the sense that I have the ability to control or determine the plethora of stimuli that impinge upon me at any and every moment throughout my life. However, the significance and meaning I give to these stimuli, the interpretation I might make of any given event, the attitude I take toward it, the values with which I invest it, the impact upon my life that I declare it to have, ultimately, *the way I am in relation with the event*, is a matter of my choice.

Even then, however, the extent of flexibility and range of interpretations we might be able to generate in such engagement is dependent upon a situated inter-relational temporal context – that is to say, when, where and how each of us 'is' within such contextual factors as time, culture and biology. Interpretative choice is not always, nor perhaps so often as we might suppose, at a level where differing meaning options are available. The given conditions of my body, my time, my culture may well impose a single option to which to ascribe meaning. In such instances, choice rests upon the choice of 'meaning A' or . . . 'meaning A'. But how can this be claimed to be choice?

Consider the following example: Jessica finds the idea of abortion to be morally repugnant. Unfortunately, she finds her self pregnant as a result of a brief fling with a man whom she has subsequently decided would not make either a good father or partner. While *in theory* Jessica might be able to choose between continuing with her pregnancy or terminating it, from the sedimented standpoint adopted by Jessica, there is a single-option choice available to her. Jessica could choose this single option. But, she could also choose what the existential philosopher Paul Tillich termed as a 'what if' option (Tillich, 1980). In Jessica's case, this 'what if' choice might be one that placed the power of choice in someone else's control, or that placed the power of choice under the control of a separate and 'possessed' Jessica, or that imbued the pregnancy with a 'special' significance, or that simply denied the pregnancy. All of these possibilities permit the appearance of a seemingly genuine alternative to Jessica's one-option choice. But, equally, they are 'false' choices in that each requires a denial either at the level of Jessica's *self-structure* (i.e., if Jessica was someone other than who she is, then other choices would be there for her) or at the event-level (i.e., if the circumstances under which the choice arose had been different, then Jessica would be facing different circumstances within which to make her choices). In general, faced with a single-option choice we can choose it, or alternatively, and perhaps more likely, we can convince our selves of the possibility of choosing a non-existent, but preferable, alternative. Considered in this way, single-option choices still require choice at its starkest level: Do I choose that which is there for me to choose? Or do I choose a non-existent alternative that is not there for me to choose but which I will choose nonetheless 'as if' it were there? Once again, it is my view that the investigation of the impact and consequences of making 'false choices' provides psychotherapy with one of its major focus points.

This view, I believe, presents the issue of choice within the actuality of lived existence. Of course, we can always play 'what if' mind games with choice, supposing that a theoretical alternative possibility was there or that we 'are always at liberty to make a change or abandon whatever lifestyle we have adopted' (van Deurzen & Arnold-Baker, 2005: 7). But such perspectives, in my view, fail to take into account the relational context within which choice is possible. Not *all* choices are available at *all* times. Rather, genuine choice can only be that which is there as 'part of the basis of our total present situation' (Cohn, 2002: 96).

Further, when the claim is made that 'I' choose X, what is being suggested is the implicit notion of a discrete 'I', whose existence is separate from that of all other 'I's, and whose choices reside or are experienced somewhere *within* the confines of its 'I-ness'. The pivotal principle of relatedness espoused by existential phenomenology challenges this perspective. Instead, it questions: 'Who *is* the 'I' who chooses?' There exists, at present, no simple or obvious answer to this question. Nonetheless, if considered from the standpoint of the worldview, any adequate answer is forced to contextualise the choosing 'I' within the self-, other- and world-constructs. In doing so, the 'I' who chooses can no longer deny either the relational grounding from which personal choice emerges or the relational consequences of personal choice.

From the standpoint of existential phenomenology, choice can no longer be exclusively viewed as an assertion of, or by, any distinct and separate individual, nor an act whose direction lies in causal events, nor an experience that reveals itself as being solely, or even primarily, pleasant or desirable. Indeed, the attempt to abdicate from, or deny, the choice before it may provide for a worldview a desired and more attractive reduction of tension. Considered in this way, Sartre's unsettling association of choice with the experience of condemnation might not be so open to dismissal (Sartre, 1991).

Freedom

> In willing freedom we discover it depends entirely on the freedom of others and that the freedom of others depends on ours . . . . I can take my freedom as a goal only if I take the freedom of others as a goal as well. Jean-Paul Sartre

Freedom and choice are often linked together conceptually. We speak of 'the freedom to choose' or we enjoin someone to 'choose freely'.

As with the brief discussion on choice from an existential-phenomenological standpoint, the sort of freedom to which the above statements refer must be *situated* within 'thrownness'. Freedom at the structural level of the worldview is inextricably inter-relationally bound to the necessity of 'thrownness'. Such freedom is not at the event-level but rather at the interpretative level. Paradoxically, the experience of freedom becomes most apparent when our stance to 'what is there' is to embrace it, accept it, 'say yes' to it, rather than adopt a stance that pretends and deludes itself into believing that 'something *else* is there for me'. This understanding of freedom has nothing to do with any passive or un-reflected acceptance of, or submission to, that which might be interpreted as wrong or undesirable or unjust. Rather, it situates the possibilities of freedom *within* those conditions that are there. Consider, for example, the unforgettable image of freedom revealed in that lone and anonymous Chinese student's placing him self directly in front of the tanks that rumbled into Tienanmen Square in 1989. Such a stance was not about any future *possibility* or gaining of freedom, it *was* freedom being lived. According to Heidegger, 'freedom . . . is only the choice of *one* possibility – that is, in tolerating one's not having chosen the others and one's not being able to choose them' (Heidegger, 1962: 331).

Equally, freedom for existential phenomenology is not at any individual subjective level but at an inter-relational level. What touched and remains with those of us who viewed that face-off between the lone student and the tanks was not a detached (if respectful and admiring) awareness of his lived freedom, but a connected experience of, and with, freedom that all could experience regardless of the plethora of differences in our life events both before and subsequent to that moment. This is not to remove the power and impact of that student's singular choice. How the student experienced freedom, and the unique invocation of freedom contained in his act is being neither minimised nor disputed. But that those who witnessed it were drawn to the act, and through it experienced their own freedom, however momentary, must also be recognised. To quote Merleau-Ponty: 'One is not free alone' (1962: 142).

But there remains another aspect to this sense of freedom that must be acknowledged. The freedom emergent in such instances as might befall any one of us reveals an embracing, no matter how brief or fleeting, of the three principles of relatedness, uncertainty and anxiety. However, *the consequence of such a completely open stance to existence is the breakdown of the worldview itself.* No meaning or security or identity as expressed within the structured confines of the worldview remains tenable. With freedom, all is flux, in and of the moment. This understanding permits the recognition that freedom is not necessarily 'good' or 'benevolent'. Those who murder wantonly, for its own sake, have also expressed views suggesting experiences of near-total freedom – as might those who witness or read about such acts. What may be so disturbingly attractive about the question of evil, for instance, may well be its connection to unbounded freedom (May, 1990; Spinelli, 2001).

This alternative view of freedom reveals its more disturbing qualities – and, once again, may assist us in comprehending the divided stance many take toward its possibilities.

Responsibility

> And when we say that man is responsible for himself, we do not mean that he is responsible only for his own individuality, but that he is responsible for all men. Jean-Paul Sartre

Responsibility, from an existential-phenomenological perspective can be understood as 'the ability to respond'. But respond to what? Obviously many differing views addressing this question exist, just as all have their philosophical, ethical, cultural, legal and personal implications. The existential-phenomenological stance emphasises the ability to respond to being itself. From Heidegger's perspective, the existence of being, as opposed to non-being, was such an unexpected and fragile event that being requires constant care and vigilance. It remains the task of humankind to 'shepherd' being.

As human beings we are responsible not merely to self, our family or others, or our faith or the achievement of 'the good life'. All of these responsibilities are contained in, but also distort, that for which we are responsible – being itself. But how can one act responsibly toward being itself? While we may be unable to quite grasp the answer to such a vast question, nonetheless, we can 'feel' our way toward it. Consider, for example, the following passage from Henning Mankell's *The Fifth Woman*:

> When I was growing up, Sweden was still a country where people darned their socks. I even learned how to do it in school myself. Then suddenly one day it was over. Socks with holes in them were thrown out. No one bothered to repair them. The whole society changed. 'Wear it out and toss it' was the only rule that applied. As long as it was just a matter of our socks, the change didn't make much difference. But then it started to spread, until finally it became a kind of invisible moral code. I think it changed our view of right and wrong, of what you were allowed to do to other people and what you weren't. More and more people, especially young people like you, feel unwelcome in their own country. How do they react? With aggression and contempt. The most frightening thing is that I think we're only at the beginning of something that's going to get a lot worse. A generation is growing up right now, the children who are younger than you, who are going to react with even greater violence. And they have absolutely no memory of a time when we darned our socks. When we didn't throw everything away, whether it was our woollen socks or human beings. (Mankell, 2002: 224)

While the passage expresses nothing directly about responsibility in an existential-phenomenological sense, at the same time it draws us toward an awareness that we permit ourselves to be and live with less than that of which we know being is capable. This view of responsibility serves to provide a *direction* to the choices available and reminds us that no expression of freedom can exclude responsibility to being in all its conditions and manifestations. This view also places responsibility within a time-frame that extends beyond the time-boundaries of any one specific existence and widens its focus into a future beyond that life's ending. Responsibility, in this existential-phenomenological sense, carries strong resonances with the ancient Hebrew notion of *Hochma* – the capacity to see and feel and then to act as if not the present but rather the future depended on us.

As might by now have been ascertained, the common thread running throughout existential phenomenology's perspective on choice, freedom and responsibility is the rejection of a persistent tendency within Western thought to isolate and contain such notions *within* some separate being whose individual presence asserts a particular and time-bound 'right to freedom' which is expressed through ever-increasing multiple choice. Instead, existential phenomenology emphasises the inter-relational and interpretative dimensions of choice, freedom and responsibility. In doing so, it reminds us of the commitment implicit in these terms and proposes that the direction of that commitment is towards being itself.

Choice, Freedom and Responsibility: the Issue of Authenticity

Only a free being can be unfree. Martin Heidegger

Such views regarding choice, freedom and responsibility also serve to clarify a persistent misunderstanding (or misuse) of the terms *authenticity* and *inauthenticity*. Unfortunately, the terms themselves are somewhat 'loaded' in that they appear to suggest appropriate and inappropriate or superior and inferior ways to be and, as well, imply a moral judgement. For many, matters of choice, freedom and responsibility would seem to be allied only to authenticity while inauthenticity suggests the loss or abdication of these possibilities. Stated simply, this is not the case.

Heidegger intended authenticity to refer to the opening-up to, or ownership of, that which presents itself to us (Cohn, 2002). Authenticity involves and implicates each being in existence. In contrast, inauthenticity is a way of engaging with existence that allows a distance or detachment from any sense of 'owned' involvement with what presents itself to a being's experience. Inauthenticity is a detached way of being. Considered from this perspective, it becomes possible to configure notions of choice, freedom and responsibility within both authentic and inauthentic modes of being. A critical difference, I believe, lies in whether the choices made and the freedom and responsibility that are sought or experienced are or are not acknowledged by the experiencing being as arising from, and contextualised within, the key conditions of relatedness, uncertainty and anxiety. Authenticity can be seen as an expression of choice, freedom and responsibility as situated within an indivisible inter-relational grounding. Inauthenticity expresses freedom, choice and responsibility as containable within an isolated being and subject to that being's dispositional stances as might be expressed in terms of moods, whims, fears and desires.

At an inauthentic level, the person's choice, freedom and responsibility is asserted as though the relational basis for such did not exist – 'as if' these were entirely in the person's control alone or, alternatively, 'as if' they were in the control of agents and forces alien to the person (what Heidegger refers to as 'the they' or what Kierkegaard labels 'the crowd' (Cooper, 2003)) Viewed from Buber's perspective, at this inauthentic level, choice, freedom and responsibility are being considered and enacted at an 'I–It' level. In contrast, an authentic stance will not permit the person to act within these 'as if' separate divides. Instead, that which is 'my' choice, 'my' freedom and 'my' responsibility requires consideration not only at the 'I' level but also, and equally, at the level of 'Thou'.

A Summary of Existential Psychotherapy's Philosophical Foundations

> Man is always something more than what he knows of himself. He is not what he is simply once and for all, but is a process. Karl Jaspers

In order to begin to address the question of existential psychotherapy in practice, it has been necessary to set out a number of key philosophical ideas drawn from existential phenomenology. While the issues that have been discussed do not begin to address the richness and diversity of themes that the study of this philosophical system provides, it remains my hope that readers will at least have become sufficiently acquainted with its major concerns so that their influence upon existential psychotherapy will be discerned with relative ease.

The overriding theme throughout this discussion is perhaps best summarised by Ronald Valle and Mark King: 'From an existential perspective, human existence reveals the total, indissoluble unity or interrelationship of the individual and his or her world. . . . In the truest sense, the person is viewed as having no existence apart from the world and the world as having no existence apart from persons . . .' (Valle and King, 1978: 7).

This foundational assumption of relatedness underpins all of the considerations given by existential phenomenology to the question of existence. Some of these considerations were subsequently reformulated in order that they might be addressed from a psychological perspective (Ihde, 1986a, 1986b; Spinelli, 2005). As a result, they entered the arena of applied psychology – whether in terms of research methodology (Crotty, 1996; Spinelli, 2006), or in psychotherapy (Cohn, 1997, 2002; Spinelli, 1997; van Deurzen-Smith, 1988; Yalom, 1980). I will now provide a brief overview of the most pertinent of these as they contribute to a theoretical basis to practising existential psychotherapy.

3

General Theoretical Assumptions Underpinning Existential Psychotherapy

HISTORICAL BACKGROUND

It is the task of existential phenomenology to articulate what the other's 'world' is and his way of being in it. R.D. Laing

As Mick Cooper has argued in his already influential text *Existential Therapies* (Cooper, 2003), no single form or interpretation of existential-phenomenological ideas has emerged as the sole or authoritative representative of existential psychotherapy. In many ways, the psychiatric work and philosophical ideas of Karl Jaspers can be considered to be among the earliest direct attempts to apply existential phenomenology to psychotherapy (Jaspers, 1963; Misiak and Sexton, 1973). As well as being deeply influenced by Martin Heidegger's philosophy, Jaspers maintained an ongoing correspondence with him. Nonetheless, in spite of (or perhaps due to) the range and originality of ideas to be found throughout Jaspers' work, the origins of a designated psychotherapeutic approach or system of ideas derived from existential phenomenology are commonly linked with the contributions of three other internationally renowned psychiatrists. Ludwig Binswanger's existential analysis (Binswanger, 1963), Medard Boss's daseinsanalysis (Boss, 1963) and Viktor Frankl's logotherapy (Frankl, 1988) can, and do, all lay claim to pioneering an 'existential' basis to psychotherapy (Valle and King, 1978). While a sound case can be made for all three, both Binswanger's and Boss's systems have the added 'authority' of Heidegger's direct involvement, even if such was somewhat limited in Binswanger's case. In addition, Frankl's system appears to have been developed outside the broad influence of existential phenomenology. While this is not to criticise it, or to suggest that this system has little to say of any existential worth, it must be noted that it is not always so evident just what its relation to other existential systems might be. Nonetheless, I must acknowledge a significant exception to this conclusion which is made apparent through the ongoing theoretical papers emerging from the International Society for Logotherapy and Existential Analysis based in Vienna (Längle, 2005). Through these, a much more obvious and creative resonance with the three inherent principles discussed in the previous chapters emerges and opens the opportunity for future dialogue.

Various forms of existential psychotherapy derived from either Binswanger, Boss or Frankl continue to retain adherents and provide formal training programmes throughout the world. More recently, North American and British expressions of existential psychotherapy have been developed and have, to some degree, re-energised both the practice of, and interest in, this unique approach. Though still deeply indebted to the philosophical underpinnings of existential phenomenology, these new 'American' and 'British' Schools are also substantially influenced by later developments in philosophy such as structuralist and 'post-modern' influences, contemporary theory and research in academic and applied psychology, and relational, social-constructionist and narrative theories that have arisen within other contemporary psychotherapeutic models and systems such as psycho-analysis and humanistic psychotherapy. The 'American School' is closely identified with the work of, among others, Rollo May (1969, 1981, 1983), Irvin Yalom (1980, 1989, 2001) and James Bugenthal (1981, 1987). R.D. Laing (1960, 1967), Emmy van Deurzen (-Smith) (1988, 1997), Hans W. Cohn (1997, 2002), Freddie and Alison Strasser (1997) as well as the present author (Spinelli, 1994, 1997, 2001, 2005) are all regarded as major contributors to the development of a 'British School' of existential psychotherapy (Cooper, 2003).

EXISTENTIAL PSYCHOTHERAPY'S CRITIQUE OF GENERAL PSYCHOTHERAPY

We all know how little skill avails, how ineffective are its artifices, in filling the lack of true artistic motivation. Mark Rothko

It is my view that in order to begin to understand the central concerns of existential psychotherapy it is essential to return once again to the three underlying principles of existential phenomenology. By doing so, it becomes apparent that a recurring critique of the dominant assumptions of contemporary Western psychotherapy runs throughout the approach and, to a certain extent, defines it. Equally, this critical attitude and its philosophical roots permit existential psychotherapy to propose a distinctively different set of principles that act as challenges to dominant assumptions regarding not only the practice of psychotherapy but also its meaning possibilities.

In an age and a culture that so values 'the expert', it is hardly surprising that when we encounter difficulties that have to do with the numerous discontents of existence, more and more people seek out *experts in living*. Perhaps it has always been so. Every culture has its wise men and women, its priests and shamans, its holy and enlightened beings who might point out 'the way' for us when it seems as though we are lost or in need of enlightenment. In contemporary Western culture, although the influence of religion has never fully died (and, in some cases, such as in what has become known as 'Middle America', continues to retain a significant socio-political influence), some part of this 'expertise' has been assumed by psychotherapists, counsellors and psychologists.

But just what is the expertise being provided?

Overall, our culture's answer, which, not surprisingly, is shared by most who label themselves as members of these allied professions, centres on issues of specialist techniques, skills and know-how. Unfortunately, as has been debated and demonstrated all too often by now, it seems evident that what specific and critical factors have been identified by experts as the necessary variables leading to a beneficial therapeutic impact upon the lives of clients tend to remain empirically unproven (Ablon and Jones, 2002; Luborsky et al., 1999, 2002; Messer and Wampold, 2002; Piper, 2004).

This is not to suggest that therapeutic interventions have no value. On the contrary, reliable evidence indicates that at both outcome and process levels therapeutic interventions are substantially effective and are more often beneficial than disruptive (Howard et al., 1994, 1996; Spiegel, 1999). Clients' reported experiential accounts and evaluations of psychotherapy suggest similar conclusions (Sherwood, 2001). However, just what the specific factors might be that provoke this overall positive evidence remain contradictory and inconclusive. Indeed, currently there exists a huge divide between what psychotherapists assume to be important and what clients report as having been of significance to them. In brief, while psychotherapists emphasise techniques and skills – the specific model-led *doing factors* of psychotherapy – clients instead place the greatest significance upon their experience of being in a therapeutic relationship and, more broadly, upon the *being qualities* that they experience as having been in some way generated within the encounter. (Anderson and Goolishian, 1992; Howe, 1993; Sherwood, 2001).

As was discussed in Chapters 1 and 2, it can be seen that the stance taken by psychotherapists is not merely an example of obstinacy. Rather, it reveals something far more significant that taps into a particular and dominant set of philosophical principles to which most psychotherapists subscribe, even if they remain unaware of their doing so. Recent and ongoing work by Alvin Mahrer has been significant in exposing to critical examination many of these assumptions (Mahrer, 2000, 2004, 2006). Mahrer, in common with the view taken in this present text, has argued that just about 'every field of study has its basic propositions, its fundamental starting points' (Mahrer, 2000: 117) – which can be characterised as that field's *foundational beliefs.* With regard to psychotherapy, Mahrer proposes, it becomes apparent that 'the field is rife with foundational beliefs that are generally presumed, assumed, implied, taken for granted, and occasionally spelled out' (ibid.). Mahrer criticises psychotherapy for relying far too much on foundational beliefs that serve as 'pleasing ideas' (or what Kagan has referred to as 'seductive ideas') which can be exceedingly well-defended and immunised against critical analysis or outright attack simply by their being assumed to be correct by the majority of psychotherapists (Kagan, 2000; Mahrer, 2000). For example, although clients' emphases upon inter-relational factors have increasingly become of interest to psychotherapists, nonetheless the persistence of various foundational beliefs whose 'seductive ideas' permit psychotherapists to maintain their primary focus upon the doing skills they enact remains dominant within contemporary psychotherapeutic research and training.

A key (or 'deeply sedimented') foundational belief has emerged to which the overwhelming majority of psychotherapists, whether they ally themselves to seemingly vastly different and competing models such as psycho-analysis and cognitive-behaviour therapy, or claim no allegiance whatsoever to any one particular model and instead adopt eclectic or integrative approaches, nonetheless subscribe. This belief expresses a philosophically derived assumption that views the world, and the relations that exist within it, from a perspective that divides and isolates subject and object such that each object of focus may be named, studied, analysed, manipulated and altered by a subject who remains scientifically detached, from the enterprise.

This is not to say that the investigating subject claims to feel nothing whatever for the object of investigation or that no moral or ethical considerations and concerns arise for the subject. Contrary to the popular stereotype of the distant and aloof investigator who cares only for his or her project or for the results to be gained from it, the great majority of investigators who adopt this philosophical stance remain greatly concerned for the overall well-being of the focus object, not least when it is a living entity. Rather, what is pivotal is the assumption that the investigating subject brings particular skills and expertise to that investigation and that it is these very skills themselves, rather than something to do with the inter-relation between the unique being qualities of the investigating subject (i.e. the therapist) and the focus of investigation (i.e. the client), which generate the impact and effects of the investigation. The key assumption here is that anyone who is able to apply these skills appropriately would provoke the same, or at least highly similar, impacts and effects. The investigating subject, in this sense, is of relative insignificance and always replaceable by another. It is the particular way of *doing* the investigation that is assumed to be critical.

This view is highly appealing to our culture and runs rampantly throughout it. It may well be the source of the great success we have had in advancing ourselves in all manner of ways, not least technologically. But, as some have suggested, it may also be the basis of our culture's increasingly experienced malaise and, ultimately, may be a pivotal factor in its downfall. Heidegger, for example, taking his lead from the work of Søren Kierkegaard and Friedrich Nietzsche, railed against the 'technologisation' of human beings and the limitations upon human relations that these permitted as attacks against being itself (Heidegger, 1977). Nonetheless, the reliance upon a philosophical stance promoting a divided view of existence remains dominant within Western culture and continues to exert its influence in all areas of knowledge and investigation.

As was discussed in the previous chapters, existential phenomenology, in contrast, proposes a perspective which, via its foundational principle of relatedness, challenges this dominant view not so much by rejecting it, but rather by repositioning it as one possible expression or consequence of relatedness. In this way, rather than create yet another contrasting duality (i.e. relatedness vs. dividedness) which, among other things, would contradict the relatedness hypothesis, it is able to subvert the assumption of dividedness as a foundational principle of existence without dismissing its felt experiential qualities and implications. Further, as well as subvert, the existential-phenomenological alternative allows us to reformulate recurring gaps, inconsistencies and contradictions arising from analyses whose implicit philosophical foundations have relied upon assumptions of dividedness.

Likewise, the existential-phenomenological enterprise as considered within the arena of psychotherapy provokes a fundamental challenge not only, or even primarily, at the level of promoting alternative ways of *doing* psychotherapy. Far more radically, this enterprise formulates a fundamental challenge to psychotherapists' assumptions regarding what psychotherapy *is*. In adopting the distinction made between Natural Science research and Human Science research, existential psychotherapy raises issues and promotes human-centred investigations focused upon matters of *understanding* rather than being centrally concerned with issues of *explanation* (Hodges, 1952; Karlsson, 1993; Kvale, 1994).

When applied to psychotherapy, existential theory approaches human nature from the assumption that it is open-ended, and capable of an enormous range of experience (Cohn, 1997; van Deurzen-Smith, 1988). Such a view rejects the still dominant tendency in psychotherapy to categorise or 'typologise' clients, or which attempts to divide and reduce them in terms of various constituents or components. Instead, it aims to remain at a descriptive and open-ended level of analysis that simultaneously acknowledges both the uniqueness of each 'being-in-the-world' and the species-shared 'givens' of being human that set the boundaries for the possibilities of each client's own particular experience of existence.

In contrasting existential psychotherapy with other contemporary approaches, it is necessary to stress its *differences* since, arising from its philosophical foundations, these are significant. Whether accepted or not by psychotherapists from other approaches, a worthwhile consequence of investigating them is that they illuminate and force critical reflection upon one's currently chosen model or approach.

Placed in this context, existential-phenomenology argues that the very enterprise of psychotherapy is principally focused upon the experience of relatedness, uncertainty and anxiety within the confines of the therapeutic encounter. This focus, in turn, discloses the client's currently maintained worldview so as to iden- tify that worldview's resonances with and deviations from the client's ongoing experience of worlding.

This stance reveals an implicit critique of the dominant Natural Science models of psychotherapy which concentrate upon what therapists *do* (partly because these factors can be measured, taught and assessed, at least to some extent). It should be clear that the situation is not necessarily an either/or one; 'being' a therapist involves 'doing' psychotherapy. Nevertheless, the existential-phenomenological stance expresses the view that if alienated from the *'being qualities'* of the thera- pist, the doing of psychotherapy becomes 'technologised' to such an extent that it distorts the therapeutic relationship in serious ways (raising, among other issues, the question of unnecessary power imbalances weighed heavily in favour of the psychotherapist) which may well be deeply antagonistic to its fundamental aims and possibilities (Cohn, 1997; Spinelli, 1994, 2005). In short, what is being argued is that these should be placed within a perspective that emphasizes 'doing' as an extension of, and not a substitute for, the therapist's 'being' in the relation.

EXISTENTIAL THERAPY AS A FORM OF PHENOMENOLOGICAL RESEARCH

The phenomenological project continually resolves itself before our eyes, into a description – empirical despite itself – of actual experience and into an ontology of the unthought that automatically short-circuits the primacy of the 'I think'. Michel Foucault

It is a basic principle of Human Science research that investigative activity 'can- not be accomplished by observing the individual as a complex mechanism geared to respond to certain conditions in regular ways; rather we have to get inside the forms of life and the socially normative regularities in which the person's activity has taken shape. This requires . . . [a]n empathic and imaginative identification with the subject . . .' (Gillett, 1995: 112). As I have argued elsewhere, existential psychotherapy might best be understood as a direct expression of Human Science research in general and of phenomenological research (a specific modality of Human Science research) in particular (Spinelli, 1994; 2006). I would suggest that the following shared aspects validate this claim.

First, the primary task of phenomenological research is to illuminate the struc- tural make-up, or way of being, of any given experience in terms of both the spe- cific as well as the universal constituents implied through that particular (Crotty, 1996). From the perspective of existential psychotherapy, the primary focus of investigation is the client's experience of inter-relational being as expressed through the presenting worldview-derived issues, disturbances or conflicts being brought to therapy. In keeping with the aims of phenomenological research, how- ever, this particular client-focused inquiry also serves to disclose the universal aspects and issues of relatedness, uncertainty and anxiety.

Second, as an extension of the above, phenomenological research assumes an inevitable inter-relationship between the investigator and his or her focus of investigation. In keeping with this principle, existential psychotherapy *implicates* the presence of the psychotherapist in its inquiry and acknowledges the (currently) unpredictable impact of that presence upon the dispositional stances maintaining the primary *constructs* of the client's lived worldview (i.e. the self-, other- and world-constructs). In like fashion, it acknowledges the (currently) unpredictable impact of the client's presence upon the dispositional stances maintaining the primary constructs of the therapist's lived worldview.

Third, phenomenological research seeks out a method of investigation which neither denies experience, nor denigrates it, nor transforms it solely into operationally (pre-)defined behaviour. Indeed, the method being sought aims to remain as adequately as possible with the presenting experience as it is experienced, and seeks to sustain contact with the statements made regarding that experience as they are expressed. In like fashion, from the standpoint of existential psychotherapy all acts of listening, challenging and interpreting on the part of the psychotherapist attempt to remain within this broadly *descriptively focused* framework. Through this endeavour both phenomenological research and existential psychotherapy avoid taking a stance that demands the rejection of some descriptively derived data in favour of others because of competing, unique or mutually exclusive variants. In phenomenological research, even the most idiosyncratic data are duly considered without the need to reject their meaning possibilities. In similar fashion, existential psychotherapy acknowledges and attempts to 'hold' the often complex, contradictory competing and complementary dispositional stances that are maintained by the client's worldview as a whole or any of its primary constructs.

Fourth, phenomenological research rejects the common notion of causality in its unidirectional, linear form. The focus of investigation is not therefore studied or understood in a manner that requires explanations derived from events or circumstances that are perceived to be unidirectional from some point in the past to the present circumstances, nor is there any assumption that a specified earlier event *caused* the latter to occur in a simple, linear. This same stance is adopted by existential psychotherapy.

Fifth, the enterprise of phenomenological research is foundationally collaborative. Researchers and the participants in their research (typically labelled *co-researchers*) are partners in the given enterprise whose meanings and purposes are openly revealed and discussed without any intent to deceive, misrepresent or obscure all or part of the process. Existential psychotherapy, too, attempts a collaborative and respectful dialogue whose concerns centre upon the investigation of the lived worldview of the client as it presents itself in the immediacy of the psychotherapeutic encounter rather than from any specific skills or learned programme of behaviours initiated by the psychotherapist.

Taken together, the above points highlight significant inter-related aims and attitudes between phenomenological research and existential psychotherapy. In brief, existential psychotherapy can be considered from a general standpoint as a particular form of descriptive investigation centred upon the key existential themes of relatedness, uncertainty and anxiety. Viewed in this way, it is hardly surprising that existential psychotherapy's stance toward the therapeutic relationship *itself* becomes a pivotal aspect of the therapeutic process.

THE THERAPEUTIC RELATIONSHIP

> I wanted to help people. Helpfulness was like a religion with a lot of us in those days. It's only in the last few years . . . that I've started to see around it. I see that helping other people can be an evasion of oneself, and the source of a good deal of smug self-satisfaction. Ross Macdonald

Perhaps more explicitly than any other current model or approach to psychotherapy, existential psychotherapy bestows an undisputed centrality upon the relationship between therapist and client. It is through this relationship *itself* that the client's issues are disclosed or 'brought forth' for examination. Broadly speaking, the therapeutic encounter is seen to be the 'microcosm' through which the 'macrocosm' of the client's stance toward the possibilities and limitations of inter-relational being in the world is both explored and expressed (Cohn, 1997; Spinelli, 1997, 2001; Strasser and Strasser, 1997).

Such a means of exploration permits an *experiential immediacy* to all discourse regarding the client's worldview. The way the client 'is' in the therapeutic relationship reveals his or her wider stance concerning the possibilities and limitations of existence. It can therefore be seen that the focus of the therapeutic relationship as understood by existential psychotherapy is always on *the-client-as-relationally-present*. It is via this first, and crucial, step of 'staying with' and 'attuning oneself to' the client's current worldview – no matter how debilitating, restrictive, limiting and irrational it may appear to be to the therapist (if not all others in the client's world, as well as the client him or her self) – that the existential psychotherapist, *simply via this client-attuned presence,* begins to challenge profoundly the client's various expectations, assumptions and concerns.

The Existential Psychotherapist's Presence

> The living moment is everything. D.H. Lawrence

The existential psychotherapist is *the present other* to the client. As this other, the therapist acts as both the representative of all others in the client's wider world relations and, just as importantly, is also the other who challenges the client's self-, other- and world-constructs simply by the inter-relational impact of his or her presence. In this way, the existential psychotherapist's related presence is in the service of an investigative focus upon the client's currently lived worldview rather than, as other systems might suggest, a hindrance to its illumination. For example, the present therapist-as-other may both clarify and challenge any number of the client's dispositional stances about how others are, how others expect the client to be, and how the client expects others to be with him or her.

On reflection, it becomes evident that any hope of achieving this enterprise requires initially the therapist's openness to, and acceptance of, the client's currently presenting worldview. To adopt any other stance which emphasises a directive or manipulative change in the client's way of being, no matter how benevolent or concerned to ameliorate the client's distress, will only serve to allow the client to continue to avoid reflecting upon, and perhaps eventually owning, his or her worldview *as it is* rather than as he or she might want or prefer it to be.

The Existential Psychotherapist's Acceptance

> Out beyond ideas of wrongdoing and rightdoing, there is a field. I will meet you there.
> Jalal ad-Din Rumi

In keeping with this stance, existential psychotherapists avoid adopting the role of a superior, objective instructor who distinguishes for the client those dispositional stances that are assumed to be 'unreal', 'false' and/or 'irrational' and who attempts to replace them with 'real', 'true' and/or 'rational' ones. Similarly, rather than present themselves as 'symptom-removers', 'treatment-providers', 'directive educators' or 'professional helpers', existential psychotherapists return psychotherapy to its original meaning: the attempt to 'stay with', 'stand beside' and 'accept the otherness of the being who is present' (Evans, 1981).

As an immediate, if disturbing, implication of this perspective, the stance of acceptance requires of existential psychotherapists the abdication of what is probably *the* foundational assumption of contemporary Western psychotherapy: that the trained and expert professional who is the therapist can know and direct the means by which the client is to be *helped*.

Instead, rather than focusing upon notions of problem-solving, goal-setting, establishing programmes for change and directing discourse, existential psychotherapists attempt a stance of *acceptance* which can be defined as the openness both to what (or who) is there in the encounter *and* how it is to be in the relationship as it is being lived within the encounter.

This acceptance is neither about approval or disapproval of what the client does or does not do, nor is it concerned with establishing a specified programme of symptom removal or reduction, nor directive attempts toward change and away from stasis. It is, rather, primarily a descriptive and revelatory enterprise. To put it succinctly, the existential psychotherapist assumes no initial understanding of the meanings, values, beliefs, fears, aspirations and so forth that are contained within the client's narrative and its associated dispositional stances, so that, through their descriptive investigation, how these serve to maintain the client's currently lived worldview can be opened to reconsideration. Such a task cannot be undertaken without the therapist's willingness and ability to 'stay with' what is present and is being presented, rather than 'moving on' to alternative ways of being that may appear to be preferable.

Equally, in assuming no prior understanding of the client's worldview, this stance of acceptance places the existential psychotherapist in a role that is at least initially akin to that of the Medieval Fool in so far as, like the Fool, the therapist seeks to clarify descriptively the client's worldview through statements and questions that would, in more normal circumstances, be deemed too obvious or too daring to voice in an explicit fashion.

In general, the existential psychotherapist's stance of acceptance toward the unknown and alien worldview of the client requires the abdication of the security that comes with assumptions such as 'doing it right', or directing change, or of 'the expert's' superiority of knowledge and status. As should now be understood, this stance has nothing to do with any perverse belittlement or rejection of more typical therapeutic enterprises. Rather, it is a necessary constituent of the specific form of investigation being undertaken.

The Existential Psychotherapist's Experiential Immediacy

A good therapist must create a new therapy with every person they see. Irvin Yalom

Through the existential psychotherapist's acknowledged presence and the expression and communication of the attempt to 'stay with' and accept the client's current way of being as it presents itself in the therapeutic relationship, clients are more likely to experience themselves as being heard and, in turn, may begin hearing themselves in a manner that is less judgemental and more accepting of the worldview they maintain. This attitudinal shift promotes the possibility of clients' greater willingness and courage to confront the fixed, or sedimented, biases and assumptions they hold within that worldview and to consider how these sedimented stances, and their parallel dissociations of incongruent experience, may themselves have provoked their current problems in living.

Once the therapist's presence has begun to provoke a more open, honest, clarifying process of worldview exploration by the client, the therapist has earned sufficient trust to be able to focus upon the client's experience of being with a particular 'other' (the therapist) so that the *experiential immediacy* of their current encounter can be considered in terms of the resonances and contrasts it provokes with regard to the client's wider worldview.

Existential psychotherapy's focus on the experiential immediacy of the current encounter reveals that its emphasis lies with the client's *conscious* experience of relatedness. While not denying that much of experience remains un-reflected, or implicit, in that it is not properly clarified and attended to, nonetheless existential psychotherapy remains cautious as to the necessity of invoking or 'working with' what is often referred to as *unconscious* material. Some existential psychotherapists retain this latter term in order to express the idea of potential awareness upon which persons cannot, or will not, allow themselves to reflect consciously (May,

1983). Others have re-stated the question of the unconscious from the standpoints of dissociation and sedimentation of the self-construct (Spinelli, 1994, 2001; Strasser and Strasser, 1997). In either case, while not denying the human ability to distort, deny or suppress conscious experience, existential psychotherapy seeks to demystify many of the underlying ideas associated with psycho-analytic notions of the unconscious which have been embraced by numerous models of contemporary psychotherapy. Lengthier discussions on this issue can be found in Boss (1963), Condrau (1998) and Spinelli (1994, 2001).

The Existential Psychotherapist's Dialogical Attitude

> In true dialogue, both sides are willing to change. Thich Nhat Hanh

This attention upon the conscious aspects of existence is further reflected in existential psychotherapy's *dialogical attitude.* The earlier discussion dealing with Martin Buber's notion of *inclusion* addresses significant aspects of this attitude. The work of the relational analyst, Leslie Farber, who was deeply influenced by Buber's ideas, reveals important possibilities and implications for this dialogical stance (Farber, 1967). Farber's emphasis on a dialogical attitude was guided by his overarching intent to shift the central enterprise of psychotherapy away from a set of inflexible methodological conditions and to re-focus it towards a *morally derived attitude* expressive of the therapist's attempt to achieve a particular way of being with others. One critical implication of this can be noted in Farber's insistence that the topic (or the 'what-ness') of therapeutic dialogue could 'be about' anything – that is to say, the content of the discussion did not truly matter. Instead, Farber's dialogical concerns centred on *a way of talking* that led both therapist and client toward a 'truthful dialogue' with themselves and one another (Farber, 2000).

This notion of a 'truthful dialogue' parallels the ideas put forward by the phenomenologist, George Gadamer (2004). Gadamer contrasted the truthfulness that emerges via a dialogue that is not pre-set in its focus and intent by any of the participants to one that has been pre-set in its intention or direction by at least one of the participants. All dialogues, Gadamer acknowledged, have – or more accurately – *find* a direction, but there exists a truthful quality to a dialogue that shapes its own form and focus that cannot be ascertained – or experienced – in a dialogue that is being actively directed toward a certain pre-set goal. One consequence of this, as Gadamer wrote, is that 'the way one word follows another, with the conversation taking its own twists and reaching its own conclusion, may well be conducted in some way, but the partners conversing are far less the leaders than the led. No one knows in advance what will "come out" of such a conversation' (Gadamer, 2004: 383). Paradoxically, this 'abdication of control' over the directive aspects of dialogue permits a greater sense of its 'ownership' by its participants.

In many ways, the views of Farber and Gadamer about dialogue hark back to Martin Heidegger's assertion that '[i]dle talk is the possibility of understanding everything without previously making the thing one's own' (Heidegger, 1962: 213.) Various existential psychotherapists have tended to interpret Heidegger's statement as an injunction to avoid therapeutic discourse that is not in some way directly significant to the client's presenting issues and concerns but which, rather, takes the form of some sort of 'gossip', 'chatter' or 'everyday discourse'. For example, they have tended to dismiss the client's statements concerning the previous evening's television programme, or a news item, or the weather as some sort of avoidance mechanism. I believe that in doing so they have misunderstood Heidegger's point, as Farber makes plain. It does not matter whether the content of the client's discourse is focused on philosophy or on *The Simpsons*. It is *how* such topics are addressed – which is to say, how 'owned' they are as expressions of the client's current worldview that is the critical factor. In addition, for the existential psychotherapist to take control of the client's subject matter by determining its appropriateness and judging its relevance not only blocks the possibility of 'dialogue-directed dialogue' as suggested by Gadamer, but, more tellingly, contradicts the very method of investigation being espoused.

In related fashion, the therapist's over-emphasis on a discourse that directs the client to the contemplation and assimilation of assumptions and conclusions that express the theoretical aspects of the therapist's preferred approach can also be recognised as an expression of Heidegger's 'idle talk'. Although existential psychotherapists are dismissive of any formal 'technique', it must be acknowledged that attempts to educate clients directly about the formal properties and principles of existential phenomenology is as much a 'technique' as is the assigning of homework or the training of clients to regulate their breathing. Once again, Heidegger made this point clear in his discussions with Medard Boss and his colleagues, alerting them to the fact that existential psychotherapy's attention was not to be placed upon the elucidation of *existentials*, or underpinning principles of existential phenomenology, in themselves but, rather, upon how those principles were given their expression through the client's therapeutic discourse (Heidegger, 2001). Explicitly, he writes, that '[existentials] are not initiating principles for the Daseinsanalytic way of seeing psychiatry. Rather, they are exactly the *content* . . .' (Heidegger 2001: 205).

Not-knowing/Un-knowing

To know what you do not know is best. To not know of knowing is a disease. Tao Te Ching

In general, existential psychotherapy is in broad agreement with current 'evidence-based' conclusions regarding the centrality of the therapeutic relationship (Mearns and Cooper, 2005; Norcross, 2002). However, as this brief discussion has hopefully highlighted, its attempt to establish a form of dialogue which expresses a 'way of being' brings a very different set of inter-relational concerns for the therapist. Karl Jaspers called the existential psychotherapist's enterprise *not-knowing* (Jaspers, 1963). More recently, I have myself referred to it as *un-knowing* (Spinelli, 1997). In either case, the terms express the aim of the existential psychotherapist as that of seeking to discern that which is *understandable within what is initially experienced as being un-understandable* – whether to the therapist, to the client, or to both.

With regard to un-knowing, I use a hyphenated spelling in order to distinguish the term from its more common associations with unfamiliarity and being unaware or uninformed. Instead, 'un-knowing' refers to that attempt on the part of the existential psychotherapist to remain as open as possible to that which presents itself as the client's narrative. Thus, it expresses the attempt to treat the seemingly familiar, assumed to be understood or understandable, as novel, unfixed in meaning and, hence, receptive to previously unexamined possibilities. The attempt to 'un-know' suggests the therapist's willingness to explore the world of the client in a fashion that not only seeks to remain respectful of the client's unique worldview, but also to be receptive to the challenges to the therapist's own meaning and narrational biases and assumptions (be they personal or professional, or both) that this exploration may well provoke. That this may often require of therapists the attempt to accept client values and beliefs that are alien or contrary to their own is a necessary condition of this enterprise. If nothing else, in striving to un-know, what the therapist is likely to experience will be similar in significant ways to that which the client is being urged to accomplish – the clarification of one's worldview.

Put bluntly, un-knowing requires the existential psychotherapist's willingness, if not eagerness, to adopt a stance of utmost receptivity to the initial novelty and mystery expressed and contained in the client's narrational statements and dispositional stances. This shift in attitude from a 'natural' assumption of shared knowledge toward that of a *phenomenological attitude* of initial openness and naivety requires the therapist to abdicate, at least for the time being, a great deal of that which might, from the standpoint of other psychotherapeutic models and approaches, be taken as the therapist's authority, expertise and interpretative power. Through this attempt, the client's embedded and often implicit dispositional stances can be opened to a revealing descriptively focused form of inquiry.

In this way, I suggest, existential psychotherapy's primary stance toward the therapeutic relationship is best encapsulated by the attitude of un-knowing. The following quote from Dave Mearns and Mick Cooper's recent text *Working at Relational Depth in Counselling and Psychotherapy* (2005) provides a sound parallel means with which to summarise the idea of un-knowing. Arguing against the focus and emphasis given to technique, they write:

> [T]echnique can make it more difficult to meet clients at a level of relational depth . . . This is for a number of reasons. First, if we try to implement a technique, our attention is likely to be on what we are doing to our client and its outcome, rather than on the particular human being present to us. In other words, our relationship with the client is no longer im-mediate [sic], but mediated by certain plans and actions. Second, if we relate to our clients through techniques and therapeutic strategies, we are less likely to be open to them as the unique human beings that they are, but will be looking for particular responses and outcomes from them across particular dimensions. And third, the more we are relating to our clients in a technique-based way, the more we lose our own naturalness, spontaneity and uniqueness and start to relate in formulaic and rehearsed ways. This, again, reduces the possibility of an immediate and direct human encounter. (Mearns and Cooper, 2005: 117–18)

EXISTENTIAL PSYCHOTHERAPY'S APPROACH TO CONFLICT, SYMPTOMS AND CHANGE

Conflict

Conflict is the beginning of consciousness. M. Esther Harding

Were it not for the client's experience of conflict, there would likely be no psychotherapy. In many ways, the differences between varied approaches to psychotherapy reflect the diversity of ways by which conflict is understood and, through that understanding, what it is that psychotherapists attempt to provide in order to reduce or remove it.

Existential psychotherapy's view of conflict once again reveals a significantly different stance from that of other contemporary approaches. It proposes that conflict be viewed as an inevitable condition of human existence and that the conflicts presented by clients arise from, and are expressions of, the client's currently maintained worldview's structurally derived distortions of, and inadequacies in reflecting, his or her lived experience of worlding. From this perspective, the client's problematic presenting disturbances cannot be isolated, or considered as distinct from, or alien to, that presenting worldview. Nonetheless, the particular expression of conflict presented by the client may be expressive of quite differing forms of tension arising within the current worldview.

In one instance, the client's experience of conflict reflects a gap or dissonance between particular sedimentations in the worldview and actual experiences of being that challenge, contradict or cannot be maintained within any number of sedimented dispositional stances – for example: the conflict that arises when my certainty about my belief in a god is eroded by the nightly television images of slaughtered innocent civilians; or, the conflict that arises when the dominant view I hold about my self as being a bad and unlovable person is confronted with the felt genuineness of another's statements about how good I am and the strength of positive feelings towards my self that this other's approval provokes for me.

Alternatively, conflict can emerge as a direct consequence and expression of the currently maintained worldview – for example: the conflict that arises when my certainty about my belief in a god creates serious obstacles in my relationship with my best friend who is an atheist; or the conflict that arises when the dominant view I hold about my self as being a bad and unlovable person leads me to experiences of unwanted loneliness or seemingly uncontrollable self-harm.

The first type of conflict can only be resolved through the re-constitution of one's divided or dissonant worldview – which may be expressed as 'change' in one's relations with self, others and/or the world in general. For example, my resolution of the conflict that arises when my certainty about my belief in a god is eroded by the nightly television images of slaughtered innocent civilians may require me to acknowledge my uncertainty about the existence of a deity or, alternatively, may require the re-defining of my concept of 'god'. Or, my resolution of the conflict that arises when the dominant view I hold about my self as being a bad and unlovable person is confronted with the felt genuineness of another's state-ments regarding how good I am and the strength of positive feelings towards my self this provokes for me may require my re-evaluation of my self as *always and only* a bad and unlovable person.

The second type of conflict is an expression of the possible consequences of an undivided and coherent, if still sedimented, stance. It is that conflict which arises *because* we are capable of choice. The possible resolution of this type of conflict has less to do with issues of overt change in the existing worldview than upon its embrace and acceptance from a more adequate or 'truthful' standpoint, such that the uneasy or unwanted consequences of that worldview are as fully owned as those deemed to be desirable and acceptable. So, for instance, I might have to extend my belief in a god to include the challenge that this belief can be main-tained in an ongoing relationship with my best friend who is an atheist. Or that my dominant views about my self as being a bad and unlovable person can also per-mit an embracing of the social world and a concern for the physical well-being of all humankind, including my self.

While the first type of conflict resolution requires a de-sedimentation of a par-ticular or set of particular attitudinal stances, the second type allows the continu-ing maintenance of such stances but demands an extension of the meaning possibilities that these stances express.

Although what resolution may be possible with either type of conflict invokes a felt sense of change, nevertheless this distinction of differing expressions of conflict highlights important variations in the kinds of beneficial therapeutic out-comes that might be both possible for, and desirable to, the client. Because the worldview is a matrix of inter-weaving and inter-related structural components, a change in any *one* component of the worldview will alter the *whole* of it. As such, any therapeutic tampering with the presenting conflict without sufficiently understanding its relatedness to the client's worldview, might well create far greater distress and unease in living than did the original presenting problem. Psychotherapists, like other self-proclaimed 'experts', have a tendency to seek the resolution of conflict only from the perspective of the first type of conflict under discussion. However, it is not unlikely that this attempt, when placed in the context of the second type of conflict might provoke a destabilis-ing of the maintained worldview, thereby generating unexpected and unwanted shifts in anxiety far more debilitating than any generated by the presenting expe-rience of conflict.

Viewed in this way, existential psychotherapy's approach to conflict is not pri-marily about its alteration, reduction or removal. Instead, it suggests that the ther-apist's task is to assist the client in focusing upon, and connecting more adequately the perceived source of conflict with, the worldview that shapes and defines it. In this way, the possibilities, limits and consequences of any attempt at conflict res-olution are more likely to be beneficial than disruptive shifts in the worldview and, indeed, may emerge simply as a consequence of the client's willingness to focus upon the worldview and its relatedness to the presenting conflict.

Any existential discussion on the topic of conflict requires an acknowledgement of its indebtedness to the work of Jean-Paul Sartre (Cannon, 1991; Sartre, 1991). Through his analyses of conflict, often lucidly brought to life through the struggles of the characters in his novels and plays, Sartre returned again and again to the theme of the inevitability of inter-relational conflict. For Sartre, the 'other' – even the other who is the therapist – remains inescapably the antagonist to one's life project. If a 'solution to conflict' exists for Sartre, it cannot be through any transcending of conflict between self and other but rather *through the mutual acknowledgement of its inevitability*. Via this acknowledgement, a co-operative possibility emerges which, while not avoiding the different and competing elements that distinguish one's life project from that of the other, also acknowledges the similarity of their aim in that all life projects seek to create and maintain the 'deceptions' of security, definability and certainty.

Sartre's ideas can be restated from the standpoint of the worldview. Although the particular components of any specific worldview are unique, all worldviews serve to secure, define and invoke tolerable levels of certitude in essence (what it is to be), existence (how being is experienced) and identity (who this being who experiences being is). In this shared attempt, all worldviews can also be understood to be deceptive and deceiving. Inter-relational conflict arises not only because of the clash of competing worldviews, but just as significantly because each worldview exposes the deceit inherent in the other's (or all others') worldview and, hence, in one's own maintained worldview. While there is no possible complete resolution to this conflict, nonetheless the willingness to embrace the mutuality of this deception permits a reciprocity between conflicting parties that is potentially transformative. This reciprocity involves both conflicting parties' simultaneous attempts to make themselves the vehicle for the other's project rather than seek to make the other the object of his or her own ends. The effect of this attempt at reciprocity cannot entirely fulfil either party's original project, but it will create a novel and more tolerable (if still ultimately deceptive) means with which to 'live with' conflict.

If we understand, as Sartre did, that 'the other' with whom one is in conflict is not only an external entity but is also 'the other who resides within each being', then the implications of Sartre's views for the forms of conflict presented in psychotherapy become much more apparent. First, Sartre's challenge forces existential psychotherapists to acknowledge that the therapeutic relationship, like all others, remains grounded in worldview-derived conflict and competing strategies. What might distinguish this relationship from others, then, would not be the *lack* of such conflict, but rather its active and unstinting recognition of this given – at first on the part of the therapist and, subsequently, via reflection, by the client as well. Second, this argument asserts that existential psychotherapy's concerns rest precisely upon the exploration of the possibilities of living *with* conflict rather than seeking its eradication. Third, this view of conflict urges the investigation of the client's experience of conflict as lived and as expressed in the immediacy of the therapeutic relationship so that its relatedness to the client's presenting worldview can be examined and, through such examination, may permit the experience of a novel stance toward conflict. And fourth, as Sartre's argument makes plain, the *means* toward this transformative possibility is through the willingness of the therapist and client to meet and engage one another as beings-in-conflict who, nonetheless, remain willing to be both revealed by the other and the means to the other's revelation.

Symptoms

> The human condition is such that pain and effort are not just symptoms which can be removed without changing life itself; they are the modes in which life itself, together with the necessity to which it is bound, makes itself felt. For mortals, the 'easy life of the gods' would be a lifeless life. Hannah Arendt

Although tending toward descriptive forms of categorisation, the various disorders of thought, emotion and behaviour that appear in widely employed clinical frameworks such as the *Diagnostic and Statistical Manual of Mental Disorders (DSM-IV)* place their psychiatric emphasis upon the diagnostic grouping of disturbances considered from a perspective of medical illness. Since the path-finding work of Karl Jaspers (1963), existential psychotherapy has generally adopted a cautious, if not sceptical, stance toward this form of diagnosis. Following Jaspers, existential psychotherapists have sought to focus upon the clients' felt sense of disabling unease by way of their self-reports and the therapist's exploration of clients' perspectives on self-awareness and perceptual processing. In many ways, these efforts express a concern that was aptly summarised by David Pilgrim: 'The psychiatric question "Is this person suffering from a mental disorder or not?" becomes transformed by a psychologist into "How do we account for this person's actions and experience in this particular context?"' (Pilgrim, 2000: 302). In addition, existential psychotherapy's adoption of the foundational principle of relatedness challenges implicit assumptions of isolated 'abnormal' factors and variables and seeks to reconsider such within the inter-related context of the client's worldview. This attitude allows existential psychotherapists to 'assume a continuity between the normal and the abnormal' (Pilgrim, 2000: 302).

This worldview-focused undertaking seeks to clarify the client's disturbing preoccupations in ways that remain attuned to the client's own descriptions and evaluations of his or her reflections upon experience, and also provides a means whereby such client-led accounts can be placed in direct relation to the implicit dispositional stances that are embedded within, and expressions of, the client's worldview so that the interplay between both can be considered and challenged.

From existential psychotherapy's inter-relational perspective, symptoms of distress and disturbance are expressions of the client's attempts to maintain the current worldview no matter how restrictive, disabling, irrational, contradictory or incomprehensible it might appear to be to the client and therapist alike, because its maintenance serves to allay the acknowledgement of intolerable uncertainty as manifested through existential anxiety. In this sense, existential psychotherapy proposes that *every symptomatic problem is also an attempted solution to the irresolvable 'problem' of existential anxiety.*

From this perspective, symptoms – whether 'neurotic' or 'psychotic' – are principally rooted in socio-ethical tensions arising from the dilemmas of relatedness and, rather than being expressions of random, meaningless illness, can be seen as revealing the client's attempts to protect the currently held worldview from overwhelming experiences of existential anxiety. Indeed, the disturbing symptoms are direct expressions and consequences of the client's currently lived worldview and, as such, are a direct means to its investigation. The client's presenting symptoms, therefore, are the starting point for existential psychotherapy's investigations in that they are the 'way in' to the client's presenting worldview, rather than alien obstacles that attack it and which require expulsion.

Any attempt to remove, reduce, amend, or 're-shape' the presenting symptoms will have its impact upon the worldview being maintained. Consequently, existential psychotherapy cautions practitioners to avoid any enterprise of 'symptom-removal' without first considering sufficiently the inter-relation between the symptom and the client's worldview, in order to minimise the all-too-likely possibility that the effects of such an enterprise may provoke for the client a far greater degree of unbearable existential tension and unease.

This view remains indebted to the still revolutionary work of R.D. Laing (1960) and the studies that he undertook together with his colleagues Aaron Esterson (1964) and David Cooper (1964). In brief, Laing argued that symptoms were most adequately understood as expressions of deeply felt and divisive unease, conflict and fragmentation of various facets of one's experience of one's own being, as expressed through one's relations with oneself and with others. These various expressions of existential disturbance can be seen to be focused upon concerns surrounding one's *essence* ('that I am'), *existence* ('what I am') and *identity* ('who I am') (Laing, 1960). Further, Laing and Esterson, argued the case that such disturbances (or, to employ Laing's term, *ontological insecurities*) arose precisely when the distinction between who one is and what one does (or must/mustn't be or do) remains unclear through one's self/world relations (Burston, 2000; Laing and Esterson, 1964; Spinelli, 1994, 2005).

To summarise, existential psychotherapists attempt neither to isolate nor pathologise the various symptoms that are expressed by the client via his or her worldview. Nor do they take the amelioration or removal of symptoms to be their primary task. Rather, together with the client, they attempt to expose and consider these symptoms as interrelated expressions of the client's wider worldview so that the implications of their maintenance, reduction or removal upon that worldview can be considered and evaluated.

Change

If my devils are to leave me, I am afraid my angels will take flight as well. Rainer Maria Rilke

As has already been noted, the descriptively focused attitude running throughout existential psychotherapy provokes significant contrasts with other contemporary approaches. Such contrasts can perhaps be best highlighted when considering the question of *psychotherapeutically directed change*.

Dominant assumptions underlying contemporary psychotherapy emphasise the goal of client change in attitude, belief and behaviour that occurs as a consequence of the therapist's skilled interventions. More specifically, the success of psychotherapy is evaluated by the kind and degree of ameliorating or curative change that is experienced by the client and that is in some way measurably demonstrable and evidence-based. Depending upon the particular model to which the therapist subscribes, beneficial change is assumed to have occurred when clients are assessed as being more rational, more 'reality-focused', more 'centred', more 'ego-reinforced', and so forth. For the great majority of therapists, the foundational aim of psychotherapy is to provide appropriate means whereby beneficial and lasting change in some aspect of the client's behaviour or worldview can be achieved. Such change is viewed as coming about largely as a result of the therapist's skills-based interventions and specialist expertise, and hence is assumed to be *directive*.

However, think of an example of significant and lasting change in your life. How did it come about? What were the key conditions and variables that allowed it to occur? What would have prevented it from happening? Like much of contemporary psychotherapy, it is likely that an underlying assumption in your response is that the key factors allowing – or preventing – the occurrence of change can be identified and perhaps even become the means to bring about further change. But is this always the case? Or even usually the case?

In contrast to generally accepted views about our ability to identify those variables and factors that generate change, existential psychotherapy is far less concerned with change-focused outcomes in general and is wary of any claims or attempts on the part of the therapist to produce direct change in the client through the use of attitude- and behaviour-shifting techniques and interventions. Indeed, it is explicit in arguing that its primary task is *not* one of seeking to direct change in the worldview of the client. Rather, existential psychotherapy's principal concerns lie with its attempts to descriptively clarify that worldview so that its explicit and implicit, sedimented dispositional stances can be re-examined inter-relationally. This enterprise is likely to reveal those disowned or dissociated experiences, thoughts, behaviours and affects that serve to maintain the client's worldview sedimentations. But here, as well, it is not the therapist's task to initiate a programme of directed change, even if these are exposed as being problematic, undesirable or debilitating for the client.

This is not to suggest that existential psychotherapists remain naive as to the change-provoking effects that their mere presence, much less any verbal statements they make, might well have upon the client. Nor should it be read that they are antagonistic to change in general, and beneficial change in particular, as experienced by the client or as subsequently identified. Rather, their attempt is to refocus their understanding and practice of psychotherapy away from the emphasis upon 'who the client might become', and instead concentrate upon 'who the client is being' and how that way of being is inter-relationally experienced and expressed. In general, existential psychotherapists deviate from dominant assumptions regarding psychotherapeutic change in four principal ways:

First, they decry the therapist's *deliberate* attempts to manipulate, induce and evoke change in the client, because to do so would run counter to the foundational inter-relational principles upon which their approach is based. Recall that the primary enterprise of existential psychotherapy is the investigation of 'that which presents itself in the way it presents itself' as an expression of relatedness. Thus, deliberate attempts to alter and manipulate, or broadly 'change' the client would defeat this undertaking. Instead, the existential psychotherapist's allegiance is toward the client who *is* present rather than to an imagined client who *might be as a result of directive change.*

Second, this allegiance cautions existential psychotherapists to bear in mind that change in any *one* aspect or expression of the worldview will alter *the whole* of it in ways that cannot be predicted. In terms of our current understanding, it remains uncertain as to how subtle or radical, beneficial or detrimental, the impact of any directed manipulation might be upon a particular client's worldview. Paradoxically, existential psychotherapy argues that it may be via the very process of assisting clients to 'stay still', so that they can clarify and challenge the presenting problems' relatedness to their currently maintained worldview, that the potential benefits of 'therapeutic change' are more likely to occur.

Third, acknowledging their cautious response to directive change, existential psychotherapists nonetheless recognise that change is an inevitable outcome of any inter-relation. However, rather than view such change as 'non-directive', existential psychotherapists assert that it is always multi-directional. Directiveness, from the standpoint of the existential psychotherapist, remains focused upon the attempt to fulfil the enterprise that has been set: namely, that of elucidating the worldview of the client as it presents itself in the therapeutic relationship. This stance on directiveness frees existential therapists from the task of setting the direction or content of the discourse itself. Instead, their focus addresses what is revealed of the client's worldview through and within the direction that the encounter takes. In permitting the therapeutic dialogue to find and direct its own way, as Gadamer (2004) has suggested, opens the possibility of change that might well impact upon therapist and client alike – even if the degree to which that impact is experienced and imbued with meaning may differ subtly or significantly for each. In this sense then, there is no need to 'induce' change, since change – however unpredictable its direction and significance might be – is a constant given of relatedness.

Fourth, while accepting this latter view of change, existential psychotherapists argue that they are nonetheless entitled to note, consider and query any detected change that might arise in and through the ongoing therapeutic encounter. Via a particular expression of therapist disclosure (as will be discussed in Part Two) this focus on change need not be restricted solely to observed changes centred upon the client but may well utilise the therapist's experience of change. The encounter between therapist and client, while undeniably focused upon the client, is, nonetheless, mutually revelatory. For both, the encounter permits a conscious reflection of 'this is what and how it is to be who I am being in this relation' and, by doing so, facilitates the experience of change.

In addition, viewed from the perspective of existential psychotherapy, any change will inevitably affect the person's currently maintained worldview. I would propose that the impact of change upon the worldview can be considered from the standpoint of three distinct levels:

Level 1 change is that change whose initial focus is upon a sedimentation existing within any one of the primary constructs of the worldview (i.e. the self-, other- or world-construct) but whose principal impact is upon either or both of the remaining constructs. Level 1 change does not directly affect or alter the sedimentation as reflected from the perspective of the focus *construct* but does, nevertheless, provoke an attitudinal and/or behavioural shift in the sedimented stance from the perspective of the remaining constructs. Consider the following examples:

- The *self-construct* sedimented stance, 'I hate my self', undergoes Level 1 change so that it now becomes: 'I still hate my self, but others can love me.' Or: 'I still hate my self, but the world won't care.'
- The *other-construct* sedimented stance, 'Others are dangerous', undergoes Level 1 change so that it now becomes: 'Others are still dangerous, and I can make myself stronger.' Or: 'Others are still dangerous, but who knows what future lies ahead for human relations?'
- The *world-construct* sedimented stance, 'Winters are always depressing', undergoes Level 1 change so that it now becomes: 'Winters are always depressing and I'll focus on finding ways to function reasonably well through them.' Or: 'Winters are always depressing but at least it keeps the "weirdos" indoors.'

Level 1 change, therefore, retains the *focus* construct's sedimentation (i.e., 'I hate my self'; 'Others are dangerous'; 'Winters are always depressing'). As such, change, at this level, does not directly challenge the sedimentation within the focus construct. Rather, Level 1 change provides the means whereby that sedimentation might not only be maintained but also, in some fashion, strengthened within the focus construct. At the same time, however, change is provoked through the effect of re-structuring the sedimentation from the perspective of either or both of the remaining constructs.

Level 2 change, on the other hand, is that change whose impact is directly upon the sedimentation *within* the focus construct. That is to say, Level 2 change acts to de-sediment the sedimentation within the focus construct and hence is typically experienced as being more significant or powerful than Level 1 change. At the same time, however, the impact of Level 2 change retains a 'dualistic divide' in its inter-relational foundation such that the acknowledged impact of its challenge remains solely within the focus construct and is not perceived to extend its effects to include the remaining constructs. For example:

- The *self-construct* stance, 'I hate my self', undergoes Level 2 change so that it now becomes: 'I don't always hate my self; I can sometimes see my self as being a lovable person.'
- The *other-construct* stance, 'Others are dangerous', undergoes Level 2 change so that it now becomes: 'Others are not always fearful beings; others can be kind or concerned.'
- The *world-construct* stance, 'Winters are always depressing', undergoes Level 2 change so that it now becomes: 'Winters can be depressing if they're treated as "failed Summers". Treated appropriately and for what they are, Winters can generate their own particular and unique pleasure, contentment and excitement.'

In each of these Level 2 change examples, the sedimented stance can be seen to undergo substantial challenge such that it may be significantly de-sedimented. Even so, however, as far as the person who maintains the worldview is aware, the experience of change remains limited to, or *within,* the focus construct; the impact of de-sedimentation does not extend directly to either or both of the remaining constructs. In this way, Level 2 change is experienced as limited or divided rather than truly inter-relational.

Level 3 change is that change regarding a sedimented stance within a particular construct whose impact extends to the remaining constructs and, hence, affects and re-contextualises the worldview as a whole. Level 3 change, therefore, provokes an interconnected shift in the self-, other- and world-construct constituents of the worldview. Level 3 change is likely to be experienced as highly powerful, meaning-altering and transformational since it provokes a direct experience of an inter-related reconstitution of the worldview as a whole.

Unlike Level 1 and Level 2 change, examples of Level 3 change are not easily summarised nor can they be expressed in a simple statement. More generally, what can be stated is that when a sedimented stance within a particular construct undergoes Level 3 change, that change is experienced directly *as equal and equally present in* the remaining construct constituents. In doing so, the whole of the worldview undergoes a radical shift whose direction and meaning opens to a multitude of unpredictable and potentially unexpected experiential possibilities. For instance, if one of the examples of sedimentation discussed above, 'Others are dangerous', is challenged so that it undergoes Level 3 change, what is being suggested is that the impact is directly experienced upon all three primary constructs. It might be the case, for example, that the shift is initiated through the challenge that if 'others are dangerous' then 'I (as an other) am also dangerous' (self-construct), and 'the world, too, is dangerous' (world-construct). Precisely how this shift would impact as a change upon the whole of the worldview is impossible to predict or specify. It might alter one's lived meaning of, and relation to, that which is defined and experienced as 'dangerous' in ways that minimise, intensify or transform its significance for the whole of the worldview. Or, it might provoke philosophical, spiritual, artistic or scientific insight regarding 'that which is dangerous'. In general, Level 3 change can be deeply destabilising and disturbing, as well as visionary and transcendent. I would suggest that significant psychological 'breakdowns' (typically labelled as psychoses) and highly creative 'breakthroughs' in artistic or scientific insights and activity share the experience of Level 3 change. Similarly, the important differences between 'breakdowns' and 'breakthroughs' can be understood as resulting from the worldview's response to the destabilising effects of Level 3 change and its subsequent ability (or inability) to reconstitute itself and its primary constructs in a novel way.

If we consider this *three-level* perspective on change from the standpoint of psychotherapy, we can see that, in keeping with contemporary Western psychotherapy's view of the client as a distinct and separate individual, most instances of therapeutic change are likely to be at Level 1 or Level 2. Level 1 change is most likely to occur when the therapeutic focus is primarily on the reduction or removal of the presenting problematic issues or concerns as separate and distinct from the worldview being maintained by the client. Level 2 change, on the other hand, is most likely to occur when the therapeutic focus is on some divided aspect of the client's worldview (most commonly, some aspect of the client's self-construct) as the source of the presenting problem. In general, Level 1 and Level 2 occurrences of change are also likely to reflect the *type* of therapeutic relationship or dialogical encounter that is being adopted or emphasised. Those therapies that are specifically goal-oriented or solution-focused in a directive process either set by the therapist or negotiated between therapist and client would be expected to provoke either Level 1 or Level 2 change.

The concerns of the whole existential-phenomenological enterprise – including existential psychotherapy – ultimately focus upon Level 3 change. As a philosophical system, existential phenomenology proposes 'a way of existing' that is highly likely to be experienced as a transformational challenge to one's previously adopted way of being. Level 3 change exposes the gap or dissonance between the experience of worlding and the structural worldview that is being maintained. Further, it offers some movement toward the bridging of the worlding experience and the worldview structure through the attempt to accept and embrace relatedness, uncertainty and anxiety as both specific and universal conditions of existence. In turn, this attempt acts to minimise the presence and impact of the sedimentations and dissociations being maintained in the worldview so that its structure is increasingly 'opened to what is there for me when it is there'.

Although existential psychotherapists, by virtue of the structured examination of their own lives which they have undertaken, may be experientially and intellectually 'closer' to this ultimate aim than their clients are likely to be, these same personal explorations will have made them aware that *any direct attempts to provoke or induce Level 3 change are dangerously unpredictable in their consequences*. In addition, as has been discussed in previous sections, any such attempts at directive change act to undermine and contradict the very enterprise of existential psychotherapy. Instead, the therapist's inter-relational focus, stance and attitude within the therapeutic relationship seeks to express existential phenomenology's assumptions and tenets in a lived way. One significant aspect of this therapeutic stance is, paradoxically, the therapist's willingness and ability to 'stay still with' the client's presenting way of being and, in this way, provide some partial context within which the client may also 'be still' in order to explore and consider his or her current way of being. In my view, Level 3 change is most likely to occur, and offer the possibility of a 'breakthrough' rather than a 'breakdown', when no direct attempts to provoke its occurrence are enacted. If Level 3 change is to occur, it will do so *in spite of* directive interventions by the therapist rather than *because* of them.

My own years of experience as a psychotherapist have led me to the conclusion that Level 1 or Level 2 change should not be dismissed or denigrated. For many clients, these levels of change are more than sufficient for their wants, expectations and ability to live more fulfilling lives. This conclusion may be particularly difficult for existential psychotherapists to accept since such levels of change address only in minimal, and likely distorted, fashion the central concerns of relatedness, uncertainty and anxiety. Nonetheless, perhaps the words of the great Buddhist Sage, Lin-Chi, might provide comfort and perseverance: 'If you live the sacred and despise the ordinary, you are still bobbing in the ocean of delusion' (I-Hsuan, 1993: 46).

EXISTENTIAL PSYCHOTHERAPY FROM THE PERSPECTIVE OF EXISTENTIAL PHENOMENOLOGY'S THREE KEY UNDERLYING PRINCIPLES

Relatedness

Every explicit duality is an implicit unity. Alan Watts

Existential psychotherapy's adoption of the principle of relatedness, that is to say the inter-relational grounding to all subjective experience, challenges a persistent assumption held not only by most of psychotherapy but, just as significantly, by our culture in general. This is the view that the person is a self-contained unit, understandable within his or her own set of subjectively derived meanings and behaviours. As has been discussed throughout, the debate provoked by these two competing views is crucial: at its heart, lie distinctly different ways of examining and understanding our selves and the world.

From the standpoint of relatedness, the problems and concerns presented by clients can no longer be seen as being solely their own, in any exclusively individualistic sense. Such a stance emphasises far-reaching challenges to our culture's, and hence psychotherapy's, dominant assumptions. For example, it suggests that 'questions of choice, freedom and responsibility cannot be isolated or contained within some separate being (such as "self" or "other") . . . . Viewed in this way, no choice can be mine or yours alone, no experienced impact of choice can be separated in terms of "my responsibility" versus "your responsibility", no sense of personal freedom can truly avoid its interpersonal dimensions' (Spinelli, 2001: 16). The implications of such a shift upon our understanding and working with the therapeutic relationship and upon the practice of psychotherapy as a whole are as plentiful as they are dramatic.

Most immediately, perhaps, the implications of this first principle lead to the conclusion that existential psychotherapy cannot be a system or approach that concerns itself solely or even primarily with the *uniquely subjective experience* of the individual client. Instead, it must concern itself ultimately with the inter-relational foundation through which the client experiences his or her unique way of being. Thus, it must *include* all of the structural constituents of the worldview in its investigations and its explorations rather than seek to *isolate* one constituent (typically, the self-construct) and *exclude* or minimise the significance of the remaining ones (typically, the other- and world-constructs).

In this sense, existential psychotherapy can be seen to be directed toward, and focused upon, not so much any particular individual who has been designated as 'the client'. Rather, its underpinning concerns rest predominantly upon *relatedness as expressed between persons*. Viewed in this way, existential psychotherapy is as much 'about' the therapist as it may be 'about' the client. While the primary focus of this enterprise obviously remains with the unease, travails and disturbances in living experienced by the client, nonetheless the exploration of such centres itself upon that which emerges experientially *between* therapist and client and what is revealed about relatedness through that particular encounter.

Uncertainty

> The quest for certainty blocks the search for meaning. Uncertainty is the very condition to impel man to unfold his powers. Erich Fromm

In approaching psychotherapy from the perspective of existential uncertainty, existential psychotherapists come to recognise that they are no longer able to be 'expert practitioners' who can offer or promise a conclusive certainty or clarity, nor a complete or final statement regarding the way of being of the client. Instead, their task becomes one that is more concerned with explicating and examining the diverse ways of being adopted by the client, be they relatively fixed or relatively open, relatively predictable as well as relatively surprising, and, hence, assist clients in becoming more accurate and honest investigators of their ways of being and how these impact upon their interactions and relations with themselves, others and the world in general.

Uncertainty within the context of existential psychotherapy is expressed through the dialogical encounter itself. In abstaining from the enterprise of therapist-directed change-focused dialogue, and instead immersing them selves in the uncertainty of a dialogue which finds its own direction and thereby opens the possibility of change whose direction and impact is unpredictable, existential psychotherapists express their willingness to face uncertainty in the presence of the client. Viewed from this perspective, the existential psychotherapist becomes an agent of uncertainty as expressed through his or her way of being with the client. Indeed the therapist, too, in opening him or her self to uncertainty is not immune to the unpredictable consequences of that openness.

How the client responds to, or makes use of this willingness on the part of the therapist is also unpredictable. Nevertheless, as the relational psychotherapist Leslie Farber proposed, this willingness on the part of the therapist may well provoke the client to experience 'pity' toward the therapist (Farber, 2000). Rather than being something to avoid, Farber asserted that it was precisely the onset of this pity that was the most reliable indicator of a likely beneficial therapeutic outcome for the client. For, in feeling 'pity', the client reached out to an uncertain – and hence imperfect – being. The impact of this upon the client, Farber suggested, was twofold.

First, via the act of reaching out to the therapist, the client simultaneously 'broke out' of his or her self-centred, self-focused, other-excluding stance and began to recognise the existence of the present other (the therapist). Second, via the act of reaching out in pity toward the therapist, the client at the same time, 'reached in' to find and accept his or her own uncertainty. By so doing, the whole of the client's inter-relational stance permitted the possibility of substantive examination and change.

As has been suggested by narrative and social-constructionist psychotherapeutic approaches influenced by existential phenomenology, psychotherapy might be thought of as a co-creation of novel meanings via mutual dialogue (Kaye, 1995). If so, the principle of uncertainty highlights a set of uneasy stances for the therapist to accept: what the emergent meanings may be, whether these will have perceived impact upon one or both of the participants, whether they may apparently resolve conflict or provoke new concerns and anxieties, and how they might de-sediment and reconstitute any or all of the primary constructs of the worldview being maintained by either or both participants prior to the discourse – all of these issues and possibilities, at present, remain unknown and unpredictable.

The principle of uncertainty reminds existential psychotherapists that rather than place themselves 'in charge' of the therapeutic encounter, they must be willing to be enfolded by it and, through this, its uncertain consequences.

Existential Anxiety

Courage resists despair by taking anxiety into itself. Paul Tillich

Unlike the majority of current psychotherapeutic approaches, existential psychotherapy argues that the experience of anxiety is neither the consequence of insufficiently met instinctual demands, nor the product of opposing drives, nor the outcome of inadequately established infantile relations, nor the distillation of misunderstood, incomplete or improper learning experiences. While any or all of the above may be ontic variables whose influence upon the primary constructs of a particular worldview may well be pivotal, existential psychotherapy asserts that anxiety permeates the structural make-up of all worldviews.

In his influential text, *Existential Psychotherapy* (1980), Irvin Yalom explores at length the various conflict-based reactions that might arise in response to existential anxiety. For example, in his analysis of death anxiety, Yalom posits two general conflict-generating modes of response. The first of these rests on the self-construct's sedimented stance of an inherent 'specialness and personal inviolability' (Yalom, 1980: 115). This stance, Yalom argues, provokes a variety of conflict-laden symptoms such as a compulsive reliance upon 'death-defying' behaviour which requires persons to both test and prove their specialness and personal inviolability by placing themselves in more and more dangerous situations. Equally, for Yalom, the symptoms of the 'workaholic' serve the assumption of personal inviolability through the 'pushing' of one's behaviour beyond ordinary temporal, mental and behavioural limits and, as well, serve the assumption of specialness in that they maintain the conviction that no one else is capable of doing the work as successfully, or knowledgeably as can the workaholic, who, therefore, must be indispensable in that the world could not possibly function adequately, if at all, were he or she to cease to be. In like fashion, current problematic 'addictions' focused upon health and virility, as well as those which seek to deny physical ageing, can be considered as further examples of this first response to death anxiety.

The second response suggested by Yalom is that which relies upon 'the Ultimate Rescuer' (Yalom, 1980). This Ultimate Rescuer may be perceived as an omnipresent supernatural entity or force which guides, watches over and protects and which often bestows ultimate reward or punishment. Alternatively, the Ultimate Rescuer might not be a supernatural entity, but another, albeit superior or charismatic, human being such as a religious or political leader – or, indeed, one who is both. In each case, the Ultimate Rescuer acts to minimise the power of death, reducing its finality to a mere turning point toward another (typically more elevated) realm of existence. In the same way, the Ultimate Rescuer fulfils the function of rule-maker, law-giver and meaning-constructor, all of which offer existential certainty and security. Death, from the standpoint of the Ultimate Rescuer, gains meaning and purpose and, as a result, is less anxiety-provoking. The problems arising from reliance upon an Ultimate Rescuer are the problems associated with the most inflexible of worldview sedimentations and the multitude of consequent dissociations from lived experience that such provoke. Various expressions of rigidity of thought and behaviour such as obsession, fanaticism, ritualised patterns of social and sexual behaviour, can be considered as problematic consequences of this stance.

A recent novel by Tim Parks, *Rapids* (2006), vividly encapsulates the above ideas in the following passage:

> [S]o many of these people who do dangerous things on rivers and mountains are afraid. It's funny, but I'm pretty sure. Afraid of dying, afraid of settling down. Afraid of life beginning really, and afraid it will never begin. These sports are something you do instead of life . . . . To feel they're really living, when they're not in danger of living at all. (Parks, 2006, quoted in Alvarez, 2006: 40)

Considered in this way, the task of existential psychotherapy is not that of providing further means to reduce the experience of anxiety but, rather, to disclose and explore the sedimented stances and dissociated experiences through which the client has already succeeded in reducing anxiety, so that the relationship between the client's debilitating, currently lived anxiety and the anxiety-reducing sedimentations and dissociations can be clarified. Readers will recall the pivotal distinction made in the earlier discussion on existential anxiety – namely, that the client's presenting anxieties are, already, essentialised 'reflections' of the inevitable existential anxiety that accompanies human existence. Such anxieties are, therefore, within the worldview and indeed may be critical components to its overall maintenance and stability. In this sense, the presenting anxieties are not only inseparable from the currently maintained worldview, they are significant 'ways in' to its descriptive investigation. Likewise, rather than treat the presenting anxieties as disorders in, or of, the client's worldview, existential psychotherapists assist their clients in exploring these as valid constituents or expressions of that currently lived worldview. Presenting anxieties, therefore, are not solely problematic, but are also the consequence of partially successful attempts to reduce or deny the unavoidable anxieties of existence. If existential psychotherapy can be said to 'treat' anxiety, its 'treatment' has less to do with the reduction or eradication of anxiety than with finding a more adequate and courageous way to acknowledge and 'live with' the inescapable 'given' of existential anxiety.

Considered together, the three key principles of existential phenomenology underpin the assumptions, values and aspirations of existential psychotherapy. Through their willingness to embrace relatedness, to stand revealed in their uncertainty, and to acknowledge the anxiety provoked through the attempt to engage truthfully with an other, existential psychotherapists can be said to embody the approach they espouse.

A SUMMARY OF PART ONE

> There aren't neat solutions to every mystery. People . . . . *complicate* everything. They do things for reasons they don't understand. They do things for no damn reason at all . . . . People are mysterious, the world is mysterious. You can't know everything. You're not supposed to. This isn't a history book. It's just the world. It's a messy place. William Landay

From its origins as a philosophical movement, existential phenomenology has provided a radical and at times disturbing view of human existence. Although its ideas confront many pivotal Western assumptions, it is only through one's attempts to engage experientially with these views that their impact upon the 'flesh and blood' of lived existence comes to the fore.

Part One has attempted a brief, and necessarily incomplete, overview of what I suggest are the three essential underpinning principles of existential phenomenology: relatedness, uncertainty and existential anxiety. Each of these principles has been examined principally from the perspective of its significance to, and implications for, any attempt to apply existential phenomenology to psychotherapy. In doing so, Part One has also provided a discussion of several corollaries arising from these key principles that impinge directly upon a general understanding of what it may be both to practise existential psychotherapy and to 'be' an existential psychotherapist.

I have proposed that existential psychotherapy is best understood and practised as a predominantly descriptively focused investigative enterprise rather than a primarily curative one. Further, this enterprise centres upon the elucidation of the client's experience of 'what and how it is for me to exist' via the inter-relational enterprise of the therapeutic encounter itself. And, further still, it addresses this investigation of the unique way of being of the client within the wider context or universal 'givens' of the 'way of being' of *all* human beings. This last aspect of the investigation highlights the presence and role of existential psychotherapists as implicated constituents of the investigation, rather than assuming their presence and role to be in some way or other detached from both the act and the consequent meanings derived from the investigation. Equally, it follows from the above statement that existential psychotherapy does not merely tolerate but, more correctly, values and embraces the diversity of client worldviews as expressed in terms of culture, race, gender and sexual orientation.

Any investigation that is situated within this set of assumptions reveals further implications for existential psychotherapy. Not least among them is the recognition that the client's experiential world is always both complex and uncertain – and can never be 'captured' in a final or complete fashion. As a consequence, while acknowledging that the therapist's own way of being will always in some manner resonate with and 'stand revealed' through the attempted disclosure of the client's way of being, just what will be disclosed or how this disclosure will occur remains both unknown and uncertain. This realisation can be both liberating and disturbing for the therapist, let alone the client. Under such circumstances, the injunction that it is not *what* you talk about but the *way* of talking that matters becomes particularly relevant for the existential psychotherapist.

Just what this particular way of talking may be provides the *structure* or set of conditions for the therapeutic encounter to which existential psychotherapists aspire. Equally, it provides the basis for all the *practice-based interventions* that the therapist might initiate or offer in response to the client's challenging presence.

In presenting this 'back-drop' to such a structure, Part One has considered many of the issues from the standpoint of my own attempts to grapple with, understand, apply and communicate a number of themes and ideas that have led me, in line with a great many other authors and psychotherapists, to declare our allegiance to existential phenomenology. In doing so, I have used a terminology that makes sense to me, both personally and professionally but which I recognise may be viewed as alien or inadequate to other authors and practitioners. For example, my distinction between worlding and the worldview (and its primary constructs), and the related discussion on the sedimentation of dispositional stances and the consequent dissociations (or dis-ownership) of lived experience are attempts on my part to interpret various pivotal insights of existential phenomenology so that I can communicate as adequately as I can to my self and others – both that which has inspired me about, and *the way* I have been inspired by, these insights. Debates will always exist as to the relative adequacy of the terminology chosen and I do not ask that others employ my personally preferred terms. Ultimately, it is what terms point us toward rather than the terms in them selves that marks their value.

Part Two extends the investigation of these terms (and provides additional ones with which readers can engage) in order to discern their psychotherapeutic implications and applications. In doing so, Part Two offers *a* structural model by which the theoretical underpinnings of existential phenomenology may find their expression through the practising of existential psychotherapy.

PART TWO

Practising Existential Psychotherapy: A Structural Model

An Introduction to the Structural Model

INTRODUCTION

On the basis of the critical underlying principles outlined in Part One, Part Two will now delineate a structural model for the practice of existential psychotherapy. This model is derived from, and is an attempt to explicate, *my own* current way of understanding psychotherapy and working as a psychotherapist from an existential grounding and perspective. This stance emphasises and seeks to express existential-phenomenology's key underlying principles of relatedness, uncertainty and existential anxiety, as have been discussed throughout this text. Nonetheless, although these principles will, I hope, be seen by the reader to underpin all of the specific components of the structure under discussion, I make no apology for the fact that none of these principles is ever addressed *explicitly* within the context of the therapeutic relationship. In taking this stance, I am, I believe, adhering to an important position addressed by Martin Heidegger in the course of his *Zollikon Seminars* with Medard Boss and his psychiatric colleagues. Heidegger states:

> The decisive point is that the particular phenomena, arising in the relationship between the analysis and the analyst, and belonging to the respective, concrete patient, be broached in their own phenomenological content and not simply be classified globally under *existentialia*. (Heidegger, 2001: 124)

This statement, as I understand it, highlights Heidegger's concern that the practice of existential psychotherapy should refrain from addressing, or educating the client toward, the direct and explicit understanding and acceptance of the key underlying ontological principles of existential phenomenology. Rather, Heidegger argues, contrasted to the client's narratives regarding the worldview as experienced in his or her 'wider world' relations.

Phase Two focuses upon the descriptive investigation of the client's inter-relational experience of co-habiting this 'therapy world' with the existential psychotherapist. This often intensely experienced examination of the client's worldview as it presents itself in the 'therapy world' may enable the implicit or covert dispositional stances that maintain the explicit or overt tensions and disturbances being presented by the client to be more adequately clarified and considered from the standpoint of their relatedness to the worldview. Since such inquiry is centred upon the immediacy of the relationship with the existential psychotherapist in the 'therapy world', Phase Two's central focus is on the client's honest examination of the challenges provoked by the therapeutic relationship itself.

Phase Three puts into practice the possibilities of reconfiguring the client's 'wider world' worldview via the incorporation of at least some of the experiential alternatives provoked by the experience of co-creating and co-habiting in the 'therapy world'. By so doing, an increased resonance between the newly established worldview and the client's experience of worlding may become possible. Through this (at least partial) *bridging* of the client's 'therapy world' and 'wider world' worldviews, Phase Three provides the means by which the temporary 'therapy world' is 'closed down' via the ending of the therapeutic relationship.

As will be discussed throughout Part Two, who and how the existential psychotherapist 'is' and what he or she 'does' with the client is substantially dependent upon which phase they are in.

At the same time, it must be stressed that explication of the practice of existential psychotherapy in terms of phases is not intended to suggest a step-by-step, or 'one-two-three' rigid formulation of process. While I am convinced that considering the practice of existential psychotherapy in a phase-like manner holds substantial explanatory and instructive value for those wishing either to develop their understanding of existential psychotherapy in practice or, equally, for those wishing to clarify, compare and contrast its practice to that of other therapeutic models and systems, nonetheless this proposed structure should not be taken for the exact equivalent of existential psychotherapy as might be offered and experienced in any actual therapeutic encounter. While the structure under consideration reflects a truthful attempt to present existential psychotherapy as *I both understand and attempt to practise it*, I doubt that any existential psychotherapist, my self included, has ever, or will ever, practise existential psychotherapy *exactly* as is being described and presented here.

In like fashion, while it is relatively straightforward to discuss the practice of existential psychotherapy in terms of three identifiable phases, it must be acknowledged that these suggested phases should not be seen to be so distinct as to be mutually exclusive of one another. In the course of an actual therapeutic encounter, some aspect or influence of all three phases will be present – regardless of whether the encounter is the very first or last in a series, or anywhere in between these two poles.

contrasted to the client's narratives regarding the worldview as experienced in his or her 'wider world' relations.

Phase Two focuses upon the descriptive investigation of the client's inter-relational experience of co-habiting this 'therapy world' with the existential psychotherapist. This often intensely experienced examination of the client's worldview as it presents itself in the 'therapy world' may enable the implicit or covert dispositional stances that maintain the explicit or overt tensions and distur-bances being presented by the client to be more adequately clarified and consid-ered from the standpoint of their relatedness to the worldview. Since such inquiry is centred upon the immediacy of the relationship with the existential psychother-apist in the 'therapy world', Phase Two's central focus is on the client's honest examination of the challenges provoked by the therapeutic relationship itself.

Phase Three puts into practice the possibilities of reconfiguring the client's 'wider world' worldview via the incorporation of at least some of the experiential alternatives provoked by the experience of co-creating and co-habiting in the 'ther-apy world'. By so doing, an increased resonance between the newly established worldview and the client's experience of worlding may become possible. Through this (at least partial) *bridging* of the client's 'therapy world' and 'wider world' worldviews, Phase Three provides the means by which the temporary 'therapy world' is 'closed down' via the ending of the therapeutic relationship.

As will be discussed throughout Part Two, who and how the existential psy-chotherapist 'is' and what he or she 'does' with the client is substantially depend-ent upon which phase they are in.

At the same time, it must be stressed that explication of the practice of existen-tial psychotherapy in terms of phases is not intended to suggest a step-by-step, or 'one-two-three' rigid formulation of process. While I am convinced that consider-ing the practice of existential psychotherapy in a phase-like manner holds sub-stantial explanatory and instructive value for those wishing either to develop their understanding of existential psychotherapy in practice or, equally, for those wish-ing to clarify, compare and contrast its practice to that of other therapeutic models and systems, nonetheless this proposed structure should not be taken for the exact equivalent of existential psychotherapy as might be offered and experienced in any actual therapeutic encounter. While the structure under consideration reflects a truth-ful attempt to present existential psychotherapy as *I both understand and attempt to practise it*, I doubt that any existential psychotherapist, my self included, has ever, or will ever, practise existential psychotherapy *exactly* as is being described and presented here.

In like fashion, while it is relatively straightforward to discuss the practice of existential psychotherapy in terms of three identifiable phases, it must be acknowl-edged that these suggested phases should not be seen to be so distinct as to be mutually exclusive of one another. In the course of an actual therapeutic encounter, some aspect or influence of all three phases will be present – regardless of whether the encounter is the very first or last in a series, or anywhere in between these two poles.

Precisely *how* existential psychotherapy provokes the possibility of shifts in the client's worldview remains, at present, largely unknown. In this, it is no different from all other contemporary psychotherapeutic approaches. Nevertheless, as with research on the effects of therapeutic interventions in general, existential psychotherapy acknowledges that the therapeutic relationship itself is a key variable – if not *the* key variable. As will be demonstrated throughout Part Two, the proposed structure that I will attempt to describe places its primary emphasis upon the existential psychotherapist's acknowledgement of, and ways of 'being in', the therapeutic relationship as a critical means through which to address, disclose and challenge the client's worldview – not least via the implicating presence and impact of the therapist's own worldview.

I want to propose that the very entry into a therapeutic relationship (possibly even the *decision* to initiate therapy) permits the client to entertain and 'try out' possibilities of being that provide a *temporary* means by which the worldview is reconfigured. The conditions within which this can occur are bounded by the physical, temporal and relational 'setting' and its agreed rules, possibilities and restrictions that contextualise the therapeutic encounter from a structural standpoint.

Considered in this way, the client and existential psychotherapist enter into, and engage with each other within, a '*therapy world*' which can be compared and contrasted to the extra-therapeutic or '*wider world*' that both client and existential psychotherapist inhabit. Through exploration of the experience of being as expressed through the worldview within the 'therapy world', the various similarities, differences, areas of dissonance and disturbance, and so forth between the client's 'therapy world' worldview and the 'wider world' worldview can be disclosed and examined.

While the directed focus of such explorations is upon the client, existential psychotherapy recognises that the therapist is neither absent from nor immune to their impact. In this acknowledgement, the strength, significance and lasting effects of these investigations upon either or both the client's and therapist's worldviews – whether in the 'therapy world' or in the 'wider world' – cannot be predetermined.

THE THREE PHASES OF EXISTENTIAL PSYCHOTHERAPY

Following on from the above points, I want to consider a structural model of existential psychotherapy that incorporates three distinct phases.

Phase One is concerned with the co-creation by the existential psychotherapist and client of a 'therapy world'. This includes making explicit and respecting the boundaries, frame and inter-relational conditions that set its parameters. By so doing, Phase One permits the initiation of an open and honest descriptive exploration of the parameters of, and explicit tensions in, the client's worldview as experienced relationally within the 'therapy world' so that it can be compared with and existential psychotherapy's focus lies with the descriptive investigation of the ontic expression of such principles as they reveal themselves 'as belonging to the actual patient . . . [and] should not be subordinated to an all-inclusive existential' (Cohn, 2002: 83).

I emphasise this point, and my agreement with it, because the structural model being presented seeks to help existential psychotherapists to maintain their descriptive focus on those concerns that directly present themselves, rather than draw attention to them through the illuminating focus of the underlying principles such that the latter take precedence over the former. I am aware that this stance opens me, and the structure being discussed, to the accusation 'of lacking philosophical depth' (Cooper, 2003: 125). I leave it to the reader to decide whether this is so.

EXISTENTIAL PSYCHOTHERAPY: WORLDING AND THE WORLDVIEW

As was discussed in Part One, worlding is the term I employ to express the ongoing, ever-shifting, linguistically elusive, process-like experiencing of being. When, as human beings, we reflect upon, contemplate and seek to discern meaning from our lived experience of worlding, we essentialise the process so that it is conceived of in a structural fashion. The resulting structure is what has been termed the worldview. The worldview, therefore, is a partial and skewed expression of worlding since, as a structure, it cannot maintain or express directly *all* of the process-like aspects of worlding. There must, therefore, always be 'gap' or dissonance between worlding and the worldview. Thus, our human attempts to access the experience of worlding through the worldview must, necessarily, remain incomplete or inadequate. Further, it can be understood that the very transformation of worlding into the worldview provides the foundation for the dissonances and disturbances in living with which we all must contend.

Existential psychotherapy takes as its primary focus the descriptive clarification of the client's currently-lived worldview. It does so in order to expose and clarify the relationally derived role and function of the client's presenting problems and disturbances as constituent expressions of, and attempts to maintain, that worldview. This structured form of descriptive inquiry is, in itself, a challenge to the currently maintained worldview. It may provoke a realignment in any one, or all, of its primary sub-structures – namely, the self-construct, the other-construct and the world-construct – and consequently upon the worldview as a whole through the impact upon the sedimented dispositional stances and dissociated experiences that maintain, and serve to define each construct. Ultimately, existential psychotherapy seeks to allow clients the means to diminish the gap or dissonance between their maintained worldview and their experience of worlding, in such a way that the worldview is a more adequate (if still incomplete and imperfect) expression of the client's direct experience of worlding.

4

An Introduction to the Structural Model

INTRODUCTION

On the basis of the critical underlying principles outlined in Part One, Part Two will now delineate a structural model for the practice of existential psychotherapy. This model is derived from, and is an attempt to explicate, *my own* current way of understanding psychotherapy and working as a psychotherapist from an existential grounding and perspective. This stance emphasises and seeks to express existential-phenomenology's key underlying principles of relatedness, uncertainty and existential anxiety, as have been discussed throughout this text. Nonetheless, although these principles will, I hope, be seen by the reader to underpin all of the specific components of the structure under discussion, I make no apology for the fact that none of these principles is ever addressed *explicitly* within the context of the therapeutic relationship. In taking this stance, I am, I believe, adhering to an important position addressed by Martin Heidegger in the course of his *Zollikon Seminars* with Medard Boss and his psychiatric colleagues. Heidegger states:

> The decisive point is that the particular phenomena, arising in the relationship between the analysis and the analyst, and belonging to the respective, concrete patient, be broached in their own phenomenological content and not simply be classified globally under *existentialia*. (Heidegger, 2001: 124)

This statement, as I understand it, highlights Heidegger's concern that the practice of existential psychotherapy should refrain from addressing, or educating the client toward, the direct and explicit understanding and acceptance of the key underlying ontological principles of existential phenomenology. Rather, Heidegger argues,

Even so, acknowledging the above limitations of introducing a three-phase perspective upon the proposed structural model, I remain convinced of the merit of treating the three suggested phases as clearly distinguishable *emphases* and *points of focus* demarcating how far the investigation of the client's worldview has advanced in terms of its descriptive adequacy and its openness to inter-relational challenge. Just as importantly, I consider the value of this proposed structure to be that of providing a means for existential psychotherapists to monitor and evaluate their interventions in terms of their appropriateness as reflected not only from the standpoint of their resonance with the underlying principles and aims of the approach but also as indicators of the degree of trust that exists between therapist and client and which determines the extent to which the therapist has earned the right to so challenge the client's worldview.

5

Phase One: Co-creating the Therapy World

PRELIMINARY ISSUES: BASIC STRUCTURAL CONDITIONS FOR PHASE ONE

Spatial and Temporal Settings for Existential Psychotherapy

Although it may initially seem too obvious to raise as a matter of concern, nonetheless I want to suggest that it remains valid to ask: 'Where and when can existential psychotherapy take place?' In principle, the most straightforward answer, I believe, is: 'Just about anywhere and at any time.' Behind this somewhat simplistic answer lies a substantive challenge for therapist and client alike. Does psychotherapy require a particular and permanent setting and time-frame? Most contemporary approaches would answer 'yes' to both of those questions, even if these might vary with regard to the specific place and time that is deemed to be appropriate.

Most typically, psychotherapy occurs within an enclosed space such as a room in an office building or within the therapist's home (the therapist's 'consulting room') and lasts anywhere between thirty minutes and one hour – with fifty minutes ('the therapeutic hour') being the most common period of time set aside per session. Meetings may take place at a time-scale that runs anywhere between daily to monthly sessions, although the vast majority of these tend to take place on a once-per-week basis.

While there may well be sound pragmatic reasons for the decision on the part of most therapists and clients to follow these standard practices, it remains worthwhile to ask: 'How did these common practices originate?' And, perhaps more pertinently, 'Is it *necessary* to remain within the bounds of these practices?'

To a large extent, many of the commonly shared assumptions about location and time-frame can be seen to have been derived from the conditions set by psycho-analysis. Historically, psycho-analysis is acknowledged to be the first contemporary model of psychotherapy, although, to be more accurate, it is the earliest model of psychotherapy that continues to be practised in the twenty-first century (Ellenberger, 1970). It appears to be the case that regardless of the concerns and critiques of psycho-analysis raised by competing contemporary approaches, the vast majority have adopted and adapted a good deal of the psycho-analytic structure and made it their own. Although there is nothing inherently problematic about this, it reveals a certain degree of unquestioning adherence to a stance that, while entirely coherent and consistent within psycho-analytic principles, may not make too much sense within the principles espoused by alternative models.

If we limit our considerations to existential psychotherapy, it can be readily seen that there is no inherent rationale that would insist that the practice of therapy must stick to these historical conditions. Even if we wished to be guided by research findings dealing with such issues, we would be hard pressed to find any evidence either of beneficial consequences arising from the adherence to these generally accepted principles or of the negative impact of alternative stances (Madison, 2002; Spinelli, 1994). Thus, there is nothing either in its theoretical assumptions or on an evidence basis at present that requires existential psychotherapy to follow other approaches in the way that it determines the broad 'setting issues' under which therapy can take place.

Yes, it remains the case that most existential psychotherapists, myself included, tend to follow 'psychotherapeutic tradition' when it comes to such matters, if for no other reason than that of convenience as well as, increasingly, client expectation. But what is critical here is the awareness that alternatives *are* possible; just because a stance has become 'traditional' does not mean to say that other stances are less acceptable or reliable or, indeed, more dangerous.

From the perspective of existential psychotherapy, no specific set of conditions regarding broad 'setting issues' dealing with time and location is deemed to be necessary for its practice. It can, and most often does, take place in a room chosen and maintained by the therapist, but there is no inherent condition arising from the foundational existential principles that would prevent appropriate therapy occurring under circumstances where, for instance, the room being used was chosen and maintained by the client, or that different rooms and different locations were set for meetings, or even that meetings did not take place within the confined space of a room but rather occurred in open or public, or, indeed, 'virtual' space. Likewise, although the most typical duration of a therapy session is fifty minutes, there is no intrinsic reason why it could not last any other length of time. In similar fashion, the frequency of meetings, and whether they are open-ended, time-limited or a 'one-off' event has no inbuilt 'fixedness'. All this is not to insist that existential psychotherapists must develop any number of possible alternatives to 'tradition', nor to suggest that these alternatives are somehow 'better than' their traditional options. Equally, it would be absurd to dismiss the rules set down by the various professional bodies who more or less regulate psychotherapy, and the necessity of existential psychotherapists' adherence to such rules and guidelines in order to be acknowledged as bona fide professionals.

Once again, all that is being raised here is that, even within the limits of current standards of practice, existential psychotherapy offers a range of possibilities regarding general 'setting issues' that is worth acknowledging and considering – particularly if the therapist is principally working in the public arena where practical issues of spatial and temporal settings are of constant concern to units and their managers. In such instances, it can be readily seen that the flexibility of the existential approach may well be more of a value than, as might initially have been assumed, a hindrance.

However, although this freedom may be a possibility, it must be acknowledged that the adoption by existential psychotherapists of a more open and flexible stance toward such matters is entirely dependent upon each practitioner's worldview regarding the twin definitions of 'being an existential psychotherapist' and of 'practising existential psychotherapy'.

One possible means of considering how existential psychotherapists come to impose limits upon the general setting possibilities available to them is through what I have somewhat facetiously termed 'the Dumbo effect' (Spinelli, 1994, 2001).

The Dumbo effect

In brief, anyone who has seen the Disney cartoon, *Dumbo* (Disney, 1941), will recall that Dumbo the elephant is able to fly because he has convinced himself that he possesses a magic feather that grants him this ability. At first, Dumbo believes in the power and significance of the feather as the only cause of his new-found ability and, as well, of his self-esteem. The loss of the magic feather during a critical sky-diving performance initially leads to Dumbo's panic. However, much to his astonishment, he discovers that he can still fly and, with that, the magic feather is recognised as possessing nothing that is inherently necessary or magical.

This allegory seems to me to encapsulate the concerns raised regarding overall frame and contractual issues for existential psychotherapists (not to mention any number of other issues to be discussed elsewhere).

With regard to the concerns under present discussion, what is being proposed is that therapists' reliance upon a particular and rigid pattern of time- and space-related concerns serves the same function as Dumbo's 'magic feather' in that while such patterns have no special or 'magical' qualities in themselves, it is therapists' *belief* in them as essential factors in their ability to 'be' a psychotherapist and to 'practise psychotherapy' that bestows their significance upon them. In addition, it may be the case that clients, too, hold values and beliefs about 'being a client' and 'experiencing the benefits of psychotherapy' that rely upon the Dumbo effect as expressed through issues of setting, frame and contract. Indeed, there may be very little in, or about, the practice of psychotherapy as a whole that is *not* a Dumbo effect.

Existential psychotherapists are no different from other practitioners in that they, too, are likely to maintain any number of 'magic feathers' as ritualistic preconditions necessary to initiate therapy. With regard to existential psychotherapy's co-creation of a 'therapy world', the lack of any evidence regarding the superiority of any particular spatial, temporal or contractual set of conditions over any other makes it plain this co-creation is, at least in part, dependent upon the Dumbo effect and its reliance upon 'magic feathers'. This conclusion is not intended to suggest that therefore 'magic feathers' are unnecessary or even potentially problematic. However, what may be a challenge to existential psychotherapists in particular is to question their reliance upon certain 'magic feathers' to the extent that they may no longer consider them to be 'magic feathers' at all, and instead have come to view them as rigidly sedimented 'truths' expressive of their worldview as focused upon psychotherapy.

Thus, for existential psychotherapists the challenge being put forward is twofold: first, to clarify what 'magic feathers' are required with regard to temporal, spatial, and overall 'setting' issues necessary to the practice of therapy. Second, to challenge the necessity of those requirements.

As the whole thrust of the existential enterprise is directed toward disclosing the structure-bound patterns of the client's worldview, it would follow that for the existential psychotherapist it becomes particularly relevant to make clearer to him or her self what current 'magic feathers' can be identified and, once identified, to consider the challenge of no longer requiring these as 'magic feathers'. I doubt that any complete or final ridding one self of the reliance upon *all* 'magic feathers' is possible, but the attempt to pursue such investigations would be in keeping with the existential enterprise.

The issue of the therapeutic setting considered from the perspective of theatre

It is by no means a novel idea to suggest a correspondence of sorts between psychotherapy and theatre (Røine, 1997). One might ask: 'What are the preconditions that alert and prepare us for a theatrical experience?' In response, one might take a traditional position and argue that a theatrical event must take place within the confines of an enclosed space, perhaps include a stage that demarcates the actors from their audience, as well as being bounded by a specified timeframe, and so forth. Radical forms of contemporary theatre challenge such fixed assumptions by, for instance, removing the spatial barriers between audience and actors so that the space between them is fluid or uncertain, or by obscuring all clues as to when the play has begun or ended. The notion of 'suspension of belief' is usually presented as a necessary constituent in order to engage with a theatrical event. I would suggest that rather than beliefs being suspended, it is more a case of the co-creation, between performers and audience, of a unique and temporary 'theatre-world', entry to which is gained via the various agreed-upon settings and conditions which, taken as whole, serve as 'magic feathers' to all participants.

My view is that, in this sense, psychotherapy is akin to a theatrical event in that each requires the co-creation of a temporary 'world' – be it the 'therapy world' or 'theatre-world' – which in various ways provokes participants to experience who and how it is to be within, rather than outside it. Considered from this perspective, the value of 'magic feathers' lies in their ability to create the 'magical' conditions and constituents necessary for the co-creation of a distinct 'world' within which all participants experience novel – as well as previously unreflected and dissociated – worldview possibilities.

To summarise: the spatial and temporal 'setting' for existential psychotherapy remains an open possibility bounded only by the combination of the therapist's and the client's belief-based assumptions and their consequent conditions, as well as any such boundaries as might be expected by professional bodies concerned with ethical guidelines designed to protect both clients and practitioners. Even so, it would be somewhat misleading to suggest that, in most instances, the setting conditions agreed to by existential psychotherapists and their clients did not follow broadly traditional patterns – which is to say, that therapy is most likely to take place in the same physical space maintained by the psychotherapist (i.e. the therapist's consulting room), at the same set day and time on a weekly basis, the duration of each session being fifty minutes.

Nonetheless, even within this most traditional of magic-feather derived set of conditions, there remains a great deal to explore and examine.

AN EXERCISE EXPLORING THE EXISTENTIAL PSYCHOTHERAPIST'S RELIANCE UPON 'MAGIC FEATHERS'

As your point of focus, imagine that you, as an existential psychotherapist, are at the very start of your very first session with a client.
  Ask your self the following questions and note down your responses to them:

1. What preparations, if any, did I make as a preliminary to this session? Are they preparations I always make before the start of all sessions? What would it be like for me if I didn't or couldn't make these preparations before a session?
2. How, if in any way at all, did I get my self 'in the mood' or prepare my self so that 'I can now be a therapist'? For instance, did I do some sort of relaxation exercise before the client arrived? Or wear particular clothing? Or rinse with mouthwash or spray on deodorant?
3. In what ways is this therapeutic relationship similar to other relationships in my life? In what ways is it dissimilar?
4. What is attractive/exciting/fulfilling about being the therapist in the therapeutic relationship?
5. What is limiting/frustrating/infuriating about being the therapist in the therapeutic relationship?
6. What do I like about my self being the therapist in the therapeutic relationship?
7. What would I want to change about my self being the therapist in the therapeutic relationship?

8. What do I want my client to note and appreciate about me being the therapist in this therapeutic relationship?
9. What would I not want my client to know about me being the therapist in this therapeutic relationship?

Discuss your responses to these questions with a partner who has also carried out the same exercise. How do you react to them? What, if anything, might they tell you about your own, or your partner's, 'magic feathers'?

AN EXERCISE EXPLORING SPATIAL AND TEMPORAL SETTINGS FOR EXISTENTIAL PSYCHOTHERAPY

1. Clarify what conditional 'magic feathers' you require with regard to questions of spatial and temporal settings for the practice of psychotherapy.
2. Challenge each of the those requirements by considering: (a) what makes them necessary for you; (b) what would be the effect of and consequences to your ability to 'be' a psychotherapist and to 'practise psychotherapy' if each ceased to be a requirement.
3. Consider how the idea of a 'Dumbo effect' might serve to reveal the flexibility or lack of flexibility that you permit in your general assumptions about and definitions of psychotherapy.
4. Explore your view on the correspondence between psychotherapy and theatre.

The Therapeutic Contract

From the standpoint of existential psychotherapy, the contract that is arrived at between a particular therapist and client attempts to capture in as explicit and straightforward a manner as possible those essential requirements and conditions that provide the entry-point to the therapy world being co-created. In addition, the contract sets the foundational boundaries – including those of spatial and temporal setting – that permit the initial experience of a novel way of disclosing and challenging the client's worldview.

The contract might include statements and rules regarding the length, frequency and overall duration of therapy sessions; their location; financial arrangements; rules of behaviour; and so forth. The contract may be quite extensive, detailing various conditions, or may be relatively brief, focusing upon those factors that are pivotal and currently fixed beliefs ('magic feathers') demanded by the existential psychotherapist or client or both and agreed to – whether verbally or in writing – by both.

In addition, it may well be necessary from a professional standards and ethics standpoint to ensure that the contract states and reflects explicitly those essential conditions and requirements for appropriate practice and ethical conduct as set by the professional bodies of which the therapist is a member or registrant. Nonetheless, whatever is contained in the contract, and how brief or detailed it may be, I would suggest that the specifically stipulated contractual conditions are, in themselves, of far less significance than is the agreement by both participants to honour them.

For existential psychotherapists, the challenge of constructing a contract is, once again, that of delineating and perhaps questioning the 'magic feathers' with which they invest their beliefs in and ability to practise psychotherapy. This process of contract creation might well assist the therapist in paring away those beliefs and views that are no longer so magically infused and hence may not be necessary to the contract.

What is essential is that whatever is included as a contractual condition must be communicated to the client in a manner that is clear, consumes as little time as necessary and allows the client to agree to the contract or to propose amendments to it that can be discussed, clarified and either mutually accepted, or rejected by the therapist. This last point acknowledges that while the contract is co-created by the therapist and client, many of the stipulated conditions of the contract are non-negotiable requirements imposed by the therapist and which may be experienced by the client as being unnecessary and unreasonable. For instance, the therapist might insist that no extra-therapeutic contact is permissible or that the client must pay for missed sessions regardless of the circumstances that forced a cancellation. Such conditions might well strike the client as being harsh or demeaning or irrational. Nonetheless, while a contractual ideal might be one where all conditions were open to negotiation, it is far more likely that a contract will reflect some negotiated stipulations alongside various non-negotiable conditions set by the therapist as essential 'magic feathers'.

The critical point, I believe, is that *whatever* the contractual conditions, and *however* these were derived, they are explicit, understood and agreed to by both therapist and client. Even if the client fails to comprehend the rationale behind some or all of the contract's stipulations, what matters is his or her understanding of, and agreement to, the rules themselves. In this, the therapy world, like the wider world of experience, reveals itself as not always comprehensible with regard to the meaning and purpose behind its rules, nor is it always in agreement with personal views, preferences, desires and predispositions. Rather, the significant difference offered by the therapy world is that at least one of its inhabitants – the therapist – remains consistent in adhering to *all* of the explicitly agreed-upon contractual conditions that make up the rules of that world. Thus, for the client, the greatest value of the contract does not lie in its specific stipulations. Nor is it the case that the contract must reflect a coherent framework which underpins these stipulations and which indicates the views, biases and preferences of all its inhabitants. *Rather, the critical worth of the contract lies in its potential for the demonstration to the client of the therapist's trustworthiness 'as one who says what he or she means and does what he or she says' through adherence to the contract's mutually agreed rules and conditions.*

Critics of psychotherapy have highlighted the 'artificiality' of the therapy world precisely because it seeks to avoid the chaos and confusion of the wider world, wherein rules and agreements are repeatedly broken or opened to re-interpretation by any one inhabitant without any communication, much less negotiation, with any other. In response to this, I would suggest that although it may make sense to argue that the attempt to adhere to the contract-derived rules of the therapy world is in various ways *different,* this is not sufficient reason to judge it as being 'artificial' (and thereby investing it with all the added implications of this term). Further, while critics have rightly pointed to the abundant evidence of some therapists' lack of adherence to their own set contractual rules and the serious consequences for their clients that the various forms of 'contract deviation' have provoked, this undesirable state of affairs demonstrates that, if anything, the experience of inhabiting the therapy world is hardly artificial (Alexander, 1995; Bates, 2004; Sands, 2000). Indeed, at an experiential level, it is not unusual to come across statements by clients and therapists alike that their experience of inhabiting and relating within the therapy world provokes a deeply felt sense and reminder of how it is to experience 'being real' (Gordon, 2000; Kirschenbaum and Henderson, 1990).

AN EXERCISE EXPLORING THE SIGNIFICANCE OF THE CONTRACT IN EXISTENTIAL PSYCHOTHERAPY

1. From the standpoint of your 'being a psychotherapist' what contractually is essential for you? From the standpoint of your 'being a client' what contractually is essential for you?
2. What is or was made explicit in the contract with your own therapist?
3. Is there or was there anything implicit in your therapeutic contract that should have been made explicit?
4. How was your therapeutic contract communicated to you? Was there any discussion or negotiation regarding any of its stipulations?
5. Have you, as a psychotherapist, ever deviated from your contract? If so, how did you alone or you and your client experience this deviation?
6. Have you, as a client, ever experienced your therapist deviating from the contract? If so, how did you alone or you and your therapist experience this deviation?
7. Following the discussion on the contract and what has emerged from doing the exercise so far, what views do you now hold with regard to the therapeutic contract?
8. Write out your version of a contract and present it to a colleague for discussion.

The Secure Frame from an Existential Perspective

Taken together, the issues regarding settings and the contract can be viewed as the primary constituents for the establishment and maintenance of what other approaches in contemporary psychotherapy refer to as a *secure frame* (Luca, 2004).

The notion of a secure frame from an existential perspective is not so much concerned with the delineation of a generally agreed-upon setting or set of contractual specifications. Rather, a secure frame for existential psychotherapy lies in the elucidation of the essential conditions and stipulations under which the client's wider world worldview may be expressed and experienced within a novel and distinct 'therapy world'.

Unlike other models' understanding of the secure frame, existential psychotherapy argues that the specified conditions and stipulations, in themselves, are meaningless in that no evidence exists to demonstrate that they, in themselves, either improve or diminish the likelihood of a worthwhile therapeutic alliance or of beneficial outcomes for the client. It is more the case that they provide a belief system for therapist and client, rather than specify what is to be believed or how such beliefs are to be enacted. This is not to suggest that there exists little, if any, import in the beliefs being maintained. As has already been argued, it is via these beliefs, or 'magic feathers', that the particular worldview possibilities within a distinct and identifiable therapy world become possible for both therapist and client. This ability to compare and contrast differing worldview experiences may well be the crucial factor determining whatever lasting benefits there may be to psychotherapy.

From an existential perspective the attempt to promote or provide security cannot be taken out of the inter-relational context that acknowledges the inevitable presence of uncertainty and the experience of existential anxiety. The attempt to provide the conditions for entry into a therapy world whose foundational rules are both explicit and maintained (initially, at least, by the therapist) should in no way be seen to be an attempt to exclude anxiety as a constituent of the therapy world. Indeed, in many ways, the clarification of, and adherence to, the inter-relational boundaries of the therapy world may well aggravate the client's experience of anxiety rather than diminish it.

As such, the notion of an *ideal* setting or an *ideal* contract – and, hence, an *ideal* secure frame – all of which implicitly suggest certainty and security makes little sense. Such 'ideals' merely reflect the conditions necessary to our magical beliefs, but we should not forget that all beliefs arise through and remain expressions of inter-relational uncertainty.

AN EXERCISE EXPLORING THE SIGNIFICANCE OF A SECURE FRAME IN EXISTENTIAL PSYCHOTHERAPY

1. From the standpoint of your 'being a psychotherapist', what constitutes a secure frame for you?
2. From the standpoint of your 'being a psychotherapist', what constitutes an insecure frame for you?

3. From the standpoint of your 'being a client', what constitutes a secure frame for you?
4. From the standpoint of your 'being a client', what constitutes an insecure frame for you?

Phase One of existential psychotherapy is most clearly identified with the co-creation between client and therapist of an experientially accessible and partially communicable therapy world. This therapy world provides the boundaries and rules through which a novel, if temporary, worldview emerges for the client which can be examined, compared to and contrasted with the client's wider world worldview. (This is not to dismiss or minimise the significance of similar emergent possibilities being experienced by the therapist and which, as will be discussed, can play a critical role in the enterprise of existential psychotherapy. Nonetheless, as will be made evident, even when the existential psychotherapist's worldview becomes the focus it remains primarily in the service of the investigation of the client's worldview.)

Thus, two people agree to investigate the worldview adopted by one of them. They agree that the primary way of attempting this enterprise is through their experience of relatedness under a certain set of agreed-upon conditions that are shared by both participants, even if these shared conditions are likely to be unequal in that their content and focus have been principally determined by one participant (the therapist), and whose underlying 'meaning' may be unclear or seem unreasonable to other (the client).

These agreed-upon conditions address issues of general setting and contractual specifications that are deemed essential to the maintenance of the therapy world. To a large extent, these have a 'magical' rather than evidence-derived basis and may have no significance in themselves other than that invested in them by the participants' beliefs.

For the existential psychotherapist, ensuring that these rules are not obscure or implicit or open to individual amendment, and adhering to their agreed-upon conditions, is critical in order to demonstrate, and for the client to be convinced of, his or her *trustworthiness*. This trustworthiness is initially communicated via the therapist's willingness both to make explicit and to stand by the agreed-upon inter-relational rules regarding the therapeutic frame.

PHASE ONE: ENTERING THE THERAPY WORLD

The Client's Journey to the Therapist

Perhaps surprisingly, it is unusual for psychotherapists to pay much attention to the steps taken and journey conditions negotiated that have enabled the client to appear at the entrance to the therapist's consulting room.

In a broad sense, such issues ask us to consider the question: 'How did the client get to me?' As can be surmised, this question concerns itself not only with matters of geography and travel but also with the broader issues of initial pre-psychotherapeutic contact.

For those existential psychotherapists who work privately, the issues here highlight such matters as whether the client selected you on the basis of some sort of personal recommendation or reference from someone else (for instance a colleague, or possibly one of your ex- or even current clients), or whether your name and details were found in a Professional Register or in the *Yellow Pages*.

For those existential psychotherapists working in the public sector, perhaps in a hospital or educational setting or as part of a GP practice, the working-out of the referred client's route to you, perhaps through a GP, a Psychological Unit, an Assessment Process or some other information-based system could prove to be of substantial value.

In either case, it would also be worth having a clear sense of the actual journey that the client makes to get from his or her residence or work-place to your consulting room and back once the session is finished. Equally, this exploration would highlight how that journey is negotiated, for instance whether by car, public transport, or walking, and how long this journey typically lasts. Further, such investigation might well consider the physical and social environment through which the client's journey takes him or her. Are there, for instance, any noticeable difficulties or dangers or tempting locales for the client to fix upon? For example, if the client's issues have to do with alcohol abuse, does the journey confront the client with numerous pubs or wine bars?

Related factors dealing with the client's journey would include *the means* by which first contact was made. Was it by telephone, letter, e-mail or text message? Was the contact directly with the therapist or indirectly through a GP or agency or some other intermediary? And equally, what was actually stated or agreed to by the end of that first contact? If it was a direct contact, what was the therapist's felt sense of that contact? Was that felt sense subsequently communicated to the client or kept to one self?

Why should such matters be worthy of the existential psychotherapist's attention?

From an existential perspective, the client's way of being as he or she progresses through the various steps to the start of a session may offer valuable clues as to the client's presenting stance, attitude, concerns and expectations regarding the process and outcome of the therapy, either of a particular session or with regard to the therapeutic relationship as a whole. These instances of 'journeying' can serve as possible expressions of the client's initial steps leading to his or her entry into the therapy world. In like fashion, they might be significant indicators of the client's *way into* the particular worldview that arises within the therapy world.

For example, one of my clients, Robert, always mentioned to me at the start of our sessions how he valued and enjoyed his journey through Regent's Park to my office. He stated that it was important to him to have a few minutes of relative isolation walking down paths where he could avoid being seen by, and having to negotiate his way through, the large number of people who might get in his way. One day, some months into our weekly meetings, Robert arrived and immediately announced that he had altered his journey. He had begun his usual route but had suddenly felt angry about his need to escape the presence of others. Now, Robert stated, the lonely path he had been taking no longer filled him with pleasure and peace, and instead served to remind him of his perpetual loneliness. Instead, he had decided to follow the most populous route and rather than avoid the presence and gaze of others he had allowed himself to make passing eye contact with several passers-by. Not surprisingly, this shift in his journey to me paralleled a broader shift in Robert's relations with others as a whole.

AN EXERCISE FOCUSED ON THE CLIENT'S JOURNEY TO THE THERAPIST

1. Pick a client with whom you are currently in a therapeutic relationship.
2. Detail descriptively the journey that this client must make to and from your consulting room.
3. What environmental landmarks might the client pass through? How direct is the client's journey? How long is it likely to take?
4. What are the final negotiations that the client must make in order to reach the door to your consulting room? For example, does the client have to speak to a Receptionist or a Personal Assistant? Or talk through an intercom? Does the client come directly to you or do you take preparatory steps to meet the client?
5. Consider what has emerged through your focus on Points 2-4 that might be of relevance both to the client's presenting issues and to your attunement with the client during your sessions. If any aspects of Points 2-4 have altered during the course of your therapeutic relationship do you have any sense of a resonance between these alterations and more general shifts in the client's worldview?
6. Consider the journey that you take (or used to take) to and from your own therapist. In doing the exercise from your own experience of being a client do you note any significant factors or resonances between that journey and the wider issues and concerns explored in your own experience of being in psychotherapy as a client?

The Initial Meeting: Greeting the Client

In my discussions with other existential psychotherapists, I have always found it somewhat odd how certain some colleagues appear to be concerning 'the rules of greeting the client' either with regard to the first session or for all sessions. Some will remain silent and refuse to reply to the client's everyday questions such as 'How are you?' or comments concerned with weather or climate or newsworthy events. Others might respond to such queries and comments only until the consulting room door has been shut and both participants are seated. Very few, it seems, just engage with their clients as one might under more ordinary circumstances.

When asked about this stance, the majority of existential psychotherapists with whom I have spoken will refer to their unwillingness to engage in 'idle chit-chat' and may even refer to Heidegger as the source for their stance. As discussed in Chapter 3, my own view is that this attitude is a serious misinterpretation of Heidegger's concerns. At the same time, as has also been discussed above, I am ready to concede that this form of initial greeting may be a necessary 'magic feather' for any number of existential psychotherapists.

Nonetheless, the question of the initial meeting captures once again the possible divergences between an existential approach and other approaches primarily influenced by psycho-analysis. In the latter, various directives are urged upon practitioners about such questions as whether to greet the client and, if so, how this might be done in an appropriately professional manner (Smith, 1991). While there is every reason for the therapist to remain appropriately respectful of, and professional toward, the client, nonetheless no formal 'initial greeting code' exists or appears to be necessary within existential psychotherapy.

Without wishing to denigrate the views of other approaches, it remains arguable that such rigid codes of conduct may serve no purpose or function in themselves other than to act, once again, as 'magic feathers' for the therapist. Hence, from an existential perspective, there is no reason to suppose that initial greetings in the therapeutic relationship need in any way be different to, or distinct from, initial greetings that might occur in *any* professional setting. In like fashion, how varied these may be in terms of physical movement such as a handshake or verbal utterances would appear to be no more or less than in any other set of similar circumstances.

Whatever is the case, what might be of importance for the existential psychotherapist in such an initial meeting is the monitoring and noting of how he or she responds in terms of greeting style to the client's presence and, in turn, what stance the client adopts in his or her initial encounter with the therapist. Rather than judge whether what occurs is or is not appropriate, it would make more sense for the existential psychotherapist simply to note descriptively his or her manner of greeting the client.

Such explorations concerning initial greetings are not intended to evaluate the relative appropriateness of the way of greeting that has occurred, nor to judge it in relation to other, once-possible, ways of greeting that might have taken place. Rather, initial greetings can be seen to be the means by which both the existential psychotherapist and the client *together agree to enter the therapy world*. Thus the initial greeting can be seen to be a means to express the wider experience of 'being with one another'. Through it, the views, values, beliefs, concerns and judgements underlying both the therapist's and the client's adopted way of being stand disclosed.

Just as *how* initial greetings are enacted may raise worthwhile questions for the therapist, such questions should not be restricted solely to *initial* greetings but can be extended to include the investigation of the therapist's way of greeting throughout the whole of the therapeutic relationship.

AN EXERCISE FOCUSED UPON THE QUESTION OF THE INITIAL GREETING

1. Consider your way of greeting your clients at the start of the initial session with them. Is your way of greeting consistent or does it vary from client to client or from session to session?
2. Is this way of greeting typical of your way of greeting someone for the first time in other circumstances?
3. If it is atypical of your way of greeting another, what makes it so?
4. Does this atypical stance seek to express something regarding 'how I am to be with this client and how I am expecting this client to be with me'? If so, what is that?
5. Is there any possible variation or flexibility in your initial way of greeting your clients? Is there any variation in subsequent sessions?
6. What do you note to your self about your client's way of greeting you? Do you evaluate it in any way? Does it provoke any particular attitude or emotion or behavioural response in you?
7. What was your therapist's initial way of greeting you? How did you experience it? Did it have any impact on the therapeutic relationship as a whole and over time?

The Initial Meeting: the Client's Opening Narratives

A significant area of concern to most therapists and closely related to the issue of the initial greeting is the question: *Who should be the first to start to talk?*

Once again, for those therapists who are influenced by psycho-analytic tradition, there is a common assumption that, other than the most perfunctory of greeting (such as 'Hello', 'Please sit down'), it is most appropriate for the client to initiate verbal discourse during the first session, and, indeed, during all subsequent ones. Something very similar to this stance is adopted by a great many existential psychotherapists, though why they should do so, other than because it serves as another necessary 'magic feather', remains something of a mystery to me.

Unlike other approaches' predominant focus upon, and interest in, the subjective world of the client, existential psychotherapy's primary concerns lie with the inter-relation between therapist and client as the focus of the descriptive exploration of the client's worldview within the therapy world. In this divergence, the existential psychotherapist can no longer exclude his or her presence from this process nor is he or she bound to a particular way of being present. Therefore, the question of who should be the first to start to talk cannot be so easily answered. What rules there may be remain uncertain and insecure – just as they are when faced with 'the how' of initiating any encounter. Each participant acts from an uncertain and uneasy space. Perhaps one or the other will speak first. Perhaps both will begin to speak at the same time. Perhaps each will refrain from speaking or have no idea what to say for some indeterminate period of time. Perhaps the client will feel hurt or irritated or unheard if the therapist begins to speak first. Perhaps the therapist may speak up because the client appears to be lost or confused or miserable. Just as, possibly, the therapist may refrain from speaking because the client appears to be lost or confused or miserable. In brief: *who knows?*

The argument being presented here is one that neither promotes a set of rules nor, in contrast, celebrates unbridled spontaneity on the part of the existential psychotherapist. Both are potentially valid just as both create limitations and possibilities in their enactment. Once again, from the existential psychotherapist's standpoint what is being urged is a non-evaluative monitoring of his or her own attitude and behaviour in the context and circumstances of being with a particular client at a specific moment in time. That the therapist may vary his or her attitude and stance toward the question of who speaks first, from client to client or from session to session, seems to be no different than what may happen in any other set of circumstances surrounding the experience of two people meeting and greeting one another either for the first time or on separate occasions under circumstances that are bounded by moral and professional codes of conduct.

In this, existential psychotherapy permits a degree of choice and freedom for the therapist that may not be as available within the dictates of other contemporary approaches. As ever, such freedom of choice has its price in terms of the uncertainty and anxiety that arise from any action taken, as well as in its consequences. It is for the existential psychotherapist to embrace such possibilities and their impact upon the relationship not so much in terms of 'could what has been co-created have been better or more appropriate if such and such a step had/had not been taken?' but rather from the standpoint of 'it is what it is and let us work with that'.

Whoever it may be who begins the dialogue between therapist and client, what remains of evident importance is *what* is said by the client as well as *how* the statements are communicated in terms of such factors as the various expressions of emphasis and nuance accompanying them.

The first things that the client says and the way they are said reveal how the client has chosen to present him or her self to the existential psychotherapist. Further, they are likely to express either directly or more subtly the client's initial stance toward, and response to, the presence of the therapist. Equally, they might contain indications of what is wanted of the therapist by the client.

From a worldview standpoint, clients' initial statements provide an early insight about their attitude and stance toward self and other being in relation. More generally, they provide pivotal initial clues as to how clients' worldviews permit them to be inter-relationally with regard to their self-, other- and world-constructs. Just as importantly, clients' first few statements serve to reveal their initial assumptions about the specific and particular therapy world that is being co-created, not least in terms of the assumptions, beliefs and expectations being placed upon its inhabitants and how they are expected to interact and relate with one another.

What is critical for the existential psychotherapist is that any client's initial statements are *always* to be treated as valid and appropriate, no matter what they express, or fail to express, as well as what views, attitudes and assumptions they may contain.

At first, this may be a difficult stance for the therapist to adopt, especially when the client's statements reveal assumptions or views that directly challenge the therapist's, either in general (e.g.: 'You're the last person left who can help me'), or in terms of a particular factor (e.g.: 'Did you watch *Lost* last night?'). This stance can be equally difficult to embrace if the client's statements are excessively critical in some aspects of the worldview (e.g.: 'I'm always going to be a loser!') or express views and stances that strike the therapist as being patently incorrect or absurd (e.g.: 'Every American film being made has sub-liminal anti-Muslim messages in it.').

Acknowledging such, it nonetheless remains the existential psychotherapist's primary task during Phase One in general, and most significantly during its early stages, to seek to attend and attune him or her self to the client's currently lived worldview as it presents and expresses itself in the immediacy of the encounter. The attempt on the part of the therapist to *stay with* the client's initial statements is by no means an abdication of challenge. Rather, this stance *permits* a powerful form of challenge which the client is likely to experience immediately: here in the therapy world that is being co-created, the first experience of 'the other' (that is to say, the existential psychotherapist) is that of *an other who does not immediately set out to transform, reject, dispute, diminish or broadly overwhelm my worldview so that it better fits that other's worldview.*

The significance of such a challenge has been insufficiently considered and addressed by existential psychotherapy in general. Even then, the inter-relational implications of this form of challenge demand further analysis and elaboration. In brief, this response on the part of the therapist serves to highlight the possible contrast between the client's experience of relatedness in the therapy world and that of the wider world. This is not to suggest that the client may immediately value and prize such possibilities as are being expressed and presented in the therapy world. On the contrary, the client may well experience disturbance, resentment and anger toward the therapist for not fulfilling his or her worldview expectations and assumptions. Equally, such reactions may provoke disturbing challenges to the client's worldview assumptions which, in turn, may demand reactions that seek to dismiss or diminish the felt impact of the therapist's challenge. Whatever the case, once again, it is vital for the existential psychotherapist to treat these as being valid and appropriate and thereby maintain the challenge.

AN EXERCISE DEALING WITH THE CLIENT'S INITIAL STATEMENTS

1. Consider the initial statements made to you by one of your clients that have struck you and remained in your memory.
2. What was said? How was it expressed?

3. What, if any, clues to the client's worldview were contained in the client's initial statements?

   • What, if any, inter-relational elements were contained in the client's initial statements?
   • What relations were presented or alluded to?
   • Where did the client place him or her self in those relations?
   • Were they predominantly concerned with the client's relations toward him or her self (e.g.: 'I dislike my self', 'I'm helpless')? Or toward others (e.g.: 'They don't appreciate me', 'They dislike me', 'They don't understand or accept me')? Or towards world-constructs (e.g.: 'When it's too hot, I lose it', 'Alcohol is a problem', 'The world is just too dangerous')?
   • Who, if anyone, emerged as the primary focus of the client's concerns?
   • What initial 'story' or narrative was being expressed or suggested through these initial statements?
   • What is the client's role within this suggested narrative? Does the client take centre-stage in the initial narrative? If not, who or what does?
   • What sort of language is being employed to convey the narrative?
   • What sort of narrative is being presented? (Comedy? Tragedy? An extraordinary epic, or a more ordinary 'kitchen-sink' drama?)

4. How did you react to the client? What brought you closer to the client? What distanced you from the client? What changes did you as therapist find yourself wanting to achieve for the client?
5. How do you react now to the client-as-recalled? What, if anything, alters your reactions?
6. Now repeat the exercise, but this time focus on a client whom you experience as being particularly problematic or difficult in some way.
7. When you compare and contrast the two examples you chose, does anything of relevance for you emerge?

While such a challenge to the client's opening statements can be both illuminating and powerful, it should not lead the existential psychotherapist to suppose that through this challenge the inter-related meanings within the client's worldview have been instantly exposed and understood. To assume so, in fact, limits and impairs whatever value this initial challenge may have, since for the therapist to assume that he or she has sufficiently understood the worldview of the client serves as a more subtle and pernicious means for the therapist to impose his or her worldview upon that of the client.

How then can the existential psychotherapist begin to discern the plethora of 'meaning factors' contained within the client's worldview?

PHASE ONE: EXPLORING RELATEDNESS

Other-focused Listening

For the existential psychotherapist, the primary task throughout Phase One is that of seeking to clarify descriptively the client's worldview as it expresses itself in the therapy world so that this worldview can be considered, compared and contrasted to the client's statements regarding his or her wider world worldview. Typically, in the early encounters during Phase One, the client will emphasise the disturbing, inexplicable or problematic conflictual relations taking place in the wider world and how these impact upon and challenge his or her worldview. In response, the descriptive exploration being attempted by the existential psychotherapist concentrates upon the clarification of:

1. the *noematic elements* of the client's narrative – that is to say, the 'story' or, more broadly, the 'what' of the client's narrative;
2. the *noetic elements* of the client's narrative – that is to say, the 'referential' elements of the client's narrative that express 'how' the client experiences that narrative via his or her dispositional stances.

This descriptive exploration initially requires the existential psychotherapist to adopt a particular stance of 'phenomenological openness' such as might be represented by terms like 'not-knowing' (Jaspers, 1963) or, as I have suggested, 'un-knowing' (Spinelli, 1997) which refer to the therapist's attempt to assume an attitude of utmost receptivity to the initial novelty and mystery of the client's worldview as expressed and contained in its narrative statements.

Other-focused listening addresses the primary consequence of the therapist's attempts at un-knowing and, by so doing, brings to the therapeutic encounter that which was perhaps most appropriately labelled by the philosopher Martin Buber as 'inclusion'.

Other-focused listening is not merely an attitudinal quality to be adopted by the existential psychotherapist in some general fashion. Rather, it has immediate and far-reaching implications and consequences regarding his or her way of being with the client, most particularly during their early encounters which set the foundation for the therapeutic relationship.

For instance, consider the example in which the client initially elects to enter the narrative being brought to therapy by adopting a verbal focus that speaks in the second ('you') or third ('they') person, and entirely avoids the first ('I'). It would not be atypical for many therapists to intrude upon this narrative and either encourage or insist that the client alter the narrative in favour of first-person ('I') statements. While such a demand might make sense for other models, it is clearly antagonistic to the existential psychotherapist's attempt at other-focused listening.

Similarly, consider the example in which much of the client's highly disturbing narrative is presented in a somewhat 'lifeless', detached fashion. While other approaches may intervene by either inviting or urging the client to repeat parts or the whole of the narrative in an increasingly loud or emotional voice, or suggesting to the client that he or she exaggerate either the dialogue or some physical movement that accompanies that dialogue, such options make no sense as expressions of other-focused listening within the first phase of existential psychotherapy.

These kinds of therapeutic interventions indicate that the existential psychotherapist has stepped away from an attempted stance of un-knowing and instead suggest a therapeutic shift toward a 'natural' attitude which assumes his or her knowledge and understanding of the meaning and function of the noematic and noetic aspects of the client's narrative. From an other-focused listening standpoint, however, the therapist cannot claim any such knowledge, nor has he or she as yet earned the right to be an active co-creator of a *novel* narrative which may arise for the client. Further, rather than seek to address and disclose the worldview of the client as it is being expressed in the encounter, such interventions express an implicit critique of the client's worldview by the therapist (who, in his/her role as *present other* in the client's *other-construct* might well confirm – however inadvertently – the client's beliefs that others are un-accepting, that others insist that they know better than the client what is the appropriate way to be, that others are demanding, or dangerous, or punitive, and so forth).

AN EXERCISE IN OTHER-FOCUSED LISTENING

1. Working together with a partner, take turns in carrying out the whole of the following:

   - Present an event that occurred today which was experienced by you as being in some way disturbing, irritating or problematic.
   - Describe the event solely from its noematic focus (i.e., describe as accurately and comprehensively as you can 'what happened').
   - Describe the event solely from its noetic focus (i.e., describe as accurately and comprehensively as you can what were the significant elements expressive of 'how you experienced the event').
   - Either have your partner re-state the event in the light of the descriptive statements generated from Points 2 and 3 or re-state your partner's focused-upon event in the light of the descriptive statements he or she generated from Points 2 and 3.

2. Discuss each other's experience of:

   - attempting to describe accurately your partner's focused event;
   - hearing your partner attempt to describe accurately your focused event.

3. Discuss with each other, what, if anything, emerged from the exercise that affected or altered your overall stance toward your own focused event.

Being-with and Being-for the Client

While the majority of contemporary approaches to psychotherapy emphasise the maintenance of a focus broadly concerned with interpretation, instruction and intervention expressed via specialist techniques, existential psychotherapy's focus calls upon therapists to respond to the challenges of openness and uncertainty that arise in the immediacy of their encounter with the client with whom the therapy world is co-created. The implications of this form of encounter can be considered from the standpoint of the therapist's attempts to *be-with* and to *be-for* the client. Although readers should not delude themselves (or be deluded by another) that either attempt is easy or straightforward, nevertheless taken together they exemplify the primary concerns of Phase One.

Being-with the client

The attempt at *being-with* the client, expresses the existential psychotherapist's respect for, and acceptance of, the worldview of their clients as revealed within the therapy world. Being-with the client is the attempt to embrace both the dispositional stances being adopted by the client and the way in which they are being given its expression such as via the language employed, the non-verbal movements and gestures that may express or accompany client statements and the chosen means of dialogue employed by them.

Being-for the client

Being-for the client expresses the existential psychotherapist's willingness to attempt an increasingly adequate 'resonance' with the client's worldview as it presents itself in the therapy world. This movement toward resonance seeks to avoid judging, overwhelming, adjusting, or 'swamping' the client's presenting worldview with an alternative that is deemed preferable by the therapist. Nor does it suggest that the therapist seeks to deny his or her 'otherness' in addressing and confronting the alien worldview of the client. Rather, it enjoins the existential psychotherapist to be an other who, in the act of embracing the alien worldview of the client, seeks to permit that worldview to co-habit the therapy world without threat of its being distorted, amended, altered or rejected by the other's (i.e. the therapist's) more powerful worldview.

The attempt to be-with and be-for the client seeks to assist the existential therapist in staying with the client's worldview on a moment-to-moment basis. In addition, it subverts his or her tendency to be the client's 'truth-bringer', 'healer' or 'helper' in any purposive or directive manner. Of course, all such may still be experienced by the client in ways that may impact both subtly and dramatically upon his or her experience. What is critical here is the therapist's abdication of any directively focused initiatives whose aim is that of altering the client's presenting worldview.

The distinction between the attempt to be-with and the attempt to be-for the client is subtle yet significant. While the former focuses on the existential psychotherapist's willingness to both discern and describe with increasingly adequate accuracy the client's presenting worldview, the latter is concerned with the therapist's attempt to embrace that worldview as currently valid and appropriate for the client. Although neither being-with or being-for the client can ever be fully achieved, and, therefore, remains an aim or attempt rather than a fulfilment, nonetheless the undertaking may well provoke, or reinforce, a challenge similar to that discussed in the previous section dealing with the client's opening narratives: the existential psychotherapist's attempts at being-with and being-for the client communicate that 'here is an "other" who, unusually, if not uniquely, attempts to embrace my way of being as it presents itself in the immediacy of the inter-relational encounter.' This challenge, in turn, may often initiate the client's own challenges to his or her sedimented stances not only toward how others 'are' but also toward how he or she 'must or must not be' in the presence of others.

The subtle power of this attempted stance has been experienced by my self, as well as by numerous other existential psychotherapists, during brief and unexpected moments in an encounter with a client that may best be expressed as *uncanny*. Such moments of intense resonance with the client's worldview may lead therapists to feel themselves to be temporarily 'lost' or 'swallowed up' in the client's world. Not surprisingly, although this experience can be exhilarating, it can equally be unpleasant, disturbing or even frightening. Nonetheless, however it may be experienced, this encounter with the uncanny, rather than create chaos or diffusion of thought and experience, can paradoxically provoke substantial clarity for the therapist with regard to the client's worldview. These experiences seem to me to resonate closely with the German term *befindlichkeit* – which Hans Cohn translates as a 'dispositional or mood-focused attunement' (Cohn, 2002: 59). Cohn argues that Heidegger chose this term in order to refer to feeling-modes that 'cannot be "split off" from the situation in which they occur' (Cohn, 2002: 61) – which is to say that they 'belong' neither to the being nor to the world alone, but to both. So is it the same, I suggest, in the existential psychotherapist's experience of the 'uncanny' possibilities of being-with and being-for? Conversely, these uncanny resonances can also be experienced by clients if they are led too forcefully or too quickly into the dominant focus of the therapist's worldview. In my opinion, the writings of R.D. Laing remain second to none in their description of what may occur when a therapist seeks to be-with and be-for a client and, in addition, when therapists, adopting a more objective model, impose their reality – or a broader 'consensus reality' – upon their clients (Laing, 1960, 1967, 1982).

Readers will recall the earlier allusion to theatre in the discussion of the therapeutic setting. It seems appropriate to reconsider such an allusion in the light of the current topic. In many ways, the existential psychotherapist's attempts to be-with and be-for the client resonate with those adopted by actors in their efforts to 'enter into their character'. Each actor attempts to discern and embrace the character's worldview *within the boundaries of dialogue and narrative set by the playwright.* The actor cannot alter such boundaries and, instead, must present an embodiment of the character through these very same boundaries. The achievement of the actor is to draw out unique, previously unforeseen interpretative possibilities for that role while respecting and adhering to its pre-set boundaries. So too, I suggest, does the existential psychotherapist, like an actor, attempt a similar enterprise of describing and embracing the client's worldview from within its current dialogical and behavioural boundaries.

AN EXERCISE EXPLORING THE ATTEMPT TO BE-WITH AND BE-FOR THE OTHER

1. Choose a client with whom you have worked as a psychotherapist (or trainee) who stands out for you as embodying attitudes, values, stances and/or beliefs which are in opposition or are alien to your own.
2. Select a specific instance or example that expresses the above differences and describe it so that the disturbing or unacceptable dispositional elements it contains are sufficiently clarified.
3. Imagine your taking on for yourself the dispositional elements highlighted in Point 2. What is it like for you to embody these dispositional elements

   - in the presence of someone whom you consider to be an intimate?
   - at your work setting with colleagues?
   - at a friend's party?
   - in a public area such as in a park or on a bus?
   - when by yourself?

4. Consider how, if at all, your attempt to describe and embrace your client's alien and undesirable dispositional elements has altered or affected your stance toward and understanding of your client.

The Existential Psychotherapist as 'the Other'

Within the therapy world, the existential psychotherapist is the presenting focus for the client's *other-construct*. As this other, the therapist is both the representative of all others who contribute to the definition and maintenance of the client's other-construct and, just as importantly, is also the other who challenges the client's current other-construct and, hence, the currently maintained worldview.

Through other-focused listening and the attempt to be-with and be-for the client, the existential psychotherapist demonstrates his or her willingness to 'stay with' and 'be attuned to' the client's worldview as it expresses itself – no matter how debilitating, restrictive, limiting and irrational it may appear to be to the therapist (if not to all others in the client's world, the client included). By so doing, the therapist begins to challenge profoundly the client's other-construct-derived expectations and assumptions regarding how others are, how others expect the client to be, and how the client expects others to be with him or her.

Via the existential psychotherapist's client-attuned presence, clients are more likely to respond to the presence of a *non-judgemental other* who attempts to describe and embrace their worldview by initiating an accepting stance toward it. This shift, in turn, promotes the possibility of clients' greater willingness and courage to access novel worldview possibilities within the secure boundaries of the therapy world and thereby confront the sedimentations and dissociations that define and maintain their wider world worldview as a whole as well as its primary constructs (i.e. the self-, other- and world-constructs).

The exploration of the 'therapist-as-other' corresponds strongly with Martin Buber's now famous contrast between *I–It* and *I–Thou* relations.

From an I-It standpoint, the therapist can be 'the other' who both experiences and relates to the client as a distinct and separate object whose meanings, values, behaviours and beliefs can be reshaped and reformulated via the imposition of the therapist's preferred meaning stance. Or, equally, the therapist can be 'the other' who is both experienced and related to by the client as a distinct and separate object whose role is to encourage and impose novel meanings, values, behaviours and beliefs that reflect the preferred meaning stance not only of the particular 'other' who is the therapist, but also of others in general. Alternatively, from an I–Thou standpoint, the therapist can be 'the other' who both experiences and relates to the client from a stance of inclusion which respects the otherness of the client by attempting to 'stand not only at his own pole of the bipolar relationship but also at the other' (Buber 1970: 178–9). In addition, this inter-relational challenge may generate the possibility of the client's embracing of inclusion within the therapy world (Farber, 1967).

Buber was careful to clarify that inclusion should not be equated with empathy. He viewed empathy, for all of its potential for warmth, care and concern toward the other, as another expression of an I–It relation. As Buber viewed it, empathy requires the therapist to treat the client as merely another version of 'I' and, thus, stays attuned only to a projected image of him or her self, thereby remaining unwilling to include the otherness of the client within the therapeutic stance. As a consequence, the client's response to the therapist's empathy is to continue to experience the therapist as an unrelated 'other'. If the I–It attitude is grounded in an insistence upon the separateness of 'the other', the I–Thou attitude promotes a reciprocity or meeting between each 'other'. The former equally objectifies both the 'I' and the 'It'. The latter reveals that both 'I' and 'Thou' co-exist as inseparable poles of interrelation.

How, then, might the existential psychotherapist seek to avoid such all-too-likely 'I–It' consequences and attempt a truly inclusive 'otherness'? In my view, the following qualities and characteristics of 'the therapist as other' permit at least a partial attempt at this possibility:

1. The existential psychotherapist is 'the other' in the therapy world whose presence attempts to reflect the client's wider other-construct.
2. The existential psychotherapist is 'the other' in the therapy world whose presence challenges the client's wider other-construct.
3. The existential psychotherapist is 'the other' in the therapy world who attempts to be adequately open and receptive to the otherness of the client so that some of the implicit components of client's other-construct can be made explicit.
4. The existential psychotherapist is 'the other' in the therapy world who is sufficiently curious to consider the possibility of being-as-the-other from a perspective that reflects the client's other-construct with increasing adequacy.
5. The existential psychotherapist is 'the other' in the therapy world who rebels at all of the above attempts and who seeks to avoid such encounters with the otherness of the client so that the polarity-derived impact of the client's explicit other-construct disclosures upon his or her own other-construct can be minimised or avoided.

6. The existential psychotherapist is 'the other' in the therapy world who acknowledges this desire to rebel as part of the polarity-derived impact of the client's explicit other-construct disclosures upon his or her own other-construct.
7. The existential psychotherapist is 'the other' in the therapy world whose inclusive otherness discloses and challenges the client's self- and world-constructs, and, hence, the client's world-view as a whole.
8. The existential psychotherapist is 'the other' in the therapy world whose inclusive otherness discloses and challenges his or her own self- and world-constructs, and, hence, his or her world-view as a whole.
9. The existential psychotherapist is 'the other' in the therapy world whose presence and impact upon both the client and him or her self cannot be fully captured through all of the above and any other statements regarding 'being the other'.

AN EXERCISE EXPLORING THE EXISTENTIAL PSYCHOTHERAPIST AS 'THE OTHER'

1. Work together with a partner in a structured session, taking turns to be therapist and client. Each session should last twenty minutes.
2. As the client, focus your discussion upon your relation to a specific 'other' in your life who is currently provoking some degree of disturbance or irritation for you.
3. As the therapist, assist the client in focusing upon his or her relationship with that other.
4. As the therapist, whenever it seems appropriate, bring the client's discussion directly into the therapeutic relationship by exploring in what ways, if any, the client's relationship with that other may be impacting upon the client's experience of being with the therapist as 'an other'.

   • How is the therapist being experienced as similar to the client's disturbing 'other'?
   • How is the therapist being experienced as different to the client's disturbing 'other'?
   • What, if anything, can the client express to the therapist-as-other that cannot be expressed, or is difficult to express, to the disturbing 'other'?

5. As the therapist, whenever it seems appropriate, monitor your experience of being with the client. In particular, consider the following:

   • What are my initial impressions of this client?
   • What are my initial expectations in being with this client?
   • What would I want to know now about this client?
   • What would I want the client to know about me?
   • What would I not want the client to know about me?
   • What is it like for me to be here in the presence of this client?

6. After the exercise has been completed by both partners, discuss with each other:

   • What it was like as a client to focus on a disturbing 'other' while in dialogue with a therapist who explicitly acknowledged and utilised his or her presence as 'an other'.
   • What it was like as a therapist to explicitly acknowledge and utilise your presence as 'an other'.

- What it was like to monitor your own experience of being the other while attending to the client. Was anything useful to the therapeutic process gained from this self-monitoring?
- What possible value or areas of concern does this focus on the 'therapist-as-other' raise with regard to the effectiveness of a therapeutic encounter?

AN EXERCISE IN INCLUSION

1. Working in the presence of a partner, count to thirty in silence.

   (NOTE: Only one of you counts, the other simply remains present and silent throughout the exercise until Point 6.)

2. Note what is the first image/word/event/sound/statement that comes to mind as soon as you have completed the counting.
3. Describe the above as accurately and descriptively as you can to your partner.
4. What feeling/thoughts/emotions are connected with it? Say something about this to your partner.
5. What is the first 'free association' that you make to it? Clarify that association for your partner.
6. Have your partner state what immediate impact upon or connection to any aspect of his or her own life experience your described 'free association' may have had.
7. Together, discuss the effect that doing this exercise has had on your relationship with each other.

   (NOTE: If you want to do the exercise from the standpoint of the 'silent' participant, it would be best to work with a different partner.)

PHASE ONE: EXPLORING THE CLIENT'S WORLDVIEW

The Phenomenological Method of Investigation

Edmund Husserl, the founder of phenomenology, initially developed what has become known as *the phenomenological method* in order that it might be applied to all forms of structured inquiry (Ihde, 1986a; 1986b). Subsequently, variations on the phenomenological method were used to address descriptively those constituents or components present in any given lived experience. It is principally with this latter focus in mind that existential psychotherapists have adopted the phenomenological method as the foundational stance or attitude for the exploration of the client's worldview as it presents itself in the therapy world. As with previous discussions (Ihde, 1986a; Spinelli, 2005), an initial description of the phenomenological method sub-divides into three distinguishable, though inter-related, steps.

Step A: the rule of epoché (bracketing)

The first step urges the existential psychotherapist to set aside any initial biases and prejudices and to suspend, or *bracket,* all expectations and assumptions regarding the client's statements and their implicit meaning. In other words, the rule of *epoché* requires the therapist to attempt to set aside any immediate personal predispositions and preferences toward any particular meaning or explanation of the client's worldview. Instead, the therapist remains temporarily open to any number of alternatives, neither rejecting any one as being out of hand, nor placing a greater or lesser degree of likelihood on any of the options available. In some instances, this bracketing may be actively practised by the existential psychotherapist via some method of focused attention or meditation that 'opens' him or her to the possibility of a phenomenological attitude. Alternatively, the existential psychotherapist may experience bracketing simply through the descriptively focused monitoring of his or her mental processing as it occurs.

For example, recall the first meeting you had with a particular client. Did you have prior information about this client such as, for instance, the disturbance that had led him or her to decide to see a therapist? If so, how were you influenced by this information with regard to how you met that client, or what expectations or concerns or ideas or doubts presented themselves for you? Had you already formulated some structure or plan or set of achievable goals for the client? And when you first encountered the client face to face, what views and values and attitudes did you hold regarding his or her appearance, age, attractiveness, facility with language, general psychological 'health', and so forth? These are just some of the many biases and prejudices with which the rule of *epoché* is concerned and which it urges therapists to bracket.

Step B: the rule of description

The second step shifts the existential psychotherapist's focus of attention away from theoretical explanations (since, for the moment, no one explanation is more adequate than any other), and, instead, emphasises the task of describing as concretely as possible that which the client presents. The essence of the rule of description is: 'Describe, don't explain' – which is to say: rather than step back from the client's statements so that they are explained, transformed or rejected on the basis of the therapist's preconceived theories or hypotheses, assist the client in carrying out a concretely based descriptive investigation of his or her currently lived experience.

For example, imagine that, in an initial meeting, your client expresses his extreme fear of rats. From an explanatory standpoint you might assume that this fear arose from some disturbing earlier experience. Alternatively, you might view the fear as irrational and the fault of some inappropriate set of learning associations. Or you might wonder whether the fear of rats expressed another 'deeper' or 'wider' fear. Or you might even consider the fear from the standpoint of existential death anxiety. All of these responses to the client's presenting statement fail the conditions of the rule of description.

Instead, in following the rule you might seek to clarify such issues as: how the client's fear is experienced and expressed: is it 'located' in any part of his body? What is the body-feeling associated with it? If the fear had a sound, what would it sound like? Is the level of fear the same in all instances of encountering a rat or does it differ? How does the client 'feel' the fear – is it awful? Does it have any pleasant aspects to it? Or, with regard to the client's focus on rats: is it a rat as a whole or a particular aspect or body-part of the rat that provokes his fear? Is it all rats or just rats of a certain size or colour? Does the location in which the rat is encountered have any significance? All of these latter questions serve as examples of the descriptively focused investigation expressed in the rule of description.

Step C: the rule of horizontalisation (the equalisation rule)

The first two steps in the phenomenological method provide a means to investigate presenting aspects of the client's worldview in a non-prejudiced and descriptive manner. The third step, the rule of horizontalisation, warns the existential psychotherapist to avoid imposing any hierarchical assumptions of importance with regard to the items of description by temporarily equalising their significance or meaning value. The rule of horizontalisation can only be applied temporarily since, simply in order to remain investigations all investigations must, at some point or other, set a pragmatic limit to its application. Nevertheless, in being willing to follow this rule to some extent, investigators reduce the likelihood of imposing unnecessary judgements or biases on their initial observations. In doing so, they increase the adequacy of their conclusions. Conversely, the failure to maintain a horizontalising attitude too soon after an investigation has begun will skew the therapist's attunement to the client's presenting worldview so the overall attunement will likely be far less adequate than it might have been.

For example, a new client comes into your consulting room for an initial session, sits down across from you and says: 'Isn't it a wet and miserable day? I'm so relieved to finally begin therapy. I'd like to take an axe to my husband and watch his brain ooze out of his skull.' Typically, therapists will focus on one of these statements, ask the client to clarify it further and in all likelihood pay no further attention to the remaining statements unless they are raised again by the client. The rule of horizontalisation challenges the therapist to avoid making such judgements regarding the relative significance of one statement over another and, instead, attempt to treat each as having equal value or significance until further information may come to reveal a hierarchical relationship between them. As a way of communicating the attempt to initially treat the statements as equal, the therapist might offer them back to the client (and thereby demonstrate that she has been heard accurately) and ask, for example: 'Do you want to explore any one of these in particular?' Or: 'If you were in my position, which of these would make the best sense to explore further?' Or: 'Do you want to stay with these three statements and explore them further or is there anything else that seems more important for us to focus on?'

Taken together, the three steps outlined above make up the phenomenological method. As should now be clear to readers, the various expressions of relatedness as discussed on pp. 106–12 above, all rely upon some or all of the 'steps' of the phenomenological method. Similarly, while the metaphor of 'steps' is useful to initially present the phenomenological method, following a strict and formal 'one-two-three' step approach would be highly artificial. Instead, each 'step' can be viewed as a particular point of focus within an inter-related set of attitudinal dispositions.

Neither the phenomenological method as a whole nor any of the identified 'steps' can ever be truly completed or reach a final all-encompassing conclusion. While it remains impossible for us to bracket all biases and assumptions, we are certainly capable of bracketing a substantial number of them. In addition, even when bracketing is not likely or feasible, the very recognition of bias lessens its impact upon our immediate experience. Similarly, no purely descriptive account is possible, since no description is altogether free of implicit explanatory components. And, in like fashion, the very act of engaging in dialogue with an other ensures that no true and complete horizontalisation of presenting statements is possible. Acknowledging such limitations does not, however, diminish the power of the phenomenological method. At the very least, the method minimises the existential psychotherapist's tendency to rely exclusively upon any self-preferred set of assumptions throughout the whole of the therapeutic relationship. Equally, while it cannot claim to lead to correct or final conclusions, the practice of the phenomenological method serves to establish and maintain a particular inclusionary relatedness within the therapy world that, in its advocacy of 'openness to that which presents itself', acts to challenge the experiential inflexibility of the client's worldview. Finally, the use of the phenomenological method provides a means for the existential psychotherapist to validate the adequacy of his or her attempts to access accurately the presenting worldview of the client. In similar fashion, the client, in turn, is likely to experience his or her worldview statements as having been accurately understood and, hence, validated. Nonetheless, to experience having one's statements accurately understood may be gratifying and reassuring, but may also be unnerving and disturbing – not least, because their implicit meanings and values may become apparent for the first time.

AN EXERCISE ON THE PRACTICE OF THE PHENOMENOLOGICAL METHOD

1. Working together with a partner, take turns in being the therapist and client. Each session should last twenty minutes.
2. As the client, select a generally provocative topic that holds some interest and significance to you and discuss its impact from your personal standpoint.
3. As the therapist, assist your client in exploring his or her relationship to the provocative topic while attempting to stay with and follow the three 'steps' of the phenomenological method.
4. After you have both completed your sessions, discuss

    - your experience as a client working with a therapist who attempted to explore the topic through the phenomenological method;
    - your evaluation of the therapist's success in attempting to explore the topic through the phenomenological method. (What instances stand out for you as examples of the therapist staying close to the method? What instances stand out for you as examples of the therapist deviating from the method?)
    - your experience as a therapist who attempted to explore the topic through the phenomenological method;
    - your evaluation of your own success in attempting to explore the topic through the phenomenological method. (What instances stand out for you as examples of your relative success in staying close to the method? What instances stand out for you as examples of your having deviated from the method?)

5. Finally, discuss with each other what benefits and limitations you suppose there might be in utilising the phenomenological method as a basis to therapeutic investigation.

Existence Tensions

As a means of clarifying the client's worldview as focused initially upon his or her self-construct the exploration of the client's *existence tensions* may prove to be useful in generating descriptive discourse. The term *existence tensions* was first proposed by Dr Bill Wahl, a counselling psychologist who aligns his views and approach to practice with those of existential psychotherapy. Wahl produced a preliminary list of existential polarities, or 'tensions', which he argued are 'intrinsic to human experience' (Wahl, 2003: 267). His list of these tensions arose through a process of qualitative archival research which drew out explicit polarities as discussed in several well-known texts by various existential psychotherapists.

Each of these conditions provokes interpretative stances toward various complementary aspects or polarities of existence, such as meaning and meaninglessness, security and insecurity, openness and rigidity, and so forth. As such, the worldview reveals where and in what way each of us locates or places him or her self with regard to these conditions of existence. Below, I have included a selective list of some of the more pertinent and apparent existence tensions derived from Wahl's initial list:

ACCEPTANCE	REJECTION
APATHY	CONCERN
ATTACHMENT	SEPARATION
AVOIDANCE	CONFRONTATION
BALANCE	EXTREMES
BODY	MIND
CHANGE	STASIS
CONTROL	LETTING GO
CONVENTIONALITY	UNIQUENESS
EFFORT	EASE
FINITUDE	INFINITY
FUTURE	PAST
HARMONY	CHAOS
HEALTH	DISEASE
HEDONISM	ASCETICISM
IDEALISM	STATUS QUO
POWER	IMPOTENCE
REASON	INTUITION
RITUAL	SPONTANEITY
SECURITY	UNCERTAINTY
SELF-CENTREDNESS	OTHER-FOCUS
SOLITUDE	SOCIABILITY
TRUST	SUSPICION
UNION	SEPARATENESS
WORK	LEISURE/PLAY

As can be readily discerned, the list is both partial and open to any number of additional polarities or alternative terms with which to express polarities. Nonetheless, it serves as a working template upon which the exploration of existence tensions can be initiated.

As I understand and employ the term, 'existence tensions' reflect dilemmas and concerns surrounding one's *essence* (*that* I am), *existence* (*what* I am) and *identity* (*who* I am) (Laing, 1960). They reveal the parameters through which the self-construct is described, maintained and verified.

The exploration of existence tensions assists investigation of the self-construct (that is to say, the 'self' that I believe or insist I am or must be) in a highly descriptive, concrete and specific fashion.

Considered from the standpoint of existential theory, the exploration of existence tensions permits a descriptive means of addressing, for example, what Sartre termed as a person's 'life project' (Sartre, 1991), the ontic constituents of existential anxiety as proposed by Heidegger (Heidegger, 1962), and the degree and expression of ontological insecurity as discussed by Laing (Laing, 1960).

What is critical to understand about the exploration of existence tensions is that they are primarily a means with which to *map* or 'to get a reading of' the client's worldview. The aim is *not* one which seeks to amend any aspects of the polarities they express. Nor is it to shift the client's position with regard to each polarity closer toward some sort of balance or equilibrium.

With regard to this final point, like many other existential psychotherapists I remain of the opinion that the enterprise towards equilibrium cannot be fulfilled. At best, our lives are composed of constant attempts which will eventually fail.

Indeed, as was discussed in Part One it may be that the insistence upon equilibrium provokes far worse expressions of disorder and disturbance than any resulting from dis-equilibrium.

With these points in mind, I would suggest that the value of the exploration of existential tensions is at the level of *description, not prescription.*

This is not to say that prescriptive aims are necessarily either incorrect or inappropriate. Rather, the avoidance of advancing a prescriptive focus via the analysis of existence tensions, particularly while in the first phase of therapy, rests principally upon the shift that such a stance would provoke with respect to the primary aim of attending and attuning oneself to the client's worldview as it is being expressed in the immediacy of the therapeutic encounter. Further, such a shift would rightly raise concerns about the therapist's potential misuse or abuse of power in the therapeutic relationship, since to utilise any discerned existence tensions prior to having gained sufficient understanding of their contextual meaning and how, in turn, such meanings serve the maintenance of the client's current worldview, would bestow upon the therapist an interpretative authority which has not yet been earned and which may prove to further debilitate the client.

The descriptive exploration of existence tensions is most typically carried out in a semi-structured fashion that is reliant upon the client's statements as the 'lead-in' to any direct inquiry. For instance:

Client:	I felt so gutted when she just left me and went to live with him.
Therapist:	What was in that sense of 'being gutted'?
Client:	Oh, lots of stuff. I guess, mainly just being rejected.
Therapist:	Is that something new for you? Or is rejection –
Client:	No, it's a recurring theme in my life. I can't stand any sort of rejection.
Therapist:	So ... OK. Let me ask you this: if we put rejection as the extreme point on a continuum between rejection and acceptance, say, am I right in thinking that you'd tend to put rejection as the more problematic polarity for you?
Client:	Oh yeah, for sure. I love being accepted.
Therapist:	And if you're the one who's doing the accepting or rejecting?
Client:	Uhmm ... Oh, that's different. Actually, then it's the other way around.

There is no inherent reason against the existential psychotherapist and client engaging in a more formal and structured exercise that presents a series of existence tensions (as above) and asks the client to 'locate' his or her current stance toward each tension either verbally or by placing a mark somewhere along the line of continuum. While some existential psychotherapists might be disturbed by, or antagonistic to, an enterprise that could be construed as a form of assessment, others might find it both an appropriate and worthwhile means to encourage descriptive inquiry and, more importantly, to address directly the inter-relational aspects of the client's worldview. Indeed, it is possible that presenting such an exercise at various times throughout the therapy (or even only at its start and completion), could highlight important factors related to shifts in the client's self-construct and worldview as a whole.

Having carried out the latter exercise with various groups of participants in a number of masterclasses that I have facilitated, I must admit to some degree of surprise as to how fruitful an exercise it was and how valuable the participants found the discussions arising from their explorations to be. Many said how powerful it felt for them to be involved in co-creating an 'inter-related overview' of the (usually) implicit attitudes, beliefs, assumptions and values that underpinned the self-construct component of worldview. Others noted that while the location at which they had placed themselves along the continuum of each separate polarity was accurate *when considered in isolation*, viewing the various polarities together and considering them in relation to one another provoked significant contradictions and unforeseen disparities in their understanding of their self-construct. For example, one participant who greatly valued 'union' but who had consistently found difficulty in initiating and maintaining lasting intimate relationships noted that she had also highlighted overwhelming tendencies toward 'suspicion', 'rejection (of others)' and 'control'. While none of these points was necessarily novel in itself, the effect of considering each inter-relationally was startling for her.

Of course, doing a structured exercise in the context of a masterclass is a significantly different enterprise from engaging in a therapeutic encounter. Acknowledging that, and also that I personally tend to distance myself from anything in psychotherapy that smacks of over-generalising assessment and evaluation models and procedures, I am prepared to accept that a structured process focused upon existence tensions, that remains exclusively descriptively focused, and is offered to the client in a fashion that permits and accepts its rejection is not inherently inconsistent with existential psychotherapy. Indeed, in the *realpolitik* of contemporary publicly funded, evidence-based provision of psychotherapy, it might make sense to explore the possibilities of descriptive structured analyses as might arise in the exploration of existence tensions.

Thus far, I have focused the discussion of existence tensions as a way to highlight the self-construct components of the worldview. However, it is vital to note that the exploration of existence tensions may also be used to assist in the concrete description of both the other-construct and the world-construct components of the client's worldview. In the same masterclasses mentioned above, for example, when the participants carried out the exercise while focusing upon the worldview of a current client who was in some way 'difficult' for them (other-construct) or considered elements of the world-construct, equally powerful and surprising connections were arrived at and discussed. Readers who attempt the following exercise may find something similar.

AN EXERCISE EXPLORING EXISTENCE TENSIONS

1. Utilising the limited list of existence tensions presented above, carry out a descriptive investigation of your self-construct by marking where along the continuum you place your self with regard to each polarity.

    *   Note any existence tensions that tend toward either polar extreme.
    *   Note any existence tensions that tend toward the centre.

2. When considered as a whole, or inter-relationally, what sense of your self-construct emerges? Is this as you would have predicted? If not, what is different?
3. Consider a current concern or bothersome issue in your life from the stand-point of the 'mapping' of existence tensions that you carried out. In what ways, if any, does this means of considering the issue provide novel and useful perspectives?
4. Focus upon a current client whom you would describe as being 'difficult' or 'irritating' in some way. Now repeat Points 1 and 2 as a 'mapping' exercise for that client's existence tensions.
5. Compare the 'map' of the self-construct and other-construct existence tensions. What, if anything, emerges when you examine where you have placed points of extremity and points of balance in each?
6. Consider one disturbing aspect of the client under consideration in relation to both the self-construct and other-construct mapping that you have undertaken. What, if anything, emerges that strikes you as worth further consideration?
7. Repeat Points 4 to 6, but this time focusing upon an example of a world-construct in your worldview.

Descriptive Challenging

As has been discussed so far, during Phase One existential psychotherapists assist their clients in examining their presenting issues and dilemmas in ways that open them to descriptive clarification. This attempt exposes in what ways the relatedness between these disturbing areas of concern and the clients' currently maintained worldview may express itself. In order to begin to explore such possibilities, clients are urged to 'remain still' with their experience of unease rather than seek out ways of distancing themselves or moving on from it.

For these reasons, the focus of existential psychotherapy during Phase One tends to avoid what might broadly be termed *analytically focused investigations* whose principal concerns lie with explanatory hypotheses about possible past or originating 'causes' of the client's current worldview. Thus, the existential psychotherapist's interventions tend to centre upon the 'what and how of experience' (that is, the noematic and noetic constituents of an experience) as exemplified through the phenomenological method. This is not to suggest, as some critics have proposed, that the existential psychotherapist cannot or should not ever ask questions focused on 'why?' However, it is clear that just as a 'why' question may serve a descriptively focused enterprise, it may also open the way to abstract explanations that distance the client from the lived immediacy of his or her experience. It is this latter form of 'why' questioning that existential psychotherapists attempt to minimise. Just as 'why-focused' questions and explanations may help clients become more aware of and connected to their own implicit meanings and truths, they may also allow them to remain with meanings and truths that, while potentially valid in their general explanatory possibilities, yet create or maintain barriers to the client's sense of connection with their own currently maintained worldview. Once again, Heidegger's warning that existential psychotherapy should focus on the client's specific ontic expression of wider or universal onto-logical 'givens' seems worth repeating. The issue, it seems to me, is not so much *that* in the course of therapy explanations may make themselves apparent for the client but rather *how* those explanations serve to assist or hinder the client's abil-ity to access the various dispositional stances of his or her worldview *as they man-ifest themselves in thought, mood, emotion and behaviour.*

Descriptive challenging is *not* the challenging of the client's worldview so that its values, logic, moral bases, beliefs and associated emotions and behaviours are criticised, approved of, rejected or provided with alternatives by the existential psychotherapist. Descriptive challenging *is* the challenging of the client's world-view so that its implicit dispositional stances are made more explicit. The more the dispositional underpinnings of the client's worldview are brought to awareness, the clearer will be the inconsistencies, contradictions and areas of tension that are con-tained within them or which they provoke for the worldview. Even then, however, the task of the existential psychotherapist is not to offer alternatives or attempt their reduction or removal but, rather, to engage with the client in the exploration of their relatedness to the presenting problematic issues.

It is evident that any hope of achieving this enterprise rests upon both the exis-tential psychotherapist's and the client's willingness to 'be still' with what presents itself, in the way that it presents itself, rather than seek to alter or move on from it. Unfortunately, one of the greatest obstacles encountered by the therapist is that the vast majority of clients neither wish, nor seem able, to 'be still' in their exploration of their worldview. Hence, the therapist's own demonstration of investigative still-ness through descriptive exploration can serve as a challenge to the client's stance, as well as provide a direct example of a potential alternative.

Of equal importance, the effectiveness of descriptive challenging rests initially upon the existential psychotherapist's willingness and ability to be *creative* in the descriptive challenges presented to the client. This creative quality is founded upon what I have termed *curiosity.* This is not to suggest any prurient focus, but rather an inquisitiveness that is eager to discern that which is being presented by the client as if it were novel to the therapist. Analogously to the behaviour of a young child interacting with a new and unknown toy, there exists a playful quality to this therapeutic curiosity that permits the therapist's descriptive challenges to originate from a stance of 'un-knowing' so that they express the investigative aims of the phenomenological method. For example:

Client:	When I think about what happened, it feels terrible.
Therapist:	What makes the feeling terrible?
Client:	That I was so stupid! That I gave up the best thing to happen in my life with-out a second thought!
Therapist:	And what is 'terrible' about that?
Client:	What do you mean? How can it be anything but terrible?
Therapist:	I was just trying to get a clearer sense of what it's like to experience feeling it as terrible.
Client:	I don't understand.

Therapist:	OK. Does the feeling have a location?
Client:	A location? Yeah. It's a tightness in my throat. Like I want to vomit.
Therapist:	Anywhere else?
Client:	No . . . Just that. And a sort of overall tingly feeling.
Therapist:	An overall tingly feeling. Right. Can you say any more about that?
Client:	It's like . . . Oh, I don't know. It's like when I used to read Spider-Man comics and he used to get this 'spider-sense' whenever there was danger. Like that.
Therapist:	So, there's something about 'danger' in the tingly feeling?
Client:	I guess so. I don't know what's dangerous, though.
Therapist:	Let's recap: 'feeling terrible' for you is a tightness in the throat and a tingly feeling all over that you connect with a warning about danger. Is that right?
Client:	Yeah.
Therapist:	Is there more?
Client:	It's funny . . . Just as you said that, I heard a sound.
Therapist:	A sound? You mean 'feeling terrible' has a sound for you?
Client:	Yeah. It's weird, but –
Therapist:	Can you make the sound?
Client:	[*makes a gargling noise*] It's like trying to speak, but you can't.
Therapist:	When you were doing that, were there any words that you were trying to produce?
Client:	I don't know. I don't think so.
Therapist:	Actually, I just wondered: did it feel like it was 'you' trying to make the sound? Or possibly anyone else whom you recognise?
Client:	Anyone else?
Therapist:	Don't worry; if it sounds like a crazy question, don't –
Client:	You know what? It does sound like someone else. It sounded like my sister when she was small and we used to play together and she'd say things like: 'I've got a really really big secret to tell you. You know what it is?' And I'd go: 'Tell me.' And she'd get right up close to my ear and then make that same damn noise with her throat! That's weird.
Therapist:	OK. So stay with that. 'Feeling terrible' has got you to hearing your sister's 'I've got a secret' noise. Let's play for a moment and imagine that it is your sister's voice and she does have a secret that she wants to tell you. Anything come to mind?
Client:	[*begins to cry*] Yeah.....
Therapist:	Do you want to say –
Client:	[*yells*] How come I end up feeling so terrible like this? What's so fucking wrong with me?
Therapist:	You want to try to answer those questions?
Client:	Yeah . . .
Therapist:	OK. So . . . have you got any clues as to why you ended up feeling so terrible as you do?
Client:	I don't know. You tell me.
Therapist:	I wish I could, but I genuinely have no idea. But, let me ask you this: What would it be like not to have this terrible feeling?
Client:	Relief, I guess.
Therapist:	OK, relief. So . . . Let's imagine that it's a year from now and the therapy's been successful and you don't have this terrible feeling any more. What comes to mind for you?
Client:	I'm normal! I'm like everyone else!
Therapist:	Ha! That's interesting. So losing that feeling allows you to be normal and like everyone else.
Client:	It's not exactly 'losing it'. It's more the way I handle it. What I can do with it.
Therapist:	Oh... So, if I heard you right: others have the feeling but they can do something with it that you can't. Is that right?
Client:	Yeah.
Therapist:	So... What is it that others can do with it that you can't?
Client:	They're not so overwhelmed. They're not so self-punishing. They can laugh a bit about it. It's not such a big fucking deal for them.

Therapist:	Great. So how come you can't do what others can? What's different about you?
Client:	It sounds stupid, but I keep going back to Christmas when I was 6 years old and I didn't get a fucking thing. Just a stupid gimpy tree with a note saying 'Sorry . . . . Father Christmas ran out of presents. He'll bring you some tomorrow.' That's the first time I just went out of control and smashed everything up and then realised how fucking stupid I was because that meant fucking Father Christmas wasn't *ever* going to come back.
Therapist:	And that's what makes you different?
Client:	Guess so . . .
Therapist:	OK. Well, Let me pose another question: Let's say it's a year later, and you're still different. And that, in fact, no matter how hard you've tried or what you do it's *never* going to go away and –
Client:	No! That's terrible! I can't accept that!
Therapist:	Wait! Stay with what you're experiencing right now. Is it like what we've just been talking about?
Client:	Yeah! Maybe even worse!
Therapist:	OK, so try to stay with it. What's happening in this experience you're having?

AN EXERCISE IN DESCRIPTIVE CHALLENGING

1. Working together with a partner, take turns in being therapist and client. Each session should last twenty minutes.
2. As the client, focus on a reasonably strong feeling that you experienced today and begin your session by just stating the feeling.
3. As the therapist, engage in a process of descriptive challenge by assisting the client in investigating the stated feeling.
4. When you have both completed the exercise, discuss what the experience of doing the exercise was like for each of you when you were being the therapist or the client.
5. What general value, if any, for the therapeutic encounter would you say that descriptive challenging might offer?

Noematically and Noetically Focused Descriptive Challenging

Although it is primarily concerned with the client's *noetic* experience (i.e., the dispositional stances that express 'how' the client experiences a narrative), descriptive challenging can be a powerful means with which to descriptively 'open up' the *noematic* (i.e., the 'story' or, more broadly, the 'what' of the client's narrative) constituents of the client's experience. Some forms of what has become known as *Narrative Theory* in psychotherapy attempt to explore clients' concerns from a standpoint that is usually referred to as 'storying' (Freedman and Combs, 1996). As with existential psychotherapy's descriptive challenging, 'storying' concerns itself with the clarification of the noematic narrative ('the story itself') in order to bring to the surface the implicit dispositional stances that are embedded within it (how 'the story' both reveals and affects the narrator). Narrative theory attempts a 're-storying' of the client's narrative through its descriptively focused, and often quite imaginative, investigation of it.

Drawing from Narrative Theory, existential psychotherapists can challenge descriptively the noematic constituents of the client's narrative by addressing such issues as:

> Who or what persons/objects/events are under focus in the client's narrative?
> Who is the most pivotal character in the client's narrative?
> What is problematic in this narrative?
> What is valued in this narrative?
> In what ways does each of the above reveal itself?
> What is being emphasised in the narrative?
> What is being minimised in the narrative?
> What gaps are there in the narrative?
> What new narrative emerges if its problematic elements are altered or removed?
> What new narrative emerges if its valued elements are altered or removed?
> What new narrator emerges if its problematic elements are altered or removed?
> What new narrator emerges if its valued elements are altered or removed?

This noematic focus of investigation provides further means with which to disclose the *noetic* aspects of the narrative. For instance, following on from the focus questions raised above, an opportunity is provided to address such noetic issues as:

> What underlying values/beliefs/views/attitudes/behaviours/felt emotions are associated with the narrative?
> How are these being communicated through the narrative?
> How do they impact upon the narrative?
> How are these being maintained?
> How are they being prevented from being altered?
> How is this problematic issue experienced by the narrator?
> How do the persons/objects/events under focus relate to the narrator?
> How do the persons/objects/events under focus relate to one another?
> How does the narrative relate to the narrator and to you as audience?
> How does the narrator experience him or her self in this narrative?
> How does the narrator experience others in this narrative?
> How does the narrator experience wider world issues and concerns in this narrative?
> How is the audience meant to respond to the narrative?
> How is the audience meant to respond to the narrator?

AN EXERCISE IN NOEMATICALLY FOCUSED DESCRIPTIVE CHALLENGING

1. Working together with a partner, take turns in being therapist and client. Each session should last twenty minutes.
2. As the client, focus on a recent event that you can communicate as a 'story' (either first-person or third-person perspectives are acceptable). Recount the narrative, emphasising its noematic constituents.
3. As the therapist, engage in a process of noematically focused descriptive challenge by helping the client to investigate the various experiential components of his or her narrative.

4. When you have both completed the exercise, discuss what the experience of doing the exercise was like for each of you when you were being the therapist or the client.
5. What general value, if any, for the therapeutic encounter would you say that noematically focused descriptive challenging might offer?

AN EXERCISE IN NOETICALLY FOCUSED DESCRIPTIVE CHALLENGING

1. Working together with a partner, take turns in being therapist and client. Each session should last twenty minutes.
2. As the client, focus on the same recent event as in the previous exercise.
3. As the therapist, engage in a process of noetically focused descriptive challenge by helping the client to investigate the various dispositional stances being expressed within his or her narrative.
4. When you have both completed the exercise, discuss what the experience of doing the exercise was like for each of you when you were being the therapist or the client.
5. What general value, if any, for the therapeutic encounter would you say that noetically focused descriptive challenging might offer?

Descriptive challenging, at its most foundational level, provides an important means by which the existential psychotherapist can directly express and demonstrate a way of investigation that remains 'still' in its focus on the the client's currently lived worldview and which, in its stillness, permits the expression of a creative and respectful curiosity. By so doing, the therapist embodies a manner and quality to his or her investigations that the client, in turn, may begin to utilise both within the therapy world and beyond its confines.

Nevertheless, any attempt at descriptive challenging directed toward the client will itself be a challenge for the therapist in that it requires the setting aside of the therapist's own desire to 're-author' the client's narrative – whether at the noematic or noetic level, or both – so that it is more in keeping with his or her preferred or 'pleasing' narrative. It is here that the existential psychotherapist's willingness to remain 'still' as an expression of his or her 'un-knowing' is put to the test.

PHASE ONE: THERAPEUTIC UN-KNOWING

As was discussed in Part One, I have coined the term 'un-knowing' in order to express the existential psychotherapist's willingness to remain receptive to, and descriptively inquisitive (or curious) about that which presents itself as the client's currently lived worldview. Throughout Phase One, the therapist's stance of 'un-knowing' is expressed in terms of *acceptance* and *curiosity*.

Acceptance

Phase One acceptance on the part of the therapist is perhaps most directly expressed as:

- You, the client, have the right to be who you are being as you are being.
- I, the therapist, have the right to be who I am being as I am being.
- We have the right to be with each other as we are being.

Taken together, these three statements set the conditions of relatedness for the therapy world. In addition, they provide an implicit challenge to both the therapist's and client's demands (be they directed toward self or other) for *perfectionism*.

Perfectionism

Recent research studies on perfectionism have associated it with excessive expressions of self-criticism and fear of failure and have highlighted its links to various personality disorders as well as specific disorders such as anorexia nervosa and alcoholism (Rasmussen, 2004). Summarising contemporary analyses, Susan Rasmussen has argued that perfectionism is 'better understood if it includes both intra and interpersonal factors . . . [s]elf-oriented perfectionism (striving for personal standards of perfection), other-oriented perfectionism (need for others to be perfect) and socially prescribed perfectionism (belief that others have high expectations of your behaviour)' (Rasmussen, 2004: 399). Similarly, perfectionism highlights a contrast between a 'want', aspiration or desire and a *necessity* (I must be . . ./ you have to achieve . . .). The psycho-analyst Karen Horney defined perfectionism as 'the tyranny of the "shoulds"' (Horney, 1991).

Viewed from an existential perspective, the demand for perfectionism *eradicates uncertainty*. To 'want' or desire opens us to the unknown: 'I may/may not fulfil my plans', 'I might/might not achieve my desire', 'Taking this step could provoke unhappiness and pain.' Perfectionism appears to provide a way out of uncertainty – but its price is significant: it is our very disconnection from desire and its uncertain possibilities.

For example, some years ago, in a discussion with a friend's daughter who had decided not to sit her A-level exams because of a diagnosed 'exam phobia', she made the following statement: 'What's the point of sitting an exam if I don't know if I will pass it?' Such a statement alerts us to a significant aspect of perfectionism – the insistence upon predictability and the intolerance of any uncertainty.

While a perfectionist attitude may be somewhat common among clients, not least those whose narratives are infused with abundant examples of 'failure' (be it their own or the failure of others), acceptance in the therapy world is directed equally to client and existential psychotherapist. The perfectionist tendency among therapists has not, in my opinion, been sufficiently examined. Nonetheless, in my own experiences of working with trainees, this (usually self-directed) demand is all too apparent. On consideration, it would be somewhat surprising that a client whose difficulties were in part expressions of an overly critical perfectionism would find the means to explore such if he or she were in the presence of a therapist who, in ways both subtle and obvious, expressed the very same demand upon him or her self. In short, the more adequate and worthwhile the possibilities of challenging and revelatory dialogical engagement in the therapy world the more necessary is the abdication of perfectionism initially by the existential psychotherapist and subsequently by the client.

Acceptance, then, challenges both the existential psychotherapist's and the client's *self-focused* perfectionism, whether in terms of 'what I do' or 'how I judge my self'. For my trainees, for example, this challenge was most apparent in their need to be sure that they could apply certain skills and techniques without concern that they 'might be doing it wrong'.

Equally, acceptance challenges both the existential psychotherapist's and client's *other-focused* perfectionism. Again, in supervision discussions with trainees who have begun their applied training in clinical placements, it is not unusual to hear complaints about clients 'who just don't do it right', or who are wrong because they don't respond to interventions in ways that were expected and predicted. This stance takes the trainees away from acceptance and its unforeseen possibilities and, instead, adopts a focus concerned with directing change, or which expresses 'the therapeutic expert's' superiority of knowledge and status. Whatever the value of such stances, their implicit relatedness to perfectionism requires attention.

Curiosity

During Phase One the existential psychotherapist's curiosity serves as the basis for descriptive challenging and can be expressed as:

- What is it like for me, the therapist, to be in the presence of this other whom I designate as 'you'?
- What is it like for me, the therapist, to attempt to embrace your way of being as you express it?
- How willing am I, the therapist, to attempt an enterprise of shifting between the polarities that are expressed as 'you' and 'me'?

Curiosity challenges both the therapist's and the client's assumptions regarding the centrality of directed change as the primary purpose and function of psychotherapy. In contrast, curiosity urges that their primary focus remain on 'what is there' as opposed to 'what once might have been there' or 'what may one day be there'. Further, curiosity challenges the technical authority of the therapist as well as the client's own demands to be the recipient of that authority.

Finally, curiosity establishes a particular way of relating between therapist and client that, while likely to be experienced as unique and different by at least one of the participants, is also experienced by both as genuine, and that expresses this genuineness through the therapist's and client's diverse experiences of both 'meeting' and 'failing to meet' one another in their dialogue. Through curiosity, the therapist cannot remain detached from the inquiry being undertaken. Equally, through curiosity, the client cannot avoid the acknowledgement of the therapist as an other who both is and is not like all others, and yet remains, nonetheless, 'real'. Curiosity serves the therapist in permitting an ever-shifting focus that explores the relatedness between the polarity of 'self' and 'other'. As a result, the therapist is better able to engage in descriptive exploration and challenge.

Existential Confrontation

Together, acceptance and curiosity, from the standpoint of un-knowing, provide a mean whereby a *confrontation* between various aspects of the client's currently maintained worldview can occur. This confrontation expresses the challenges that the therapeutic encounter has provoked to the adequacy, or 'fitness', of the client's worldview in reflecting worlding as it is experienced. The following confrontation questions permit an exploration of this dissonance and can be presented by the existential psychotherapist through the stance of un-knowing:

- What fits/does not fit between the being you say you are and the narratives you provide regarding that being?
- What fits/does not fit between the being you say you are and the being who is in or embodies this current relation?
- What fits/does not fit between your stance regarding the others you say exist 'out there' and this particular other who is in or embodies this current relation?

This confrontation, in turn, begins to expose that which has remained unarticulated, covert and implicit regarding the client's worldview as it is expressed via the self-, other- and world-constructs. By so doing, a number of sedimentations within each construct, as well as their concomitant dissociations, which, together, both define and maintain each construct, can begin to be identified. Critically, the existential confrontation provoked by the therapist's adoption of a stance of un-knowing permits a preliminary means through which the descriptive investigation of the client's presenting concerns and disorders – as might be experienced, for example, in terms of either a general or a localised sense of 'stuckness', or conversely as a 'lack of control' – can be considered in terms of their *relatedness* with the currently maintained worldview.

It remains to be stressed that during Phase One existential confrontation should remain *solely* at the level of identification and clarification of dividedness or 'split'. While it is always a possibility that a divided stance is transformed simply through identification, or, equally, that the client's *own* confrontation with a maintained 'lack of fit' in any one or all of the three inter-relational areas summarised above provokes a movement toward self-challenge, nonetheless, *any directive interventions on the part of the existential psychotherapist to alter or 'heal' any exposed aspects of the client's divided stance would be incongruent with the overall aims of this Phase.*

TWO EXERCISES ON UN-KNOWING

EXERCISE 1

1. Write out the lyrics to a song that you would classify as one of your favourites.
2. Explore the lyrics while practising un-knowing, as described above.
3. Consider and evaluate what impact the above exploration has had on your relationship to the song.
4. Repeat the above but this time select the lyrics to a song that irritates you or to which you would not choose to listen.
5. Consider and evaluate what impact this second exploration has had on your relationship to the song.
6. Repeat the steps 1–5, but this time begin by writing out the initial problematic narrative presented to you by one of your clients.
7. Consider and evaluate what impact the above exploration has had on your relationship to the client.

EXERCISE 2

1. Working together with a partner, take turns in discussing and exploring a difficult or problematic therapeutic relationship that each of you has experienced with a client.
2. In each instance, with the partner's descriptively challenging assistance, focus on the stance taken toward acceptance/perfectionism, and the way of working adopted with regard to curiosity and existential confrontation as was expressed in this problematic relationship.
3. On the basis of these explorations, how did the ability, or inability, to stay with an attitude of un-knowing contribute to the difficult or problematic aspects of this therapeutic encounter?

A SUMMARY OF PHASE ONE

It can now be understood that the major concern requiring the existential psychotherapist's attention during Phase One can be encapsulated as the attempt to adopt an attitude of 'un-knowing'.

Initially, it is the therapist who seeks to embody this attitude via his or her *way of relating* with the client. This way of relating aims to communicate a foundational respect toward the client's worldview as it presents itself in the therapy world. Thus, the existential psychotherapist's investigations are not so concerned with any form of directive change in the worldview but are, rather, descriptively attuned toward its disclosure. This world-disclosing enterprise brings into focus the client's dispositional stances as currently maintained within and between the self-, other- and world-constructs as they express themselves in the immediacy of the therapeutic encounter itself.

This process of disclosing 'what is there' for the client is the primary challenge set by the existential psychotherapist during Phase One. As a challenge, it should not be undervalued or underestimated in its potential impact. For the client, it may be the first experience of a reasonably secure inter-relation with an other who is neither overtly nor covertly expressing a critique of his or her currently adopted worldview nor demanding that it be altered or defensively protected.

If the existential psychotherapist's way of relating is experienced by the client as being sufficiently accepting, and if the inter-relational setting within which this way of relating occurs is both clear and consistent, the client may begin to experience relatedness in novel ways that can be compared and contrasted to his or her more common or habitual ways of relating. Once again, the challenge provoked is likely to be neither minimal nor superficial. The client's shifts between 'what and how' it is to relate within the boundaries of the therapy world challenge the worldview being maintained in that the self-, other- and world-constructs are opened to descriptive inquiry which may begin to expose any number of dispositionally-maintained sedimentations as well as the concomitant dissociations that define them.

Considered as whole, the therapeutic process during Phase One attempts to establish a relationship that is experienced by the client as being increasingly *trusting and trustworthy*. While this sense of trust may be limited exclusively to the therapy world, nonetheless *that* it is experienced as such permits a degree of honest and challenging exploration that he or she might not otherwise be willing to undertake.

The establishment of trust rests to a substantial degree upon the existential psychotherapist's ability and willingness to embrace with increasing adequacy the client's worldview as it presents itself in the therapy world. As well as being open to its being tested by the client, the therapist's attempts to *be-with* and *be-for* the client generate a movement toward *immediacy* in the therapeutic encounter. Once again, this immediacy allows the client to examine critically his or her worldview as maintained in the therapy world and to consider this in relation to his or her wider world worldview narratives. As well, this immediacy admits a felt sense of relatedness that is neither detached nor easily disowned through abstraction. Rather, *immediacy re-connects that which is being stated with the being who is making the statement*. By so doing, it provokes yet one more challenge to examine critically the currently maintained worldview.

As the reader may have become aware, the discussion of Phase One has been somewhat lengthy. I have opted to discuss it in such detail for two main reasons.

First, because, in my view, whatever therapeutic 'success' may emerge from existential psychotherapy it requires the establishment of that particular relatedness that is the *sine qua non* of Phase One. Whatever value the subsequent Phases may have to the whole of the therapeutic process, it is dependent upon the inter-relational possibilities experienced by the client during Phase One. Second, it is also my view that the experience of relatedness that is possible during Phase One, and the challenges that are provoked from this experience, may themselves be sufficient for the client's experience of genuine and lasting therapeutic benefit. Indeed, as is suggested by the number of increasingly reliable research studies on the central significance of the therapeutic relationship itself (regardless of the model being espoused) as *the* critical variable determining beneficial outcomes, my personal suspicion is that the majority of beneficial therapeutic outcomes may well be the product of therapists' and clients' (often inadvertent) experience of Phase One relatedness. It is likely that, for many clients, simply the validation of their narrative is all that is required to provoke meaningful and lasting therapeutic benefit. In such instances, which in my view are common, the therapist's attempt to establish a Phase One therapeutic relationship takes on a significance that perhaps has not been sufficiently examined or acknowledged.

INDICATIONS AS TO THE APPROPRIATENESS OF A THERAPEUTIC SHIFT FROM PHASE ONE TO PHASE TWO

As will be discussed below, Phase One and Phase Two of existential psychotherapy reveal substantive differences in their focus on and possibilities of relatedness. What then might indicate to the existential psychotherapist that a shift toward Phase Two has become possible? I would suggest the following critical factors:

1. The content of the client's narrative is increasingly concerned with addressing and investigating his or her immediately lived worldview as experienced within the co-created therapy world and as contrasted with and compared to that of the wider world worldview narratives (and their problematic focus) that have been previously identified.
2. The client's *way* of being present with and in the presence of the therapist is suggestive of the establishment of a sufficient degree of trust in the therapist as a responsible and valued 'other'.
3. The client shows increasing willingness and ability not only to respond non-defensively to descriptive challenging but also to initiate it at times – whether within or beyond the confines of the therapy world.
4. There is a noticeably growing ease in the client's engagement with the therapist at a level of immediacy.
5. There is greater willingness on the part of the client to challenge some aspects of his or her own habitual stances and statements regarding the currently maintained worldview.
6. There is greater willingness on the part of the client to challenge the therapist's statements regarding some aspects of the client's currently maintained worldview.
7. There is an increased willingness to employ and respond to humour in the therapist's and client's discourse which suggests a greater degree of relational openness and respect.

FACTORS THAT PREVENT A THERAPEUTIC SHIFT FROM PHASE ONE TO PHASE TWO

Just as there may be various indications that the therapeutic relationship is at a point that will permit a shift from Phase One to Phase Two, so is it equally the case that this shift may have occurred too soon in that the foundational conditions of Phase One relatedness have not been sufficiently established. In such cases, attempts at Phase Two relatedness are likely to be at best ineffective and, at worst, may have the effect of disabling any further attempts at descriptive challenge. The following are likely to be the most common underlying factors indicative of this possibility:

1. The inter-relational frame conditions are either insufficiently clear or are not being followed consistently by the existential psychotherapist.
2. The inter-relational frame conditions are being consistently challenged or broken by the client.
3. The existential psychotherapist's statements and descriptive challenges are not adequately attuned to the client's presenting worldview so that they fail to generate sufficient trust.
4. The existential psychotherapist's statements and descriptive challenges do not follow directly from the client's statements, or the initiatives leading to the statements are not made clear to the client, so that they provoke incredulity, unease, distraction, irritation, suspicion or even fear.
5. The existential psychotherapist's statements and descriptive challenges are too misdirected, too infrequent or too 'parrot-like', so that they are limited in their impact and worth.
6. The existential psychotherapist's inability or unwillingness to accept the client as he or she is being in the therapy world is expressed through a stance that is anonymous, distant and self-conscious.
7. The existential psychotherapist's inability or unwillingness to accept the client as he or she is being in the therapy world is expressed through the attempt to change, cure, improve, educate, heal, help or make the client more 'real', more logical or more 'authentic'.

In the event of the occurrence of any of these factors, it is critical for the existential psychotherapist to acknowledge the tensions in the relationship, to be willing to hear non-defensively whatever critical statements the client might make, consider with the client what options there may be to deal with the situation, if necessary re-formulate the relational frame and, most importantly, re-initiate the attempt to establish Phase One relatedness.

6

Phase Two: Exploring the Therapy World

INTRODUCTION TO PHASE TWO

Phase One of the structural model for existential psychotherapy that is being presented permitted the establishment of a therapy world. During that phase, the primary task of the therapist was to assist the client in initiating a descriptively focused investigation of his or her problematic concerns as relational expressions and consequences of the worldview as adopted and embodied within the therapy world. The principal 'skills' used by the therapist in this task centred upon the adoption and demonstration of various *being qualities* associated with what I have termed a broad attitude of 'un-knowing'. In this, the *way of relatedness* adopted by the existential psychotherapist emerged as *the* pivotal means to both expose and challenge the client's worldview.

Phase Two continues the enterprise initiated during Phase One in that its aim is that of further challenging those dispositional stances that underpin and maintain the client's worldview so that the presenting problems that led the client to therapy can be considered in relation to these. Again, as in Phase One, the existential psychotherapist's principal 'tools' or 'skills' are the *being qualities* that he or she brings to the therapy world.

What distinguishes Phase One from Phase Two is that while during the former these qualities served to allow the existential psychotherapist to be 'the other' who sought to attune him or her self to the client's presenting worldview, in Phase Two the therapist's attempts to 'stand beside' the client are primarily expressed by challenges that are drawn from the worldview *differences* that are also expressions of the therapist's 'otherness'. In other words: consider two people in dialogue with one another. For each person, there exists 'a self' who engages with 'the other'. Person A's 'self' is Person B's 'other', and vice versa. In Phase One, the existential psychotherapist's aim was to engage in dialogue with the client in such a way that the therapist's 'self' undertook the attempt to attune itself as accurately as possible to 'the other' (the client). In this way, the client's experience of the existential psychotherapist as 'other' was also partially the experience of the therapist 'as-the-other-who attempts-to-reflect-the-self-I-am-being'.

Now, during Phase Two, the task of the existential psychotherapist becomes increasingly that of engaging in a dialogue with the client that stands at the 'self' end of the therapist's self/other polarity and which simultaneously stands at the 'other' end of the client's self/other polarity. In this way, the client's primary experience of the therapist is as an 'other' who asserts that 'otherness'. A pertinent quote by the psycho-analyst Hans Trüb captures much of the focus towards which Phase Two gravitates: 'The analyst must change at some point from the consoler who takes the part of the patient against the world to the person who puts before the patient the claim of the world' (Hans Trüb, quoted in Friedman, 1964: 520).

What may be the value in such a shift? In brief, through it the client can begin to engage in a novel way of dialogue which permits the exposure and challenging of any number of foundational components of the currently maintained world-view and, in particular, those components impacting upon the self-construct and other-construct.

Thus, Phase Two focuses upon the descriptive investigation of the client's experience of co-habiting in the therapy world with the existential psychotherapist. Through this, the inter-relation between the explicit tensions presented by the client and the implicit components that generate and maintain these tensions can be more adequately disclosed via the resonances, divergences, challenges and conflicts that arise as expressions of the 'self/other' polarity experienced in the immediacy of the therapeutic encounter .

Phase Two focuses upon the investigation of the existential possibilities inherent in honest and trustworthy self/other dialogue initially within the therapy world, and the potential for permitting some extension of these possibilities into the client's wider world relations.

From an experiential perspective, Phase Two relatedness is likely to be intensely felt and challenging to both therapist and client. Equally, in its emphasis upon the experienced immediacy of encounter that exists between them, Phase Two relatedness is largely unsharable with others in both the client's and the therapist's wider world relations. Hence, Phase Two relatedness can be beguiling, uncanny, liberating, disturbing, desirable and undesirable both for and between the therapist and the client. Because of the likely intensity of the therapeutic relationship during Phase Two, much of the existential psychotherapist's expertise throughout it rests upon his or her ability and willingness to be active and involved in the therapy world. At the same time, he or she must also always be able to 'step back' from it, or to leave it behind at the conclusion to each therapeutic session. In this way, the existential psychotherapist's entitlement to address issues from the polarity of his or her 'otherness' during Phase Two proves to be of valuable assistance to the achievement of this latter skill.

As should now be apparent, whatever therapeutic value or benefit Phase Two may have to offer the client, it is entirely dependent upon the foundational qualities of relatedness established during Phase One. Without these, not only is Phase Two unlikely to be effective, but its potential for deleterious impact upon the client and/or the therapist becomes a very real possibility.

PHASE TWO: LISTENING TO AND CHALLENGING THE CLIENT'S NARRATIVE

Throughout Phase One, the existential psychotherapist's general 'other-focused' stance informed a way of listening to and challenging the client's narrative that sought to adhere as closely as possible to investigations centred upon what was stated explicitly by the client. Phase Two listening and challenging, in contrast, encourages the therapist to initiate a mutual exploration of what remains implicit or unstated in the client's narrative.

Equally, Phase One remained primarily at the level of overt clarification so that the client might experience the 'otherness' of the existential psychotherapist attempting adequate attunement with the client's worldview. This attunement was neither critical of the currently presented worldview, nor asserted its authority and superiority through demands that it be altered. During Phase Two, however, the existential psychotherapist has earned the right, through his or her proven trustworthiness, to express that 'otherness' which may be discordant with the client's worldview and whose challenges reveal alternatives to its currently maintained stances.

Nonetheless, the overall task of Phase Two listening and challenging remains that of continuing to assist exposing and exploring 'what is there' for the client as expressed via the currently maintained worldview. Therefore, the shifts in listening and challenging that are characteristic of Phase Two require continuous scrutiny as to the impact they may be having upon the client's experience of sufficient security within, and trust of the other who co-habits, the therapy world. As one option, the existential psychotherapist can always *monitor* the client's experience through straightforward inquiry (e.g., 'Are you OK with this?' 'Is it all right for me to push you a little more here?'). A second option is for the existential psychotherapist to adopt an overtly *invitational* stance to all such investigations so that they proceed only if agreed to by the client (e.g., 'I'd like to offer an alternative here – is that OK with you?' 'Can I suggest something? If you don't like it or want it, that's fine').

Three useful and straightforward, yet surprisingly powerful, means for existential psychotherapists to express Phase Two listening and challenging are addressed below.

Shifts between the Particular and the General

This first aspect of Phase Two listening and challenging invites the client to re-consider those narratives focused upon a particular experience from a perspective that opens the experience to its more general experiential possibilities. Conversely, this mode also invites the client to re-consider those narratives that are focused upon a general experiential stances from a perspective that opens these to focus on a particular instance. For example:

(From the General to the Particular)

Client:	I just can't stand it when people are so phoney!
Therapist:	Can you give me an example?
Client:	An example?
Therapist:	Yeah . . . Tell me about the most recent time that this happened.
Client:	Uhm . . . The waitress at the restaurant last night. It was that phoney 'I'm having an orgasm just because I'm so pleased to serve you' look.
Therapist:	And what is it that you couldn't stand about that?
Client:	Well, it's such an obvious lie, isn't it? She didn't give a fuck about me. She was just after a big tip.
Therapist:	And what was it about her wanting a big tip that got to you?
Client:	It wasn't that she wanted a big tip! I could understand that. It's the way she did it. Like she was saying: 'You're such a nobody and an idiot that I'm going to actually convince you that you mean something special to me when you clearly don't.'

(From the Particular to the General)

Therapist:	So when you say that you can't stand people who are phoney, what's in that is that it feels to you like you're being taken advantage of, that your intelligence is being dismissed, that you don't mean anything to them as a person?
Client:	Yeah. And also the way they look at me. That's a big part of it.

(From the General to the Particular)

Therapist:	Think of that look that they give you. Anyone come straight to mind?
Client:	Oh yeah . . . When my son looked at me like that, like I'd let him down. I felt like I was totally worthless as a human being.
Therapist:	That was the same look?
Client:	Yeah.
Therapist:	So you're saying that your son is another phoney?
Client:	Uhm . . . No. No, I was the phoney that time.
Therapist:	You were the phoney.
Client:	Yeah . . .

(From the Particular to the General)

Therapist:	OK. Stay with the 'I was a phoney'. Can you make any other connections to it? Has anyone else ever given you a look that makes you the phoney?
Client:	Yeah . . . My grandmother when she caught me taking money out of her purse.
Therapist:	OK. Anyone else come to mind?

Client:	I don't know. Maybe an old friend of mine, Jimmy, when he saw me act like a real jerk with my then girlfriend.
Therapist:	So... Your son, your grandmother and your friend Jimmy all gave you a similar look. And did that look make you feel like a phoney in all instances?
Client:	Oh, yeah. And just worthless.
Therapist:	Worthless. Just like the look that the phoney waitress gave you last night.

Shifts from the Explicit to the Implicit

Throughout Phase One, the existential psychotherapist's focus centred upon the clarification and challenge of the client's *explicit* statements. During Phase Two, the existential psychotherapist's focus rests more directly upon that which *implicitly* underpins the client's explicit statements. This focus attempts to disclose the underlying, unstated dispositional stances through which the explicit statements emerge so that the client is challenged to address and explore that which was previously left implicit and on the fringes of his or her awareness. As an example of this, let us continue with the previous client/therapist dialogue:

Therapist:	Can we look at this sense of 'being worthless' a bit more?
Client:	Yeah, whatever.
Therapist:	This may sound stupid, but what's so bad about being worthless?
Client:	You're right. It does sound stupid! It's obvious what's bad about it.
Therapist:	OK. It's obvious and maybe I'm just thick, but what makes it so bad? I mean, hear yourself say: 'I'm worthless.' What's being said in that?
Client:	That . . . that I don't live up to expectations. That I'm a failure.
Therapist:	OK. So 'being worthless' for you is not fulfilling expectations, being a failure. Let me try out something here: 'I tried and I failed. So, I'm worthless. Even if I gave it my best shot, I'm still worthless because I didn't succeed.'
Client:	Yes.
Therapist:	So anything other than being perfect in that I always succeed, is to be condemned as worthless.
Client:	Yeah.
Therapist:	So when your son and your grandmother and Jimmy all gave you that look that made you feel like a phoney, would it be right to conclude that their 'look' was basically saying: 'We've found you out! You're not perfect! And therefore you're worthless.'
Client:	That's right.
Therapist:	OK. And let me try this out as well then: what made the waitress a phoney was that you found her out. She was faking perfection and you saw through it.
Client:	You know... that feels right. It's about perfection. And not getting there.
Therapist:	So who, quite literally, is saying to you: 'You're either perfect or you can only be a worthless phoney?'

The Existential Psychotherapist's Use of 'Self-as-Other'

As in Phase One, the exploration of the contrast between the client experience of co-habiting the therapy world and that of being part of the wider world beyond its boundaries can offer a valuable means to the clarification and challenging of the client's worldview. Readers will recall that a significant consequence of these explorations could be that of an experiential shift towards *immediacy*. Now, in Phase Two, the exploration of immediacy within the therapy world can be extended to include directly the client's experience of engaging with the existential psychotherapist as 'the other in the therapy world' who both stands in for, or represents, all others in the client's other-construct, and whose way of being 'the other in the therapy world' is a challenge to the client's other-construct, and, through it, the whole of his or her worldview. In my own experience of this way of listening and challenging, I have found it additionally powerful for the existential psychotherapist to adopt a 'first-person' ('I') mode of speaking when reflecting back the client's self-construct narratives. Instances of this appear in the continued therapeutic dialogue example:

Client:	I guess that somewhere along the way, the world taught me that you can only be either perfect or a phoney.
Therapist:	So, what about here? Does that rule still hold true?
Client:	You mean me here with you?
Therapist:	Yeah. Imagine asking your self: 'Can I only be either perfect or a phoney when I'm here with Ernesto?'
Client:	Uhm... I don't know. Probably. I don't know. It's difficult –
Therapist:	Can I ask you this: Is this your experience? 'Ernesto's demanding that I be perfect because otherwise he'll judge me to be a phoney?'
Client:	No.
Therapist:	So what's different about Ernesto, or about this experience of being with Ernesto, that this world-rule gets broken?
Client:	[laughs] What's different? Well, I pay you for one thing –
Therapist:	You paid the waitress as well, but that didn't break the rule.
Client:	Yeah, but you're not a waitress, are you? You can't compare her to you.
Therapist:	OK, aside from the obvious physical differences, what's different between the waitress and Ernesto?
Client:	Well, she's a phoney.
Therapist:	So does that mean: 'Ernesto's perfect'?
Client:	[laughs] No!
Therapist:	So 'Ernesto's not perfect and Ernesto's not a phoney.' How can that be? Within the scheme of things that's been laid out, there's only one or the other.
Client:	Yeah, but this is different. We're doing therapy here.
Therapist:	Oh . . . So, does that mean that 'Ernesto doesn't have to see me as either only perfect or only a phoney'?
Client:	No, I guess not.
Therapist:	So, let me ask you this as though it was you asking it and see what comes up for you: 'How is Ernesto experiencing me right now?'
Client:	You know what? It's like you couldn't care less as to whether I was perfect or a phoney. It wouldn't make any difference to how you relate to me.
Therapist:	And what's that feel like from your side?
Client:	It's great. It's freeing . . . Liberating. I want to take a deep breath [*breathes deeply*]. I don't feel worthless. But I also don't feel perfect.
Therapist:	And you're not insisting that I also have to be perfect or else be judged by you as worthless?
Client:	Nope.
Therapist:	So what's different here – about me, about you, about us – that we can be other than perfect or worthless?

AN EXERCISE IN PHASE TWO LISTENING AND CHALLENGING

1. Working together with a partner, take turns in being the therapist and client. Each session should last twenty minutes.
2. As the client, select a recent encounter that has provoked you in some way. Begin the session by describing the encounter and discussing its impact from your personal standpoint.
3. As the therapist, listen and challenge the client from a Phase Two level by making use of (a) shifts between the general and particular, (b) shifts from the explicit to the implicit, and (c) bringing into the discussion your presence as 'the other'.
4. After you have completed the exercise, discuss how you each experienced the encounter from each perspective and what it was like for you to listen and challenge or to be heard and challenged at the Phase Two level.

Phase Two listening and challenging acknowledges that the existential psychotherapist has earned the right to enlarge the focus of his or her attunement so that it increasingly encompasses views and possibilities that extend beyond the client's perspective and express more of the therapist's own dispositional stance.

Nonetheless, the shift to Phase Two listening requires caution and respect for the client's focus. Its challenges to the client's worldview can be unpredictably powerful and disturbing and may, in turn, provoke responses from the client that weaken both the trustworthiness of the therapy world as well as the trust that has been established in his or her inter-relation with the therapist. As a way of attempting to offset such an eventuality, the existential psychotherapist's expression of an openly invitational attitude prior to any direct challenge allows the client the option to experience the challenge as something that he or she has chosen or permitted.

PHASE TWO: EXPLORING THE WORLDVIEW

While Sigmund Freud, the founder of psycho-analysis, employed the analogy of archaeological 'digs' in order to express the psycho-analytic aim of bringing up to the surface of consciousness the deeply buried artefacts of the unconscious (Ellenberger, 1970; Gay, 1988), for Ludwig Binswanger, one of the first psychiatrists to employ a form of existential analysis, a more appropriate analogy was that of anthropology. The expertise of the anthropologist lies in the exploration and elucidation of differing, often novel, cultures in terms of their beliefs, aspirations, interactions, societal structures, artistic expressions, public and private behavioural codes of conduct, as well as many other socio-cultural features. For Binswanger, the task of the existential psychotherapist held close parallels. Each of his patients could be understood as an initially unknown and novel 'culture'. The therapist who enters and explores this novel culture must remain open both to its particulars and to the universal concerns that these particulars express. In brief, Binswanger sought to carry out an 'anthropological analysis' of his psychiatric patients' various relations through a world-dimensional investigation focused upon the patient's engagement with (a) the natural world with its physical, environmental and biological dimension (the *umwelt,* or *'with-world'*); (b) the world of everyday, public social relations with others (the *mitwelt* or *'around world'*); and (c) the world of private and intimate relations both with them selves and with the significant others or significant meanings in their lives (the *eigenwelt* or *'own world'*). Further, Binswanger argued that the exploration of these world-dimensions, the relative value ascribed to each by the patient, and the possible tensions arising between them provided a useful means with which to expose the implicit, and often unconsidered values, attitudes and beliefs that underpinned and maintained each of these world-dimensions on its own and in relation to the others (Binswanger, 1963; Stadlen and Stadlen, 2005).

In many ways, Binswanger's focus corresponds closely with the exploration of the client's worldview as discussed in Phase One. Unlike Binswanger, however, who concluded that an alignment of, and balance between, the various world-dimensions was the key to mental health, the structural approach being outlined in this text makes no such claims. This is not to say that Binswanger's hypothesis is either incorrect or inappropriate, only that it deviates somewhat from a number of the implications of the key defining principles of existential phenomenology that were discussed in Part One and which Heidegger was the first to point out (Valle and King, 1978).

Even so, there is a great deal that remains from Binswanger's ideas that is of value to the investigation of the client's worldview. Some existential psychotherapists such as Emmy van Deurzen, for example, continue to use a variation of Ludwig Binswanger's world-dimensions in highly creative ways (van Deurzen and Arnold-Baker, 2005). Indeed, van Deurzen has added a fourth world-dimension – the *uber-welt* (or *'over-world'*) – which seeks to make explicit those factors concerned with the person's relations to the ideals and aspirational aspects of living which were implicitly presented in Binswanger's discussion of the *eigenwelt* (Binswanger, 1963; van Deurzen-Smith, 1988; van Deurzen & Arnold-Baker, 2005). Other existential psychotherapists, such as Naomi Stadlen and Anthony Stadlen, however, take issue with this perspective, arguing that Heidegger's original use of the term *mitwelt* was not intended to imply 'just one "world", or "dimension", among others. Mitwelt needs no supplementing with [the other world dimensions] for the simple reason that it includes them . . . . Being-in-the-world with others is not one "dimension" of being human. It is what being human *is*' (Stadlen and Stadlen, 2005: 135).

My own approach to the debate about the world-dimensions is to offer an alternative to what they seek to express through the analysis of the worldview and its primary constructs. I take this stance for the following reasons: first, because I am convinced that these latter construct distinctions are more immediately accessible to clients; second, because I think that the demarcations between them are less obviously structurally artificial and more distinctively apparent to clients; and third, because the embedded sedimentations and dissociations that both maintain and define each construct are more clearly discernible.

Nonetheless, whatever the existential psychotherapist's preference, the exploration of the client's worldview throughout Phase Two continues the process begun during Phase One in that it seeks to disclose that worldview to descriptive investigation and challenge.

As a brief recap of what was discussed in Part One, readers should recall that the worldview expresses the way each of us constructs all facets of our reflectively lived and embodied way of being – my awareness and definition of self, of others, of the world as a whole, and the way that relations between them are both possible and impossible. Equally, the worldview seeks to provide and maintain for each of us a 'groundedness' in a time, location and narrative so as to make the continued experience of being at least a more tolerable option than that of non-being. The self-construct component of the worldview expresses the sum total of all the dispositional stances being held regarding the construct labelled as 'self' or 'I'. The other-construct component of the worldview expresses the sum total of all the dispositional stances being held regarding the construct labelled as 'others', be it any particular or specific 'other' or of 'others' in general. The world-construct component of the worldview expresses the sum total of all the dispositional stances being held regarding the construct labelled as 'the world', be it in terms of its living and non-living components and/or its physical, environmental, biological, social, cultural, moral and spiritual dimensions.

During Phase One the various elements and constituents that make up and maintain each of these three primary constructs of the worldview have been sufficiently examined and challenged *within* the parameters of each construct. What is distinctive about Phase Two inquiry regarding the primary constructs is that the existential psychotherapist is now more concerned with the exploration of the inter-relation *between* them so that the client's ongoing problematic concerns can be more adequately considered in terms of their impact upon the worldview as whole.

For instance, how and in what ways does a particular identified dispositional stance from the self-construct manifest itself in the other-construct? Or in the world-construct? Further, when its manifestation in the latter two constructs is highlighted, in what ways might this clarify that stance's meaning, function and significance within the self-construct? Equally, when all three dispositional stance manifestations are considered *in relation to one another* what might be further clarified about the worldview as a whole and the client's presenting problem's relatedness to that worldview? As further clarification, consider the following brief case vignette.

Dora sees herself as being a warm, caring, bright and attractive person. However, all of her relations with men, whether intimate or at a social or public level, are judged by her to be 'total failures'. How can she find a way to success with men in general and with a male life-partner? One of the focus points to which Dora constantly returns is her body. She is able to speak of it in a fairly detached and distanced fashion, relating what 'it' wants, how 'it' does or does not function properly, how 'it' is one of the main sources of her troubles and difficulties.

From the self-construct perspective, Dora's statements regarding her body include: 'I keep myself in good shape through exercise', 'I have most of the features that would define me as physically attractive and I believe my self to be so', 'I enjoy sex', 'I can't see a problem with my body, but I must be avoiding that.' When these statements are explored further in order to disclose more of the values, beliefs and assumptions that infuse these statements, what emerges is a strong critical, if not punitive, stance: Dora *must be* physically attractive and the only evidence that matters for her to 'prove' that she is 'has to be' the establishment of a lasting relationship with a man.

From the other-construct perspective, Dora's statements regarding men's (as representative 'others') stance towards her from a body-focused standpoint include: 'Men demand perfection: perfect bodies, perfect sex, perfect everything', 'When men get to see me as a body, they like what they see but they don't "handle with care"', 'When I think of how I'm letting a man invade my body when we have sex, I feel pretty disgusted.' Again, when these statements are challenged in order to discern something of their underpinning dispositional factors, Dora becomes agitated and angry. She finds it difficult to say anything other than 'I love men's bodies, it's the creeps inside them that I can't stand!'

From the world-construct perspective, Dora's statements regarding her body as a physical, material 'thing' or 'object' inhabiting the world include: 'It's like a cat. It only relates to you on its own terms', 'It's very jealous and wants all of my attention', 'It's entirely unpredictable as to what will please or satisfy it.' With further probing of these statements, Dora is very specific in her felt sense that her body is too much like the men in her life: it is always threatening to do something awful to her, it constantly betrays her and yet she can't live without it and what it provides.

In terms of the exploration of Dora's overall worldview, consider the following:

When Dora and the therapist take major elements from each construct and consider these together and in relation to each other, one example of what emerges is:

- I must be physically attractive and the only suitable evidence to prove that I am must be that I am in a lasting relationship with a man (self- construct).
- I love men's bodies, but can't stand the beings 'inside' them (other-construct).
- My body, like a man, does awful things to me, betrays me and is essential (world-construct).

What immediately stands out from these three statements is that the other-construct and the world-construct together make it unlikely that the aims and aspirations of the self-construct can be fulfilled. From her focus on bodies, the statements suggest the importance that Dora gives to bodies in general, and that nonetheless she must pay a price – including betrayal – for this importance, in that the ultimate cost to her of being recognised as physically attractive is to be with a man who, 'as a man' – aside from his body – can only repulse her. If we then consider this as a general worldview stance, the possibility emerges that one of the critical assumptions that underpins and maintains it is that Dora must want and recognise how essential it is to her to be in a lasting relationship with a man *and* that it is equally essential that she fails to get what she wants. Can Dora's presenting problems now be re-considered in the light of this? Is it not possible that the 'problems' actually serve, and express, the divided demands of her worldview? Would not the 'solving' of the problem actually serve to destabilise that worldview?

When we take a statement that arose from her self-construct and reconsider it within either or both of the remaining constructs, what might emerge? For example, from a self-construct perspective, Dora states 'I enjoy sex.' What emerges when this statement is placed within the other-construct? Immediately we are presented with a possible contradiction: Dora enjoys sex *and* feels repulsion at the thought of a man invading her body. Together, these statements require further clarification on Dora's part. It is not necessarily that the two don't 'fit' with each other, only that it is not yet understandable what that 'fitness' is for Dora. Equally, if we consider any of Dora's world-construct statements and place them within the framework of her other-construct, what emerges? Is Dora suggesting, for example, that 'bodies-as-things' are more 'man-like' or more allied to men than they are to Dora? And, if so, does this help to clarify Dora's self-construct view that the unknown problem with regard to her body is that it is 'man-like'? What might be the implications of this with regard to Dora's presenting problems?

Obviously, there is far more that is open to exploration regarding the worldview and the inter-relation of its primary constructs in this example. Readers are invited to pursue its many possibilities on their own or in group discussion. What needs to be stressed here is that, just as in Phase One, the clarification of these various inter-relations and their implications emerged entirely from *descriptively focused inquiry*. No analytic interpretations were required, no statement was treated initially as being any less – or more – significant than any other, nor were any assumptions made regarding the greater or lesser 'truthfulness' of any statement *even when apparent contradictions arose*. In Binswanger's sense, this exploration of the worldview adopts an anthropological attitude even if it does not directly apply the same world-dimensional distinctions. I leave it to readers to determine their personal preference.

AN EXERCISE ON THE EXPLORATION OF THE CLIENT'S WORLDVIEW

1. Select a client whom you have worked with as his or her therapist.
2. Select a specific focus-topic related to that client's presenting problem or issue.

3. What statements regarding the self-, other- and world-constructs as expressed through that presenting problem have been made by your client?
4. As with the example of Dora discussed above, explore the various inter-relations between the three constructs.
5. How does this exploration add to and clarify with greater adequacy the related-ness between the client's presenting problem and his or her worldview?

(Although you may do this exercise on your own, it is recommended that you work together with a partner and take turns in facilitating the exploration of each other's client's worldview.)

PHASE TWO: EXPLORING SEDIMENTATIONS AND DISSOCIATIONS IN THE CLIENT'S WORLDVIEW

As has been stated elsewhere, the worldview, both as a whole and as considered from the standpoint of its three primary structural constituents – the self-, other- and world-constructs – is in part maintained by its dispositional stances which serve to define it and locate it spatially and temporally.

As was discussed in Part One, while some components of the worldview remain relatively flexible and open to reconstition and redefinition in response to experiential challenge, it is also the case that many – perhaps the great majority – of components, in response to challenge, resist redefinition and remain fixed or inflexible to alteration. These typically recurring, fixed dispositional stances or *sedimentations* provide the worldview with a sense of (relatively) fixed and permanent essence. Many sedimentations in the worldview – or in each of its primary constructs – remain resistant to challenge and reconsideration by the client regardless of the restrictions upon the client's inter-relational experience of being that their adoption imposes. Via the clarification of the client's sedimentations, various emergent distorted and disowned or *dissociated* experiences of being can begin to be identified. *Dissociation* refers to that 'splitness in reflective being' that arises when the worldview's response to the challenges of meeting the world is that of denying or 'disowning' those challenges in order that the current sedimentations that define it can be maintained. Dissociation 'blocks' or avoids the assimilation of challenging inter-relational experiences whose impact and 'ownership' would alter or fragment the worldview.

Nevertheless, although dissociations, like sedimentations, also serve to maintain the stability of the worldview, their impact imposes experiential limitations upon it such that various lived experiences, and their associated dispositional stances, must be 'disowned' by, or 'split off' from, the worldview, even if the consequences provoke problematic, undesirable or even seriously debilitating symptoms. For example, dissociations as experienced by the self-construct permit the possibility of meaningful statements regarding: 'who I believe I am (and am not)', 'who I can (and cannot) be', and 'who I must (and must not) be)'. However, the implicit dissociations required to allow sedimentations to remain meaningful ensure that those statements that fail to 'fit' (for example as might arise when I am being who I am not, or cannot be, or must not be) remain 'split off' from or disowned by the self-construct. Examples focused upon the other- or world-constructs would reveal the same.

Even so, dissociations should not be seen to be inherently problematic, or at least no more problematic than the sedimentations in the worldview itself. As should be clear, no coherent, definable or meaningful worldview would be possible without its constituent sedimentations and dissociations. For example, if at the self-construct level the statement 'I am Ernesto, the author of this book' is to have any meaning whatsoever, then the 'Ernesto who I claim to be' must believe himself to be distinguishable from the plethora of potential 'non-Ernestos'. Sedimentations and dissociations validate the claim to 'be Ernesto' who can be distinguished from his 'non-Ernesto' alternatives.

The problems that arise through sedimentation and dissociation, in so far as they are of relevance to psychotherapy, can be briefly summarised: *the degree to which we sediment is paralleled in the extent to which those experiences that challenge the sedimentation must be dissociated.* In the West, perhaps as a consequence of our elevation of the individual and the subjective, the demand for stable and inflexible sedimentations – and their corresponding dissociations – is extensive. Given the option of either 'de-sedimenting' inadequate sedimentations so that more of the previously dissociated experiences can be 're-owned', or maintaining the inflexible sedimentation even if it requires ever-increasing dissociations of experience, our culture typically opts for the second strategy. If there is a 'madness' in this method, it would appear to be that 'madness' which reflects a cultural bias toward fixed and certain meanings and which avoids, or cannot easily tolerate, those meanings that maintain the complementarity that permits the 'truthfulness' of competing claims. We in the West appear to be overly enamoured of 'either/or' and far too wary of 'both/and'. As examples of this, consider the many assumptions of 'superiority' (whether it be of political system, ideology, religion, class, intellect, gender, race, sexual preference and so forth) that have guided and impacted upon our culture and protected it from the destabilising challenges of different perspectives that were deemed 'inferior' at best, 'dangerous' or 'unnatural' at worst.

The adoption of the first strategy of de-sedimentation provokes an increasing inability to sufficiently contain and define the worldview. The more open and flexible the worldview is to 'owning' and defining itself on the basis of its direct reflective experience of worlding, the less temporally fixed become its sedimentations and, as a consequence, the less definable or identifiable the worldview becomes – thereby provoking increasing levels of uncertainty and anxiety. Taking up the second strategy in a rigid fashion designed to stabilise over time the boundaries and meanings of the worldview creates ever-increasing dissociation from all those lived experiences that threaten destabilise it. This, in turn, is likely to be experienced as restrictions in dispositional stances related to thought, affect or behaviour that also provoke anxiety though it is the anxiety that arises from the attempt to avoid or reject the uncertainty of worlding. The first strategy risks destabilising the whole of the worldview since, through the inter-relatedness of all of its aspects or constituents, the de-sedimenting of any one will impact upon all the others in ways that cannot (at least at present) be adequately foreseen or predicted. The second strategy maintains the current worldview but, again, because of the inter-weaving of all its constituents must of necessity increasingly rigidify and force dissociations even upon those sedimentations that were once reasonably flexible and open to maintaining ambiguity and complementarity in their meanings.

The examination of the client's worldview throughout Phase Two permits both the existential psychotherapist and client to identify the sedimentations and dissociations that present themselves through the descriptive investigation and challenge being undertaken. In addition, as well as identifying these, Phase Two challenges to the worldview allow the clarification of the depth or rigidity of the sedimentations (and the parallel strength of their concomitant dissociations). Together, these investigations can more adequately place the client's presenting problem *in relation to the worldview* rather than consider it as separate and alien to it. Equally, the presenting problem can be better understood as expressive of either:

(a) the attempt to maintain the worldview; or
(b) the expression of disturbing instability in the worldview; or
(c) the unwanted and unplanned consequence of a rigid, yet positively valued, set of sedimenta-tions upon previously more flexible and experience-receptive constituents of the worldview; or
(d) the unwanted and unplanned consequences of desired de-sedimenting of a previously fixed sedimentation upon other sedimentations that were once fixed and that the client desires to remain fixed.

As an example of (a), let us return to Dora's body-focused dilemma and con-sider this in the light of sedimentation and dissociation. Dora's presenting problem is that it is an essential need for her to be in a lasting relationship with a man, but she constantly fails to achieve this. However, readers will recall that a significant possibility that emerged from the previous analysis regarding the inter-relation between the primary constructs of her worldview was that as well as Dora want-ing and recognising how essential it was to her to be in a lasting relationship with a man, it was *equally* essential to the maintenance of her current worldview that she failed to get what she wanted. Thus it can be seen that the immediate sedi-mentation presented by Dora that 'there must be a problem with my body (even if I cannot identify what it is)' serves the maintenance of the current worldview in that it permits the continuing desire to be in a lasting relationship but also creates the obstacle to its achievement (via the 'currently unidentified problem' that is preventing this). Equally, in placing the avowed source of the problem within the self-construct ('I must be avoiding seeing something') Dora permits her other-construct-derived awareness that 'the men' who inhabit desirable male bodies disgust her to remain dissociated from the self-construct, thereby maintaining the self-construct sedimentation.

As an example of (b), consider my client Philip's presenting problem: 'I don't know who I am any more.' Philip holds the deeply fixed sedimentation that 'I must always be 100% honest in all of my relations with others.' At the same time, Philip is in a difficult work situation that has convinced him that he will soon be fired from a position he has maintained all his working life. In reaction, he has begun to steal various items of office stationery and has recently also been 'raiding the office kitty'. As a result Philip has discerned a dishonesty that cannot be maintained by his sedimented worldview. Hence, the presenting problem partly permits the maintenance of that sedimentation but also expresses his growing awareness that the current sedimentation cannot be maintained and is becoming increasingly unstable.

As an example of (c), consider the dilemma posed for Geraldine whose presenting problem is 'my colleagues are jealous of me and are trying to ruin my career when I'm only trying to do my job.' Geraldine who has worked as a teacher in a Further Education College for fifteen years, was, until recently, well-liked by her colleagues, and was strongly supported by them when the opportunity arose for the appointment of a new Head of Department. Geraldine applied for the post and was awarded it. Unfortunately, Geraldine holds extremely rigid views about 'being an authority' and has begun to behave in ways that are excessively demanding of her colleagues. Increasingly, the 'free and easy' relations that she had previously maintained with them and which she values as a desirable aspect of her self-construct have begun to be overwhelmed by the strict sedimented stance regarding 'being an authority'. Geraldine's presenting problem, although focused on her other-construct, expresses the increasingly restrictive impact of a rigid sedimentation which has extended on to previously more flexible aspects of her worldview.

As an example of (d), consider my client, Armand. Armand has had great difficulties throughout his life in trusting other men and developing close friendships with them. Increasingly unhappy with what he saw as a 'gap' in his life, he had attended an intensive group process restricted to men and which was intended to 'celebrate manhood'. The group experience had been dramatic and highly significant to Armand and, as a consequence, he felt that he had 'broken through' his uneasiness in being around and close to other men. Thus, Armand has successfully challenged a rigid sedimentation. When Armand comes to see me, his presenting issue is 'I feel lost. I think I may be gay and need to explore this. But if I am, my marriage and family fall apart and I don't want this to happen.' Through our discussions, it becomes more evident that Armand's life-altering experience in the men's group has allowed the de-sedimentation of his previous reluctance to be close to men. In doing so, however, his experience of the possibilities of 'being close' and developing friendships with men has also stirred previously dissociated stances regarding his possible sexual attraction to, and desire for, other men. Prior to this, Armand had seen himself as a 'heterosexual male' and had developed a close and harmonious life with his wife, Julie, with whom he continues to have an enjoyable and active sex-life. The recent de-sedimenting of Armand's self-construct-focused dispositional stance toward men in general has had the undesired effect of also de-sedimenting Armand's self-construct-focused dispositional stance regarding his sexual orientation, which he did not actually want to de-sediment. Once again, his presenting problem encapsulates this dilemma.

During Phase Two, the existential psychotherapist and client work together on various aspects of the client's worldview. In doing so, any number of sedimentations and dissociations that maintain the worldview become exposed to inquiry and disclosure. While it is of great value to consider these sedimentations and dissociations in the light of the client's presenting concerns, it is also vital that the therapist carries out these explorations with great care since their relatedness to, and impact upon, other – possibly problematic, possibly desirable – client-held sedimentations and dissociations cannot be known in advance. Once again, the existential psychotherapist's focus on descriptive clarification and challenge is likely to decrease the probability of unexpected and overwhelming upheavals in the client's worldview, though, whatever approach to therapy is taken, such circumstances always remain as a possibility.

TWO EXERCISES EXPLORING SEDIMENTATION AND DISSOCIATION

EXERCISE 1

1. Working with a partner, take turns in being the therapist and client. Each session should last twenty minutes.
2. As the client, focus on your self-construct and select an example of 'someone I could never possibly be' (for example: 'I could never possibly be someone who lies to her friends' or 'I could never be a committed member of X political party') that you feel sufficiently at ease to explore with your partner. Focus your exploration on the following: 'Who would I be if I became the person I could never possibly be?'
3. As the therapist, help your client to explore his or her presenting situation by challenging its impact upon the client's wider worldview. In doing so, pay particular attention to the examples of sedimentation and dissociation that might become apparent.

EXERCISE 2

Working with a partner, take turns in exploring the presenting problem of one of your clients (or a client from a published case study) from the focus-point of how, and in what ways, the presenting problem might be expressing issues of sedimentation and dissociation in the client's worldview.

PHASE TWO: THE INTER-RELATIONAL REALMS OF ENCOUNTER

Broadly, Phase Two utilises various structured forms of inquiry which help existential psychotherapists to clarify the implicit structural components that maintain and define their clients' currently lived worldview. A particular approach
toward such investigations, the primary advantage of which lies in its focus upon
the immediacy of relatedness as experienced within the therapy world, has been
suggested and developed by the present author in various papers and texts
(Spinelli, 1994, 1997, 2001, 2005). This approach focuses upon four distinct
inter-relational realms. I have labelled these the *I-focused, You-focused, We-
focused* and *They-focused* realms of encounter. I now want to propose that the
first three of these realms are of particular significance to the aims of Phase
Two (the fourth, the They-focus will be considered as part of the discussion on
Phase Three). Each of the first three realms can be briefly distinguished in the
following way:

The I-focused realm of encounter attempts to describe and clarify the dispositional stances that arise through 'my experience of being "my self" in any given
relationship'. It asks, in effect, 'What do I tell my self about my current experience
of being me in this encounter?' The following are dialogical examples of an
I-focused realm of encounter: 'I'm scared', 'I wish I was more interesting', 'I am
being punished and I deserve it because I was not good to my parents.' In general, I-focused therapeutic inquiry considers those dispositional stances that
express the client's experience of being him or her self in the current encounter
with the therapist.

The You-focused realm of encounter attempts to describe and clarify the dispositional stances that arise through 'my experience of the other in any given
relationship' *as well as* 'my experience of the other's experience of me in any
given relationship'. It asks, 'What do I tell my self about my experience of you
in this encounter?' *and* 'What do I tell my self about your experience of me in
this encounter?' The following are dialogical examples of a You-focused realm
of encounter: 'I trust you', 'I don't like the way you dress', 'You don't seem
terribly interested in what's being said', 'You're trying to hide your sadness',
'You find me boring', 'You like me', 'You laugh at my jokes as though I need to
be humoured.' In general, You-focused therapeutic inquiry considers those
dispositional stances that the client both imposes upon the other and assumes
exist for the other (the therapist) in relation to him or her self (the client) in the
current encounter.

The We-focused realm of encounter attempts to describe and clarify the
dispositional stances that arise through each participant's experience of 'us
being in relation with one another'. It asks, 'What do I tell my self about the
experience of being *us* in the immediacy of this encounter?' The following
are dialogical examples of a We-focused realm of encounter: 'My sense is
that we really seem to be connecting right now', 'As I see it, even though neither one of us is saying anything at the moment, it feels like we're

communicating in important ways', 'It feels like we keep missing each other and this makes us over-cautious in what we end up expressing.' In general, We-focused therapeutic inquiry concerns itself with that which is being experienced 'in the moment' or in the immediacy of engagement *between* client and therapist. As such, it expresses explicitly that inter-relational grounding which exists (and is more implicitly expressed) in I-focused and You-focused statements.

While existential psychotherapy attempts a descriptive exploration of all three realms of encounter, throughout Phase Two an explicit and overriding emphasis is placed upon the third (We-focused) realm of encounter (Spinelli, 1994, 1997, 2005). The existential psychotherapist's willingness to examine and consider what emerges experientially through this realm as being real and valid (rather than sub-stitutive, symbolic or 'transferential') serves to place his or her active presence within the immediacy of the interactive relationship with the client. Further, this focus serves to expose and clarify in that immediacy the self-same inter-relational issues that clients express as being deeply problematic within their wider world relations.

As an example of how these realms can be explored and their potential value to the therapeutic process, let us return to a previous example regarding the existential psychotherapist's and client's exploration of 'the phoneyness of others' and consider their dialogue from the perspective of these three realms:

Therapist: Look, I wonder if I can interrupt you here for a moment. I'm trying to hear what you're saying and getting some sort of fix on it, but I am also wondering: have you any thoughts or feelings or some sort of sense of how it is for you to be telling me this?

Client: How I feel about what I'm saying?

Therapist: Yeah. For instance, I'm wondering if you are hearing yourself make any private statements about your self while you're speaking?

Client: You mean like judgements or criticisms?

Therapist: Are there judgements or criticisms?

Client: Sure. Plenty. All of the time.

Therapist: OK. So . . . 'When I'm talking about something I said or did to someone, I am also privately judging and criticising my self' [**I-focus**]. Is that right?

Client: Yeah. And I bet you want to know what they are, right?

Therapist: Sure. Of course. But before you tell me, can I ask you if any of those judgements and criticisms are directed toward the people you're talking to? Or are they just focused on your self?

Client: What a weird question. [*Pauses to consider it.*] They're mainly toward me. But they're also directed outward. It's like I criticise them for the words they're using, or how they've dressed that day, or any old thing. I never thought about that. Weird.

Therapist: So, in the private judging and criticising that you're doing *here* are there any statements you're making privately about me?

Client: You? [*Pauses*] Well . . . Yeah. Sometimes you say things in a complicated way [**You-focus**]. Like now, when you asked the question. It made me feel like I had to talk 'posh' [**I-focus**]. Don't get me wrong, I appreciate what we're doing here [**We-focus**].

Therapist: Thank you. I really value it, too.

Client:	[*touched by the therapist's statement and also angered*] See? There it is again! As soon as you said that, I thought: 'what a phoney!' [**You-focus**]. But I don't believe that! You're not! [**You-focus**].
Therapist:	Was it what I said that triggered that private judgement? Or the way I said it?
Client:	No! No! It was the look you had on your face when you said it.
Therapist:	And the look said: 'Ernesto's a phoney' [**You-focus**].
Client:	Yeah . . . But . . . No. It did say that. But mainly it said that *I'm* the phoney [**I-focus**].
Therapist:	So we're both phoneys? [**We-focus**].
Client:	[*laughs*] Yeah! We're both phoneys! [**We-focus**]. But I'm the 'phonier' phoney! [**I-focus**].
Therapist:	OK. Let's keep the focus on your self-directed judgements.
Client:	Chicken! [**You-focus**].
Therapist:	Yeah . . . I admit it. So . . . 'I'm a phoney' [**I-focus**]. Can you make any other connections to it?
Client:	Yeah. That phoney waitress from last night. It was like she could just see through me [**You-focus**].
Therapist:	OK. Let's stay with that for a minute. Am I another person who can 'just see through you?'
Client:	You? Well... You see through me at times, that's for sure. But it's different [**You-focus**].
Therapist:	How's it different?
Client:	I don't feel like you're seeing me as a phoney [**You-focus**].
Therapist:	I agree. I don't feel like either one of us is ever being a phoney [**We-focus**].
Client:	Yeah, I feel the same, even though we're such different people [**We-focus**]. But, you know I just realised that although I believe in what I just said, and I'm not ever being phoney here, I can still hear this voice inside saying 'But I *am* a phoney!' [**I-focus**].
Therapist:	OK. Stay with that. Hear that voice inside saying: 'But I *am* a phoney!' [**I-focus**]. What's your reaction?
Client:	When I hear you say it, I get suspicious about you. I'm wondering whether you're playing some sort of therapeutic game with me and that in spite of what you say, you really do believe I'm a phoney. I don't trust you [**You-focus**].
Therapist:	Thank you. You sounded really honest to me [**You-focus**]. It doesn't sound at all like something a phoney would say [**You-focus**]. What's it like for you to hear me say that?
Client:	[*shows facial signs of being affected by the therapist's statement; becoming tearful*] I didn't mean it when I said I didn't trust you. I do [**You-focus**]. I just felt threatened in a weird sort of way when you said that you didn't experience me as a phoney [**You-focus**].
Therapist:	What was that sense of feeling threatened? Do you feel it now between us? [**We-focus**].
Client:	No. But you know what I wanted to say before? I wanted to say: 'How dare you? How dare you just sit there and pontificate about whether I am or am not a phoney? [**You-focus**]. Who do you think you are? [**You-focus**].
Therapist:	What's it like to say that, what you just said?
Client:	I feel shit-scared! [**I-focus**].
Therapist:	Because . . .
Client:	Because I realised that it's what I wanted to say to that waitress. And to my grandmother, and Jimmy and Luke. [*Turns to face away from the therapist; shakes his fist; grimaces.*] How dare you! [*Faces the therapist again.*] But I couldn't. I was terrified it would destroy our relationship. And now I've said it here and I'm just as terrified about what it'll do to *this* relationship [**We-focus**].
Therapist:	So what do you think? What has saying it done to you? [**client's I-focus**]. To me? [**client's You-focus**]. To us? [**We-focus**].

TWO EXERCISES ON THE EXPLORATION OF THE FIRST THREE INTER-RELATIONAL REALMS

EXERCISE 1

The I-Focus

1. Together with a partner take turns in completing the following statement *'What I am telling my self about me right now is that I . . .'*
2. After you have both completed the statement, repeat the exercise and continue to do so for five minutes. Try to avoid pauses or the preparation of completing parts to the statements.

The You-Focus

1. Together with a partner take turns in completing the following statement *'What I am telling my self about you right now is that you . . .'*
2. After you have both completed the statement, repeat the exercise and continue to do so for five minutes. Try to avoid pauses or preparation of completing parts to the statements.
3. Now, together with a partner, take turns in completing the following statement *'What I am telling my self right now is that you are experiencing me as . . .'*
4. After you have both completed the statement, repeat the exercise and continue to do so for five minutes. Try to avoid pauses or the preparation of completing parts to the statements.

The We-Focus

1. Together with a partner take turns in completing the following statement *'What I am telling my self about us right now is that we . . .'*
2. After you have both completed the statement, repeat the exercise and continue to do so for five minutes. Try to avoid pauses or the preparation of completing parts to the statements.

Discussion

1. Discuss with your partner what the experience of doing all three parts of this exercise was like for you.
2. What general value, if any, for the therapeutic encounter would you say that any aspects of this exercise might offer?

EXERCISE 2

The I-Focus

1. Working together with a partner, take turns in being therapist and client. Each session should last ten minutes.
2. As the client, focus on a recent encounter that has provoked you in some way. Begin the session by describing the encounter and discussing its impact from your personal standpoint.
3. As the therapist, assist the client in exploring his or her experience of the encounter and its impact *by restricting all your statements and interventions so that they are attempts to disclose the client's I-focused realm.*

The You-Focus

1. Working together with a partner, take turns in being therapist and client. Each session should last ten minutes.
2. As the client, continue to focus on the encounter described above.
3. As the therapist, assist the client in exploring his or her experience of the encounter and its impact *by restricting all your statements and interventions so that they are attempts to disclose the client's You-focused realm.*

The We-Focus

1. Working together with a partner, take turns in being therapist and client. Each session should last ten minutes.
2. As the client, continue to focus on the encounter described above.
3. As the therapist, assist the client in exploring his or her experience of the encounter and its impact *by restricting all your statements and interventions so that they remain at the We-focus realm of encounter.*

Discussion

1. Discuss with your partner what the experience of doing all three parts of this exercise was like for each of you.
2. What value, if any, for the therapeutic encounter would you say that any aspects of this exercise might offer?

PHASE TWO: WORKING WITH DREAMS

Working with clients' dreams has been a major area of interest to numerous approaches within contemporary psychotherapy, in particular those approaches that have been most influenced by psycho-analysis. The dreams recounted in therapy by clients often involve events and images that might appear to be highly unusual, absurd and/or disturbing, suggesting the need for an interpretation that will transform these so that they can be made meaningful. Similarly, many psychotherapeutic approaches consider dreams to be laden with symbolic material whose hidden significance requires at least the assistance of an expert (the therapist) for the dream's meaning to be discerned.

Without wishing to suggest that the strategies summarised above are of no value, existential psychotherapy adopts a very different approach to dream material. While dreams are acknowledged to often be puzzling, existential psychotherapy proposes that '[t]hey are not puzzles to be solved but openings to be attended to' (Cohn, 1997: 84). Medard Boss, who was originally a psycho-analyst and a Jungian analytical psychologist, was one of the first existential analysts to argue against what he saw as the unnecessary emphasis being placed upon 'the interpretation of the unconscious' as a means to the understanding of dreams (Boss, 1957, 1977). Greatly influenced by Heidegger, Boss became convinced that dreams expressed a form of lived reality that demanded it be approached from the standpoint of what was being presented to the dreamer rather than 'looking behind or beneath' their given statements. The exploration of dreams became, for Boss, a descriptively focused examination of the dreamer's experienced relationship to the dream. Rather than focus on symbols and analytically derived forms of dream interpretation which assumed that the manifest material of the remembered dream had been disguised in various ways which now required 'un-disguising', Boss argued that the 'dream world' was to be treated as equally valid and straightforward as the 'waking world'. Instead of demanding interpretation, dreams addressed the issues and concerns of our lived experience, using the dreamer's own private language which, presented in stark fashion and in ways that did not focus on its relatedness to the dreamer, could appear to be absurd or obscure. In acknowledging the relatedness between the 'dream world' and the 'waking world', each could shed light on the other through the content of the dream. In this way, the dream content, rather than disguising meaning could be treated as 'the bridge' that interconnected the two worlds.

Working with dreams in existential psychotherapy can be a very stimulating and creative enterprise. It provides the opportunity to explore and play with experiential possibilities that might not otherwise be open to the client's consideration. Like Boss, my own way of working with clients' dreams is to avoid treating them as some sort of substitutive 'stand-in' for hidden concerns or revelations. Instead, I encourage the client/dreamer to place him or her self 'in' the 'dream-world' and initiate a process of descriptively focused clarification and challenge. In general, I view working with dreams in existential psychotherapy as a co-operative inquiry which parallels the therapeutic relationship as a whole, but which can reveal the greater possibilities of honesty, play, mutual respect and shared openness to the novel experiential options being presented in the dream.

To a large extent, I have concluded that dreams allow the dreamer to challenge the currently maintained worldview, particularly in terms of its currently problematic sedimentations and dissociations, by providing 'dream world' descriptions, alternatives or challenges to that worldview for the dreamer to experience, explore and 'play with'.

Although existential psychotherapists can, and do, work with dreams during any Phase of the therapeutic relationship, such work is particularly powerful and worthwhile during Phase Two because the relationship that has been established between therapist and client permits an immediacy in dialogue as well as ways of helping the client relate the dream material to waking life and hence lends itself very well to the overall aims of Phase Two.

In general, the following statements and example of a dream by one of my clients, Tom, provide a brief account of my approach to working with dreams:

1.   Allow the client to recount the remembered dream in his or her own initially preferred way.

> I was at my desk, attempting to write my report when I suddenly had the urge to suck the ink out of my pen. It tasted surprisingly sweet. I looked in the mirror and saw I had ink all over my mouth and shirt. I suddenly thought: 'Mom's going to kill me!'

2. Invite the client to offer any additional information that seems immediately relevant to the remembered dream.

> The night I had the dream, I had avoided writing the report because I was bored with it and just wanted to relax and watch some television. When I went to bed, I was glad to have done that but also felt a bit guilty and was dreading what I'd have to do the next day to make up for it. I think I did suck ink out of a pen once when I was a kid, and it didn't taste sweet at all! When I woke up, I felt sad and sort of weepy because mom's been dead for three years now and I don't really have anyone in my life, other than my self, to sort of 'kill me' when I do something stupid.

3. Invite the client to consider a number of descriptively focused clarifications intended to contextualise the dream. For instance:

   (i) *Spatial contextualising*: was the 'dream world' room Tom was in the same as that of his 'waking world'? Or was it a room and a desk from another time in Tom's 'waking world' life? Or was it a room belonging to someone else? Or an imaginary room?

   (ii) *Temporal contextualising*: did the dream occur in Tom's 'waking world' present time? Or was it in the future? Or the past?

   (iii) *Contextualising dream world objects*: what did the pen look like? Is it a pen Tom uses today? Or another pen that he recalls? And the desk? What was the report? Was it the same as the one he didn't write in his 'waking world' or another report of some kind?

   (iv) *Contextualising the dreamer in the 'dream world'*: is Tom the same age in the 'dream world' as he is in his 'waking world'? Are the clothes he was wearing the same or different from those he'd worn during the day prior to the dream? If not, what was different about them?

   (v) *Contextualising key behaviour*: when Tom, following the suggestion of his therapist, mimics the act of putting a pen in his mouth and sucking out its ink, as in the 'dream world', what does this look like? Does the act provoke any thoughts or feelings connected to the remembered dream? Equally, when Tom repeats aloud the 'dream world' statement 'Mom's going to kill me!', how does he do it? How does he sound? Does the act provoke any thoughts or feelings connected to the remembered dream?

   Anything that arises from this descriptive disclosing of the dream can then be further clarified and considered.

4. Following these initial steps, invite the client to repeat the dream, but this time expressing it in the present tense.

> I'm at my desk, trying to write my report. I pick up my pen. I am sucking the ink out of it. It's sweet! I'm looking into the mirror. I see ink all over my mouth and shirt. 'Mom's going to kill me!'

5. As the therapist, repeat the dream for the client staying in the present tense, using the first person ('I') throughout and imitating key behaviour as has been previously demonstrated by the client.

6. Has the repetition of the dream provoked any further thoughts or remembrances about the dream for the client?

> It feels very kid-like, even though I'm an adult in the dream. Sucking out the ink is very enjoyable. Maybe even erotic. My mother keeps coming back to me. I wish she was still alive. I miss her. We had such great times together and she was as much a friend as she was a mother.

7. Highlight the key elements of the dream from an inter-relational perspective and centred upon the dreamer.

   (i)   Tom and the room.
   (ii) Tom and his desk.
   (iii) Tom and the unwritten report.
   (iv) Tom and his pen.
   (v)   Tom and the act of sucking ink.
   (vi) Tom and the statement 'It's sweet.'
   (vii) Tom and the mirror.
   (viii) Tom and his inky mouth.
   (ix) Tom and his ink-stained shirt.
   (x)   Tom and his mother.
   (xi) Tom and the statement 'Mom's Going to kill me!'

8. Explore descriptively with the client each of the above inter-relational dream elements. Or, if there are too many, ask the dreamer to select those that provoke the greatest interest or curiosity. The descriptive explorations are intended to focus on the various dispositional stances that emerge when the inter-relational associations between the dreamer and the dream-content element are considered.

   For instance, in Tom's case, his relationship to the unwritten report (element iii) provoked for Tom the realisation that in the 'dream world' Tom was enjoying the act of writing the report – something that was an entirely alien experience to his attempts to write reports in the 'waking world'. This led Tom to wonder what the topic or content of his 'dream world' report might be and various challenging possibilities arose for him to consider. Similarly, the exploration of Tom's relation to the statement 'Mom's going to kill me!' (element xi) provoked a very powerful and painful, yet much appreciated, emotional reaction. Tom was reminded that this phrase evoked all manner of significant memories for him that, while tinged with some degree of fear, were also expressions of his deep love and respect for his mother. At the same time, Tom realised that within the 'dream world', it was fear alone that he associated with the statement. This awareness challenged Tom to look again at his relationship with his mother so that the fearful aspects of this relationship could be more acknowledged. Through this, Tom began to see his mother as 'more human' than he had previously allowed her to be.

9. Explore the potential inter-relations between the dream-content elements while keeping in mind what has been discerned from the previous step (8) above.

   For instance, when Tom places together 'Mother' and 'sucking ink,' does any meaningful connection occur? Or when he connects together the statement 'It's sweet' with the statement 'Mom's going to kill me!' does any novel meaning come to mind? If so, how might these relate back to the dream as a whole? For example, following the points discussed above, when Tom considered the possible relation between the unwritten report and his statement 'Mom's going to kill me!', he connected the feeling of pleasure to that of overwhelming fear. Staying with the content elements but now adding the noetic constituents of fear and pleasure, Tom was further enabled to investigate his relationship with his mother, as well as his own failed attempts at both 'mothering' him self and finding a 'substitute mum' in the relations he had formed with various women.

10. Explore what has emerged from the above points in relation to the presenting problem with which the client has been grappling in recent therapy sessions. Does anything emerge through this exploration which sheds light on both the dream and the problem?

   Tom had initially come to therapy because of an overall sense of disinterest in, and detachment from, living. He was not suicidal; he just didn't feel 'alive'. What interests he conjured up in his work, his social and romantic relationships just seemed to 'fizzle out' after a while. At the same time, he was dissatisfied with him self for allowing him self to become, as he termed it, 'a bystander on life's highway'. The dream proved to be significant for Tom in that it demonstrated to him that he could still experience intense feelings – pleasure and fear – even if only in his 'dream world'. Although there was a great deal of material relevant to his often-troubled relationship with his deceased mother, it was primarily this rich, felt sense that he could still experience something that he'd felt had been forever lost to him which he most valued about this dream.

11. Explore what has emerged from the above points in relation to whatever sedimentations and dissociations in the client's worldview had been previously discerned and/or have been mentioned in the course of the investigation of the dream. Does anything emerge that suggests a relation between the dream and these sedimentations and dissociations?

> Tom's primary sedimentations, in relation to his presenting problems, rested upon dispositional stances related to (a) his disinterest in everything and (b) his inability to complete that which he initiated, simply out of boredom (but, also, implicitly, because he feared the judgement of anything he'd completed far more than he feared the complaints that arose as a result of his unfinished work). Although Tom's report was also unfinished in the dream world, what was of significant difference was his acknowledged sense of enjoying its writing. This dream world experience directly challenged Tom's sedimentation of 'disinterest'. Similarly, the enjoyment of sucking ink from his pen, even if the act led to significant fears, nonetheless also challenged this sedimentation. Moreover, Tom also saw that the act of sucking ink out of the pen was a 'completed' act, and although it generated fear (as his sedimentation had 'predicted'), nonetheless his pleasure could not be denied or dismissed. Thus, the dream also challenged the second dispositional stance not by challenging its validity, but by revealing to Tom that this validity was only part of the narrative regarding his experience of 'an act of completion'.

As the above example should indicate, working with dreams from an existential perspective follows the same descriptive focus as applied throughout the whole of the therapeutic encounter. The client is challenged through clarification and descriptive challenging. At no time is there an attempt on the therapist's part to add to, distort, transform or assume any symbolic aspects to the dream material.

Although it may consume a good deal of time and attention, working with dreams can be highly rewarding and challenging for the client. My personal view is that dreams permit clients to address difficult concerns and issues from the initially more secure and distanced 'third-person' perspective of 'the dreamer in the dream'. In this partially dissociated manner, views, values, fears, beliefs that would otherwise be difficult, if not impossible, to 'own' in the client's 'waking-life' worldview are permitted their expression and exploration. In the course of working on the dream with the existential psychotherapist, it may become more possible for the dream's de-sedimenting challenges to the 'waking life' worldview to be explored and considered.

In many cases, the therapeutic session focused on a dream may simply initiate something that the client could be encouraged to continue outside the therapy world. At least as importantly, working together on the client's dream often permits an intimacy between client and therapist that expresses the client's experience of both the trustworthiness of the therapy world and his or her trust of, and ease in being with, the therapist. These, in turn, allow the therapist to further clarify and challenge the client's worldview and its relatedness to the client's concerns.

AN EXERCISE ON WORKING WITH DREAMS

1. Working together with a partner, take turns in exploring a remembered dream, or, if it is too long, a section of it that most intrigues, surprises or disturbs. Each session should last thirty minutes.
2. As the client, initially recount the dream, or the section of the dream, in your own preferred way.
3. As the therapist, follow the investigative sequence outlined above to help you and your client explore the dream.
4. When you have both completed the exercise, discuss what personal value, and what value, if any, for the therapeutic process you have found in working with dreams from this perspective.

PHASE TWO: WORKING WITH INTIMACY

Intimacy: Therapist Disclosures

Although many of the more strident objections toward therapist disclosures have eased somewhat over time, and, consequently, have been the subject of critique and reformulation (Rowan and Jacobs, 2002), many of these attitudes and regulations remain fixed areas of concern, in some form or other, for the vast majority of psychotherapists, regardless of the model they espouse. Even existential psychotherapists who have consistently criticised and rejected most of the theoretical assumptions of psycho-analysis in particular, and of many subsequent psychotherapies in general, have, on the whole, retained and advanced these same concerns with little hesitation or question. As I have argued elsewhere, the most recurrent arguments both for and against disclosure fail to take into account the inter-relational factors that are so central to an existential approach to psychotherapy. As a result, many of the concerns expressed don't really touch on those issues that are most pertinent to existential psychotherapy (Spinelli, 2001).

My personal view is that the issue of therapist disclosure, considered from the perspective of existential psychotherapy, touches upon issues relevant to the *immediacy* of the therapeutic relationship in general, and in particular to the three inter-relational realms discussed above. Most pertinently, I believe, it is the We-focused realm that is critical with regard to the question of disclosure. Let us reconsider this realm from the standpoint of the existential psychotherapist.

At the We-focused realm of relation, I, as existential psychotherapist, experience my 'self-being-in-relation-with-the-client' and note what emerges, or is disclosed, through the interaction between us. This could include my reflections upon what it is like for us to be with one another in this currently reflected moment, my sense of what we might be sharing at an experiential level, and what may be being expressed by us in an indirect, or metaphorical manner that is resonant with our current way of 'being together'. It is here, I would argue, that the possibility of disclosure on the part of the existential psychotherapist becomes most apparent. Indeed, such disclosures may be both appropriate and beneficial to the client.

However, the question arises: what is the existential psychotherapist attempting to promote or achieve through disclosure? Clearly, various models and approaches in psychotherapy may have clear-cut answers to this question that might be valid to their system. But what might these be for existential psychotherapy? My view is that the critical issue concerning the use of disclosure for existential psychotherapists is straightforward: *Does this disclosure remain within the over-riding aim of seeking to bring into focus and reveal the implicit dispositional stances of the client's worldview that maintain his or her sedimentations and dissociations?* If so, then it seems to me that disclosure is a valid means of descriptive clarification and challenge, as well as a powerful expression of the We-focus. On consideration, I would suggest that two forms of disclosure are available to the existential psychotherapist: *covert* and *overt disclosures.*

Covert disclosures are those whereby the existential psychotherapist makes use of his or her own lived experiences in order to clarify and challenge the client's worldview statements, but does so in a way that does not directly reveal the source as being the therapist's personal material. For example:

Client: When he finally told me that he didn't want to stay in the marriage and that he'd found a new life-partner, I just felt so sick and angry. I hated my self more than I hated him.

Therapist: Can you say a bit more about what it was like for you to hear him say these things? How was that sense of feeling sick and angry, for instance?

Client: I can just feel it, you know? It's hard to put words to it.

Therapist: [*accessing his own experiences of being rejected and the feelings that arise in him regarding this*] Would it be OK for me to try to speak the words?

Client: Yeah . . .

Therapist: Now, I'm just guessing here. So anything I say that feels wrong to you, that's fine. You let me know. OK, so what I'm imagining when I put myself in your experience is: I get an overwhelming dizziness; a tightness in my gut; a restriction in my throat so that I can't even reply to him; I see flashes of all sorts of earlier moments in our life together: happy moments, sad ones, silly ones, private ones; and as I see them I hear his voice saying over and over: 'It's finished. This is the end.' I feel a rage that is almost murderous directed toward him, but oddly it's also directed toward my self. How's that so far? Is it at all close to your experience?

Client: Yes, a lot of it is. But as you were talking, what mainly came up for me was a sense of failure. That was the main thing. 'I've failed and I'm not worthy.'

Therapist: OK. So let's stay with that. 'A lot of those statements Ernesto made are correct and they've provoked my overwhelming sense of failure.' Are you feeling it now?

Client: Yes.

Therapist: So what's it like to feel it right here with me present?

Client: It's like I felt with Harry when he told me he was leaving me.

Therapist: OK. So that feeling with Harry is right here in the room with us. Can you access any words for that feeling?

Through the use of *covert disclosures,* the existential psychotherapist carries out an act of personal revelation but in such a way that the material is not explicitly presented as 'belonging' to him or her.

Overt disclosures also make use of the existential psychotherapist's personal 'material' in order to clarify and challenge the client's worldview. However, they are explicit in acknowledging their source as the therapist's own lived experience. For example:

Client:	I felt like such a complete fool! I thought that she'd been attracted to me because we'd got on so well together. But I was completely wrong! She started laughing at me! Can you believe that? Do you have any idea how something like that could feel?
Therapist:	Tell me.
Client:	I can't! It's just so painful. [*Begins to cry.*]
Therapist:	OK. I want to ask you if you'll let me try something here. As you were speaking, I began to remember an incident in my own life that maybe evoked similar feelings to your own. I wonder whether it would be OK for you if I gave you a sense of it and focused on what it evoked for me so that we can see whether your experience and mine share anything in common. But if you think it's pointless, just say so. Or stop me at any point.
Client:	No, go ahead. I'd appreciate that.

[*Therapist recounts his experience of being rejected, focusing on the dispositional factors accompanying it.*]

Therapist:	Was any of that at all like what went on for you?
Client:	Yeah. It brought a lot of my feelings back up.

[*Client discusses the points of connection that have been made, as well as new noematic and noetic factors that have emerged with regard to his experience.*]

Therapist:	What was it like to know that it was *my* story and not yours?
Client:	Well, I knew it was your story. But it also felt like mine.
Therapist:	And what's it like to know: 'It was Ernesto's story, and that it also feels like mine?'
Client:	Well, it doesn't make it feel any better. But I don't feel so alone in my stupidity.
Therapist:	So . . . 'The fact that my therapist also got rejected and feels stupid about it, stops making me feel alone?'
Client:	[*laughs*] Now you're reading my thoughts.
Therapist:	[*laughs*] Maybe you're reading mine.
Client:	I wish I could.
Therapist:	Oh? What would you like to read about my thoughts?
Client:	Whether you feel I'm an idiot for over-reacting so much.
Therapist:	I wouldn't mind reading your thoughts about the very same thing.

Covert and overt disclosures during Phase Two acknowledge the existential psychotherapist's presence in the therapy world as genuine and immediate. While the primary aim of the therapist does not deviate from that of helping the client explore, clarify and challenge his or her presenting worldview, these disclosures rely upon the therapist's own experience as an additional means with which to pursue this aim.

As the above examples indicate, disclosure, from the perspective of existential psychotherapy, has little to do with permitting the therapist to express him or her self in order to be 'congruent' or 'real' (as in 'I am feeling really bored right now'). Rather, the existential psychotherapist's use of disclosure provides another way into the clarification and challenge of the client's worldview and permits a dialogue that in its immediacy opens up the therapeutic possibilities of discourse at the We-focused realm of encounter. As the above examples attempt to demonstrate, all such disclosures focus predominantly upon the description of the *noetic* elements of the therapist's personal narrative and, in turn, are followed by the therapist's explicit invitation to the client to examine his or her (the client's) experiential response to the therapist's disclosure in the immediacy of their dialogue. It is in this latter part of the disclosure process that most of its potential worth as a form of descriptive clarification and challenge can emerge.

At the same time, as can also, I hope, be seen from the examples above, the existential psychotherapist's use of disclosure always seeks to remain both *tentative* and *invitational*. The genuine opportunity for the client to reject such an invitation must be part of the process. Equally, whatever the client takes from such disclosures, including that they bear no relation at all to the client's experience (or, indeed, as may sometimes occur, that they provoke the client's anger in that the disclosure is seen to misunderstand, demean or minimise his or her experience) cannot be disputed by the therapist nor be responded to in a possessive and defensive manner which rejects the client's reactive stance.

There is a real risk involved in the existential psychotherapist's use of disclosure. Disclosures may miss the mark, confuse or burden the client. Equally, they may enfold the therapist in the feelings and memories they contain and, in doing so, deflect inquiry from focusing upon the client's worldview. At the same time, disclosures can provide a powerful means for the client to access elements of his or her own experience that might otherwise have been minimised or missed.

My personal view is that both covert and overt disclosures are best offered during Phase Two, where the existential psychotherapist's presence and 'voice' within the therapy world are more explicitly focused on his or her 'otherness'. If employed during Phase One, covert disclosures are more likely to be experienced by the client as 'uncanny' ('How on earth could the therapist have known *that*?') and in turn may add unnecessary imbalances to the power aspects in the relationship. Equally, overt disclosures offered during Phase One may seem to the client to be implicit directives to change, or may swamp the client's own explorations. Both covert and overt disclosures made during Phase One run the risk of focusing too soon upon the more implicit dispositional stances of the client's worldview and, as a consequence, may serve to counteract their intent by provoking unease as well as suspicion and distrust of both the existential psychotherapist and the therapy world.

TWO EXERCISES ON THERAPIST DISCLOSURE

EXERCISE 1

1. Working together with a partner, take turns in being therapist and client. Each session should last fifteen minutes.
2. As the client, focus initially on a recent event that has provoked a strong reactive response from you.
3. As the therapist, assist the client in exploring his or her relationship to the focus topic *but only in such a way that all your interventions are at the covert level of disclosure.*
4. When you have both completed the exercise explore the experience of utilising covert disclosures and what value, if any, they have to the therapeutic enterprise as a whole.

EXERCISE 2

1. Working together with a partner, take turns in being therapist and client. Each session should last fifteen minutes.
2. As the client, focus initially on a recent event that has provoked a strong reactive response from you.
3. As the therapist, assist the client in exploring his or her relationship to the focus topic *but only in such a way that all your interventions are at the overt level of disclosure.*
4. When you have both completed the exercise explore the experience of utilising overt disclosures and what value, if any, they have to the therapeutic enterprise as a whole.

Intimacy: Daniel Stern's 'Present Moments in Psychotherapy'

A recent, and already invaluable text by Daniel Stern, entitled *The Present Moment in Psychotherapy and Everyday Life* (Stern, 2004), focuses upon 'present' or 'now' moments of meeting 'in which therapist and client know and feel what the other knows and feels' (Mearns and Cooper, 2005: 46). For Stern, this is a 'shared meaning voyage' (2004: 172) which also encapsulates a significant shift from a 'one-person' to a 'two-person' psychology (ibid.) – which is to say, that its focus is upon inter-relatedness rather than upon an isolationist subjectivity. Exploring recent research data (including that of mirror neurons as was briefly discussed in Part One), Stern maintains that there is now sufficient evidence to indicate the existence of a foundational species-based system for inter-subjective (or inter-relational) knowing whose aim is achieved in those instances of 'present moments' (ibid.).

Stern's 'present moment' rests upon his phenomenologically derived understanding that 'we are psychologically and consciously alive only now' (Stern,

2004: xiv). In taking this view, Stern acknowledges his indebtedness to the ideas on temporality advocated by existential phenomenology in that the 'present moment' is infused with, and structured by, both retentive (immediate past) and protentive (anticipated future) horizons (ibid.). The spontaneity of the 'present moment' – a shared laugh, a touch of the shoulder, a glance that connects – cannot be initiated in some directive fashion and thus runs counter to any emphases given to technique.

From a psychotherapeutic perspective, 'present moments' often occur at crisis points in the therapeutic relationship when the client and therapist are disconnected or 'missing' one another or, alternatively, when they are together 'in' the intensity of their meeting. Such instances can often express themselves as direct challenges to the therapist by the client which require the former to respond to the immediacy of the inter-relational encounter in a way that reveals his or her willingness to meet the latter in a spontaneous self-revealing response, rather than falling back on a 'formulaic role-based one' (Mearns and Cooper, 2005: 134). For Stern, such therapist responses that remain at the immediacy of the 'present moment' are far more valuable and beneficial both to the ongoing process and to the outcome of the therapeutic encounter than are the theory-laden interpretations with which therapists might feel more at ease (Stern, 2004).

During Phase Two of existential psychotherapy, instances akin to those highlighted by Stern as the 'present moment' can indicate to the therapist the degree to which the focus taken on the exploration of the client's worldview is open to the immediacy of encounter. The existential psychotherapist's openness to disclosure and to We-focused discourse is likely to promote psychological and relational conditions sympathetic to the experience of the 'present moment'. In my view, one relatively common phenomenon associated with the 'present moment' is that of the therapist's spontaneous completion of the client's statement as it is being uttered. Such moments require the therapist to be attuned to the client in a highly 'connected' or intimate manner. While they can generate a sense of closeness and trust, they can also be jarring and disturbing in their 'quasi-telepathic' appearance.

Readers may have noticed from the examples above that, as with previous session extracts, a number of therapist reflections are in the first person ('I') rather than in the second person ('you'). For example:

Client: I don't know whether you've understood me or not and I'm feeling anxious about that.

Therapist: Let me see if I got what you said: 'I can't be sure as to whether or not Ernesto's understanding me and that makes me feel anxious.'

On the basis of what clients and trainees have recounted, I suspect that as well as allowing the client to be more directly confronted with his or her statements in a fashion that makes plain their ownership at the first-person level, this way of reflecting may also facilitate the experience of 'present moments'.

AN EXERCISE ON THE 'PRESENT MOMENT'

Together with a partner, discuss those instances of the 'present moment' that you have experienced both within the therapeutic relationship and in other non-therapeutic encounters. Explore the felt sense of these experiences. What was their impact upon your relationship with the other with whom the experience occurred?

As a therapist, how have you responded to those 'present-moment' challenges presented by the client? What were the consequences to the therapeutic relationship of your response?

As a client, how has your therapist responded to those 'present-moment' challenges that occurred in the course of your therapy? What were the consequences to the therapeutic relationship of these responses?

What value, if any, do you place on 'present moments' in therapy?

Intimacy: General and Erotic Attraction

Because of the sometimes intense focus on the immediate relationship taken throughout Phase Two, it is not overly surprising for a deeply felt sense of closeness and connection to develop between the existential psychotherapist and his or her client. This movement toward intimacy might be expressed in terms of a growing sense of care and respect toward the client by the therapist which also, at times, may be mutual. Often, this sense is associated with notions of friendship; less often, as erotic attraction. Equally, such intimacy may provide the means for clients to experience and express 'explosive', highly charged feeling-focused reactions that may be centred upon anger and aggression or combinations of love and hatred directed toward the therapist.

From the perspective of many of the current models of Western psychotherapy, such experiences are usually 'explained' as instances of *transference* and *counter-transference*. I have explored these terms critically elsewhere (Spinelli, 1994), but for present purposes let me simply state that, in my view, they are of little value to existential psychotherapists in that, in their reliance upon a hypothesised secondary mental system (the unconscious), which is claimed to be their source, they deviate from the primary focus on the immediacy of the current encounter. In addition, their explanatory value obscures what there may be of value to understand about the currently felt attraction in and of itself and its possible relation to the client's worldview as expressed in the therapy world. Most significantly, they impose an element of unreality and inappropriateness upon such experiences that hampers the existential psychotherapist's attempt to stay with that which presents itself, as it presents itself, in the therapeutic encounter.

That the great majority of therapists *do* experience attraction towards their clients is beyond doubt. A 1986 survey revealed that 87 per cent (95 per cent of male therapists and 76 per cent of female therapists) of all therapists who participated in the study admitted to feelings of sexual attraction to clients at some point in the therapeutic relationship, even if the vast majority did not subsequently go on to have sexual relations with their clients (9.4 per cent of male therapists and 2.5 per cent of female therapists did do so). Equally, many therapists felt guilty, anxious or confused about their experience of attraction but did not seem to find the means of resolving such feelings. Only 9 per cent reported that their training or supervision was adequate to deal with such (Pope, 1990). In a study reported in 2001, Giovazolias and Davis investigated UK counselling psychologists' experiences of sexual attraction toward their clients. As well as confirming that sexual attraction toward clients was a common experience, the study argued that such feelings were not necessarily detrimental to the therapeutic process. Indeed, approximately 50 per cent of those who disclosed these feelings of attraction to their clients reported a positive impact on the therapeutic relationship (Giovazolias and Davis, 2001).

Nonetheless, the experience of attraction – be it specifically erotic or more diffuse in that the therapist is attracted to the person, his or her personal beliefs and qualities, shared interests and social attitudes – can surprise, disturb and confuse. Therapists may experience guilt, fear of discovery by other professionals or of losing control of their desires, and, in turn, may experience or express anger and blame toward the client for somehow having provoked these feelings (Pope et. al., 1993).

How are existential psychotherapists to deal with feelings of both general and erotic attraction? When I have raised this in seminars and lectures, the most common response has been that existential psychotherapists 'somehow should be able to eradicate [it] from their thoughts (by means of some form of determined willpower)' (Spinelli, 1994: 112). Unfortunately, such strategies tend to fail and, instead, provoke reactions all too similar to those generated when we tell our selves, or are told, 'Whatever you do, don't think of the colour red.'

Instead, as I have suggested elsewhere, 'rather than seek to deny or suppress such feelings, or, alternatively, to "transform" them or minimize their impact by invoking such terms as "counter-transference", therapists might do better to *acknowledge* them as being present in their experience of, and relationship with, their client' (Spinelli, 1994: 114). This acknowledgement of 'what is there for me' enables existential psychotherapists to place this particular aspect of their experience of relatedness alongside whatever other experiential factors may be present, just as would be the case in attempting the Rule of Equalisation. Rather than be oppressed by such experiences, the therapist might then include them in his or her ongoing clarification and challenge of the client's worldview. Through this accepting stance, that which was previously experienced as being problematic might well be transformed into something both appropriate and advantageous to the therapeutic process.

Thus, in dealing with attraction by first acknowledging it, existential psychotherapists can remain *within* the lived conditions of the therapy world. This stance requires the shift from considering something that is initially experienced as being in some way problematic – and hence, unwanted or not permitted to be present – to that of being open to its actuality and, through that, avoiding the experience of being 'swamped' or overwhelmed by this one dispositional focus of experience. In this way, the experience of attraction, while by no means denied, is nevertheless prevented from distracting the focus of attention away from the client. Equally, in the choice of acknowledging 'what is there' for them, existential psychotherapists might discern relevant aspects of the client's worldview that had been previously set aside or left unconsidered. Further, in their acceptance of attraction within the therapy world, existential psychotherapists (and clients as well) may find that, in many instances, such intense feelings often simply reside within the confines of that world and either do not extend beyond it, or dissipate once they have stepped out into the wider world. Perhaps most significantly, in their attempt to adopt this open and receptive stance toward that which would otherwise be avoided or shunned, existential psychotherapists can *embody* their theory and, by so doing, become living expressions of a way of being that the client, in turn, may experience and consider.

As to the question of whether existential psychotherapists should or should not voice their experiences of attraction to their clients, I refer readers back to the previous discussion on disclosure and suggest that there is nothing inherent in the question of attraction that demands an alternative to, or rejection of, the proposals set forth therein.

AN EXERCISE ON ATTRACTION

1. Working together with a partner, take turns in exploring an example of how you have experienced and worked with general attraction in the therapeutic relationship, both as a client and as a therapist.
2. Working together with a partner, take turns in exploring an example of how you have experienced and worked with erotic attraction in the therapeutic relationship, both as a client and as a therapist.
3. On the basis of your discussion, take turns in examining how you would work as a supervisor with a supervisee who came to you concerned that mutual erotic attraction had developed between him or her self and a client.

Intimacy: Rollo May's Hypothesis of the 'Daimonic'

The American existential psychotherapist, Rollo May, suggested that the expression of both creative and destructive dispositions is a universal aspect of human existence (May, 1969; Hoeller, 1996). Because the experiences associated with each disposition can often express themselves as uncontrollable, assertive demands that appear to spring from a source that is not directly identified with the person's personal worldview as a whole or with any of its primary constructs, May adopted the term *daimonic* as a descriptive means with which to express this ontological 'given'. Rather than view the creative and destructive as separate and distinct tendencies, the daimonic expresses them as inter-related polarities expressive of a single urge to assert one's being in, and upon, the world.

In cultures where the daimonic is suppressed or identified only with the undesirable or evil, it finds various 'underground' means through which to express itself. May argued that the daimonic 'comes to the fore in times of transition in a society' (May, 1969: 129) and, in such instances, is revealed both in movements of novel and challenging expressions of creativity – whether artistically or scientifically focused – and in reactive and assertive aggression, hostility and other forms of destructiveness. So, too, from an individual perspective, the daimonic urges of creativity and destruction can be directed toward self, others or the world. In all such instances, the daimonic reveals an accompanying ambiguity in meaning and identity. In that transitional moment when the daimonic erupts, all is uncertain.

One cultural example of what May is suggesting might be seen in the explosion of the underground 'rave' culture of the 1990s. Through their use of dance, music and drugs, 'raves' offered a communal experience of connectedness, trust and affection among participants which served as counter-example to the 'overground' culture's elevation of unbridled egoism and the worship of 'the individual'. In this way, the underground culture of 'raves' challenged in a daimonic fashion that which the 'overground' culture had dismissed as irrelevant or non-existent. Following May's argument, such expressions of the daimonic emphasise the interconnectedness and co-existence of the creative and the destructive, not only in the 'underground' rave behaviour, but also in the attitudes and biases of 'overground' culture. May argued that the daimonic must be channelled, structured and integrated so that the potential for creating anew is not overwhelmed by the potential for only destroying that which is present. In order for such to occur, society must be brave enough to welcome the daimonic and recognise the necessity of its presence and expression.

From a more individual perspective, May viewed psychotherapy as one of the few remaining ways in Western culture of allowing the individual's daimonic eruptions their expression under structured conditions by which these would be sufficiently harnessed, to increase the likelihood of a reconstructive rather than a merely destructive set of circumstances. For May, the provision of psychotherapy had little to do with the attempt make people happy; rather, therapy was in the service of their potential for freedom (May, 1981). Paradoxically, May suggested that the personal confrontation with the possessive forces of the daimonic provides a pivotal means for individuals to experience the freedom inherent in their existence (May, 1969).

May's hypothesis remains controversial for many existential psychotherapists, not least because of his tendency to present the daimonic both as an entity and as a somewhat vague biologically in-built force which serves as the existential equivalent to psycho-analytic drive theory. Nonetheless, even if the notion of the daimonic were to be considered solely as a metaphorical expression of the human potential for creation and destruction, much of the substance of May's proposal remains. For example, the daimonic can be seen as as a way of expressing the tension between 'being-as-process' (worlding) and 'being-as-structured-essence' (the worldview). When the worldview reveals its sedimented and dissociative limitations, the ensuing struggle between the attempt to maintain the existing worldview and the 'push' to reconstitute it parallels the depersonalised (or dissociated) possessive force of the daimonic. In such instances, the consequences of this struggle remain unpredictable. They may destabilise the worldview, thereby provoking extreme forms of unease that are subsequently expressed in various aggressive or destructive tendencies focused upon self, others or the world. Alternatively, they may either generate a creative reconstitution of the worldview in that it more adequately expresses the person's ongoing process of worlding, or they may provoke temporary creative dissociations which generate the experience of possession, diminution or transcendental expansion of one's 'self'. If the person's experience of worldview ambiguity is contained within a suitably adequate structure that allows it to be embraced, explored and 'worked through', then it is more likely that both the process and its outcome are primarily creative and reconstitutive rather than destructive. Structures such as prayer or meditation, artistic expression, research-focused inquiry and body-focused activities such as dance, running or exercise, can all provoke the 'possessive' experience of the daimonic while harnessing it within an adequate structure intended to meaningful, life-enhancing and creative outcomes. So, too, can psychotherapy.

Psychotherapy's structure, the co-created therapy world, provides the baseline conditions within which emergence of the daimonic can be both embraced and contained. Indeed, it is likely to be the case that the client has turned to therapy *because* he or she experiences some disturbing ambiguity in the currently maintained worldview. Existential psychotherapy's explicit focus upon the investigation of the client's worldview under circumstances where the client experiences it to be in at least partial transition provides further conditions that encourage the expression of the daimonic. In this sense, existential psychotherapy can both assist the expression of the daimonic and offer inter-relational possibilities that may help the client to direct the encounter with the daimonic in such a way that its consequences are more likely to be predominantly creative rather than destructive. Considered from the perspective of Phase Two of existential psychotherapy, the daimonic is likely to occur as a direct consequence, and expression, of the exploratory focus being undertaken and the inter-relational intimacy within which such exploration is channelled and contextualised. Therefore, at any point throughout Phase Two, the existential psychotherapist should be prepared for those indications of the client's movement toward, or immersion in, the daimonic. Such are likely to be expressed via intense feelings that 'spring up' for the client in ways that may surprise, shock, disturb, excite, repel or dismay him or her. These may be directed toward the client him or her self, toward others in the client's wider world of inter-relation, toward beliefs, values and aspirations associated with the client's challenged worldview, and, just as likely, toward the therapist who, in turn, may experience some equivalent to any and all of these as challenges to his or her own worldview.

Rather than seek to dissolve, reduce, intensify or explain these daimonic explosions, it remains the task of the existential psychotherapist to attempt to 'stand beside' the client throughout their appearance and to pursue their investigation through descriptive clarification and challenge. The sharing of these moments can be intensely intimate and may involve a minimal exchange of verbal discourse. It is during such confrontations that existential psychotherapy's emphasis upon the embracing presence of the therapist within the co-created confines of the therapy world, and the possibilities of this particular stance toward truthful and trusting relatedness, truly come to the fore.

AN EXERCISE EXPLORING THE DAIMONIC

1. Together with a partner, take turns in exploring a personal instance of a confrontation with the daimonic.
2. Examine what were the circumstances that provoked this from the standpoint of the worldview that was then currently maintained. What were the effects of this encounter with the daimonic upon the then current worldview?
3. Discuss how the notion of the daimonic might impact upon your practice as a psychotherapist.

PHASE TWO: RECONFIGURING THE SETTING, FRAME AND CONTRACTUAL CONDITIONS OF THE THERAPEUTIC RELATIONSHIP

In the earlier discussion focused upon Phase One, the existential psychotherapist's strict maintenance of the setting, frame and contractual conditions for the co-creation of a therapy world were highlighted as key factors in the establishment of a trustworthy therapeutic relationship. Having read the discussion on Phase One, readers will, I hope, have had the opportunity to consider and better understand the importance of this stance with regard to the overall enterprise of existential psychotherapy.

While it is entirely possible, if not highly likely, that these same conditions will remain in place throughout Phase Two as well, it is my view that a reconfiguration and renegotiation of the setting, frame and contractual conditions is also possible and may, in some instances, even be desirable within the specific circumstances of each particular and unique relationship between therapist and client. Let me highlight some possible instances where the existing conditions may be opened to renegotiation:

1. The intensity of the Phase Two relationship is such that the client requests, or the therapist offers, the possibility of either an increase in the frequency of meetings or an extension of their duration.
2. The intensity of the Phase Two relationship is such that the client requests a decrease either in the frequency of meetings or in the duration of the existing meetings.

3. The intensity of the Phase Two relationship is such that the client requests the possibility of being able to contact the therapist by telephone, e-mail or text messaging during times beyond those set in the agreed contract.
4. For reasons of convenience or owing to changes in life conditions, either the client or the therapist requests a change in the times or location of meetings or of the fee-structure that had been agreed.

All of the above examples are likely to occur at various points throughout an existential psychotherapist's professional career and are neither highly unusual nor unexpected possibilities. In each case, unless previously specified as potential options within the agreed-upon contract, it is important to approach the potential change in conditions as *a request that either party is entitled to refuse.* At the same time, any amendment proposed by the client deserves consideration and descriptively focused exploration, even if the therapist is in no position, or has no desire, to agree to the proposal.

Let us now consider some less common instances relevant to a reconfiguration of any or all of these conditions:

1. The client requests that the therapist suggest some other sources, such as books, films or music, that might serve to further challenge issues and concerns that have been discussed in the therapy world.
2. The client offers the therapist the opportunity to read a book, listen to music or watch a film that means a great deal to client and which might help the therapist to better understand some aspects of the concerns and issues raised by the client in the therapy world.
3. The client proposes that either one or a set number of sessions are focused upon a meaningful item in the client's life, such as a particular piece of music, or an extract from a novel, or a painting or photographs relevant to a particular topic of therapeutic discussion that, the client believes, will assist its exploration. For example, one client who had been examining the effects of the sudden and unexpected death of her younger brother upon her life, requested that she be permitted to bring in photographs taken of their relationship from its earliest period, when they had both been children, right up to the photograph she had taken of his corpse.
4. The client puts forward the idea of an extension of the therapy world such that it can now exist within a different space as well as the current one. For instance, one of my clients proposed that I see him for several meetings in his office space since he felt that this would allow him to 'tap into' his 'way of being a manager', and the concerns we'd discussed about this, in a much more immediate way that would assist him. Another client expressed the desire to have a session with me outdoors, in the public space of the park surrounding my office since, for her, the sense that being in a space unrestricted by walls and permitting physical movement seemed a matter of some significance, even though she could not state why.
5. The client suggests the possibility that someone else be temporarily admitted into the therapy world. For example, one client requested that he be allowed to introduce his boyfriend to me at the start of the subsequent session because so much had been said about me by my client to his boyfriend that it would resolve a great deal of curiosity (and possible jealousy) if I could just meet him. Another client requested that she be allowed to bring her dog to one session because she felt that it was only in her dog's presence that she could begin to broach a particularly painful topic.

All of these examples, and many more that would arise upon further consideration, express the intent to alter the existing agreed-upon relational conditions necessary to the identification and maintenance of a clearly designated therapy world. Rather than focus upon questions regarding the relative appropriateness, or lack of it, in either acceding to or rejecting any of the amendments proposed above, I simply want to suggest that there is nothing within existential psychotherapy during Phase Two that would automatically demand the rejection of any of these requests. Nor is there anything in existential psychotherapy that would automatically require their agreement.

As was discussed in the section dealing with the setting, frame and contractual issues during Phase One, unlike other contemporary approaches, existential psychotherapy's 'rules' seek to express, and are derived from, a pivotal focus dealing with the investigation of relatedness. Considered from this perspective, so long as they exist within the 'givens' of codes of professional practice and ethics, there can be any number and variety of possible, and appropriate, frame conditions. The one proviso is, as was discussed earlier, that both existential psychotherapist and client must 'own' whatever conditions arise as appropriate and sufficient to maintain their 'magical beliefs' about when and whether a structured relationship is or is not 'a therapeutic relationship'.

Even so, it remains to be asked: even if all of the above is accepted, what value would there be in re-appraising a frame that has demonstrated its reliability in fulfilling these inter-relational requirements and possibilities?

An answer that has infused my own thinking on this issue is the recognition that shifts in the worldview can often occur because those aspects of worlding that the worldview was intended to reflect from a structural perspective are no longer being adequately reflected. In this sense, *the currently maintained worldview has become a hindrance to its own enterprise.* In the same way, is it not possible that the various setting, frame and contractual conditions that provide a structure for the therapy world and that so adequately reflected that world during Phase One may also have become inadequate in that they impose unnecessary and undesirable limits to the exploratory possibilities of the currently lived Phase Two experience of relatedness between therapist and client? Alternatively, permitting a reconfiguration of setting, frame and contractual conditions (whether permanently or temporarily) may more adequately reflect emerging or newly emerged inter-relational possibilities and, hence, restructure the therapy world.

In many cases, I suspect, Phase One to Phase Two shifts in the therapeutic frame may never occur or be requested. It is not that such shifts are necessary, only that they remain a possibility that may be both appropriate and desirable within existential psychotherapy.

This discussion of the possibility of structural shifts in the therapy world during Phase Two brings to mind a common fear expressed by trainees and practising psychotherapists alike: the unexpected meeting of a client outside the therapy world, such as in a supermarket or at a party. In such circumstances, it is not unusual for therapists to seek to avoid all contact or to deny any acknowledgement of their own, or their client's, presence. Indeed, these instances are often considered as a danger to the established frame and, depending upon the model that the therapist adopts, may be viewed as anything from a minor infraction to a cataclysmic deviation from the frame. As these concerns are also often expressed by existential psychotherapists, it seems worthwhile to consider such instances in the light of shifts in the setting, frame and contractual conditions in the therapy world.

As was discussed in Part One, existential phenomenology is explicit in acknowledging a basic 'given' of uncertainty. At any moment the circumstances of life might alter everything any one of us held as being secure, valid and meaningful. When confronted with such instances, the worldview is challenged. As has already been discussed, it may respond to such a challenge in two broad ways: either via the dissociation of the experience so that its threat to the worldview is controlled or minimised, or via the de-sedimentation of the worldview followed by the reconstitution of a novel worldview. If we consider the currently existing therapy world structural conditions as aspects of the therapy world worldview, it becomes clear that the avoidance response of existential psychotherapists in such circumstances parallels the strategy of dissociation. Alternatively, accepting the event and attempting to incorporate it into a newly reconstituted therapy world structure can be seen as an act of de-sedimentation. Either option has its desirable features as well as its limitations and risks. Equally, the consequences arising from either strategy cannot be entirely predicted in terms of their subsequent impact upon the therapeutic relationship. Once again, both the therapist and the client are confronted with uncertainty.

My own most common stance with regard to these instances is to opt for the less typical strategy of permitting the challenge to the therapy world structure and seeking to remain open to its unforeseen consequences and possibilities. In the event of an unexpected contact with a client (whether current or past) I initially acknowledge his or her presence in some non-verbal fashion, such as a slight nod or a smile, and then leave it to the client to determine whether he or she wishes to approach me or, alternatively, prefers to keep our relationship unacknowledged within a public arena. This strikes me as a way of remaining professionally respectful of the client's right to anonymity as well as being open to the possibility that the client wishes to express publicly in some fashion the existence of a professional relationship between us. Should the client decide to engage in a conversation, I have found it to be always possible to ensure that its content remains at a level that retains the privacy of our professional relationship. In fact, my experience has been that clients are as concerned and responsible about this as I attempt to be. What does seem to me to be of importance – particularly with current clients – is that our meeting, as well as our separate reactions to it, are addressed in some way during the subsequent therapy session.

For me, personally, this stance seems a truthful one to adopt in relation to how I currently understand and seek to practise existential psychotherapy. Nonetheless, in taking this stance I am also aware of its inherent and unavoidable uncertainty. And, as well, that other responses to such instances are possible and may be more appropriate in that they more adequately reflect the particular relational stance of the therapist. Nonetheless, it would seem to me that, whatever stance was taken, a discussion during therapy acknowledging such an event and the client's experience of it would be appropriate.

AN EXERCISE ON RECONFIGURING THE FRAME

1. Together with a partner, discuss what you believe to be the pros and cons of reconfiguring Phase One structural conditions of setting, frame and contract during Phase Two. What would be the circumstances, if any, that you would deem to be appropriate for such reconfiguration? As therapist, how would you go about addressing this reconfiguration to the client?
2. Together with a partner, focus on the specific examples of potential therapy world reconfiguration summarised above. How do you each personally respond to these possible instances of reconfiguration? How would you respond to your client's request that the structural conditions be reconfigured on the basis of any one of the stated possibilities?
3. If it has happened to you during your practice, describe an incident of meeting a client outside the therapeutic environment. How did you react? How did the client react? Following the discussion presented on this issue, how do you now evaluate your reaction? If such an incident were to occur again, what would be the differences, if any, in your way of responding to it?

PHASE TWO: UN-KNOWING

The existential 'given' of uncertainty seems to me to encapsulate what is possibly the key practice-focused theme underpinning all of the Phase Two interactions that have been discussed. Considered from the standpoint of un-knowing, Phase Two demands of the existential psychotherapist a willingness to embrace the uncertainties that arise in the therapy world as both an expression and a consequence of the often intense and intimate relatedness between therapist and client that is characteristic of this Phase. Throughout Phase Two, the otherness of the existential psychotherapist, while still seeking to 'stand beside' the client, nonetheless stands out as well as a distinct presence which can speak on its own behalf and thereby challenge the client through its difference. The impact of this shift, I believe, intensifies the experience of relatedness in so far as it is a relatedness that, as well as acknowledging care and acceptance and truthfulness, now also acknowledges difference. In highlighting this, the possibility that Phase One qualities of un-knowing will be either nurtured or disturbed by Phase Two's addition of difference as a quality of un-knowing remains uncertain for both client and therapist.

Perhaps the following quote by Vaclav Havel begins to capture something of the uncertainty that exists in all of the existential psychotherapist's attempts at un-knowing throughout Phase Two:

> There are no exact guidelines. There are probably no guidelines at all. The only thing I can recommend . . . is a sense of humour, an ability to see things in their ridiculous and absurd dimensions, to laugh at others and at ourselves, a sense of irony regarding everything that calls for parody in this world . . . . Those who have retained the capacity to recognise their own ridiculousness or even meaninglessness cannot be proud. (Havel, 2000: 20).

Overall, Havel's insights serve as an apt summary of Phase Two.

INDICATIONS AS TO THE APPROPRIATENESS OF A THERAPEUTIC SHIFT FROM PHASE TWO TO PHASE THREE

What indications might there be for the existential psychotherapist that a shift toward Phase Three has become possible? I would suggest that at least the following would be reasonably apparent:

1. The client has begun doing most of the therapeutic work. That is to say, a challenging focus on the worldview is increasingly being adopted by the client such that, in many ways, the client has begun to be his or her own therapist.
2. There are substantive indications of an experiential and dispositional shift in the client's stance toward the sedimentations and dissociations that have been investigated throughout Phase One and Phase Two.
3. In line with point 2, there are substantive indications that disturbing ambiguities in the client's worldview are either no longer so disturbing and can be better 'owned' by the client, or that some aspects of those ambiguities have been challenged and the client's worldview has shifted in some discernible ways.
4. The client's narrative is increasingly concerned with the consideration of novel possibilities. Often, this is expressed by the client as reaching a point where decisions can be made as to various novel ways of being outside of the therapy world.
5. The client's narrative is more focused on the explication and investigation of his or her experience of 'testing out' ways of being outside of the therapy world.
6. The client's narrative is increasingly future-directed.
7. There are frequent indications of the evident ease with which the client engages with the therapist at a level of intimacy.
8. The client's *way* of expressing his or her narrative is suggestive of the initial establishment of a sufficient degree of resonance between the client's therapy world worldview and that worldview which is maintained in the client's wider world relations.

FACTORS THAT PREVENT A THERAPEUTIC SHIFT FROM PHASE TWO TO PHASE THREE

Just as there may be various indications that the therapeutic relationship is at a point that will permit a shift from Phase Two to Phase Three, there may also be indications that the intimacy established during Phase Two is, itself, provoking previously unforeseen issues and concerns for the client. Once again, the uncertainty that accompanies a growing sense of intimacy may well impact upon the client's worldview in any number of unpredicted and surprising ways so that, although the client's initial presenting concerns have found some sort of acceptance or resolution, nevertheless the stability of the worldview has been threatened or novel ambiguities have arisen such that the client experiences disturbing or intolerable levels of tension in the worldview that had not previously been apparent. If so, the following are likely to be indicators of the client's unease with, and lack of preparedness for, a shift to Phase Three:

1. The client expresses a reluctance in contemplating possibilities that might extend the experience of relatedness within the therapy world beyond its boundaries and into the client's wider-world relations.
2. The client is able to contemplate ways of enacting novel possibilities of relatedness beyond the therapy world but makes little or no attempt to do so.
3. The client characterises the experience of co-habiting the therapy world as being so interesting or so noticeably real in comparison to its alternatives that an explicit or implicit desire to maintain their distinctiveness is expressed.
4. The client's experience of intimacy remains substantially dependent upon the presence of the therapist or upon the therapist's initiatives in investigating it.
5. In the course of discussion with the client, new concerns arise, or unforeseen aspects of previously discussed concerns emerge.
6. The client returns regularly to the expression of, and confrontation with, various intense and explosive feelings directed toward self, others beyond the therapy world, or the therapist, but appears unable to consider and use these as exploratory challenges to the currently maintained worldview.

All of the above suggest that significant constituents of the client's worldview as a whole, or of the inter-relations between its primary constructs, have either been missed or have not been sufficiently investigated. If so, these require further exploration within Phase Two. Equally, however, such instances may also reflect insufficiently explored client tensions or unease with aspects of the therapy world – including the client's relationship with the existential psychotherapist – that would suggest that the move to Phase Two had been premature and what is now required is the re-establishment of the conditions of the therapy world at the Phase One level.

7

Phase Three: Closing Down the Therapy World

INTRODUCTION TO PHASE THREE

Phase Three of existential psychotherapy primarily concerns itself with the ending of therapy and the dissolution of the therapeutic relationship. Viewed from the perspective adopted throughout this text, the ending of therapy can be equated to the closing down of the therapy world. Of what does this 'closing down' movement consist?

First, and most obviously, the closing down of the therapy world refers to the completion of all contracted arrangements, and their inter-relational conditions, between existential psychotherapist and client. The therapy world that has been co-created by them and which has served as the principal structure within which to disclose and challenge the client's worldview must formally cease to exist. As such, Phase Three addresses the relevant issues surrounding the question of endings as understood by existential psychotherapy.

Just as significantly, however, the closing down of the therapy world also refers to the consideration and implementation on the part of the client of those possibilities of relatedness as experienced and examined within the boundaries of the therapy world extending beyond its boundaries and into his or her wider world of relations. In this sense, Phase Three is concerned with the exploration of the potential 'bridging' between the therapy world and the wider world worldviews. This latter set of possibilities reveals the wider implications of existential phenomenology's key underlying principles of relatedness, uncertainty and existential anxiety, and brings to existential psychotherapy a novel means with which to address and respond to the persistent critique regarding contemporary Western psychotherapy's tendency to both isolate and elevate the individual.

Because so little has been stated explicitly regarding this latter point, I will focus my initial discussion upon it and then return to the question of therapeutic endings.

PHASE THREE: THE THEY-FOCUS

As was suggested in Part One of this text, the great majority of contemporary Western approaches to psychotherapy explicitly promote notions of freedom, choice and responsibility as aspects of both the process and the desired outcomes of therapeutic interventions. What is evident about therapists' typical assumptions underpinning these notions is that they tend to be viewed exclusively from a perspective which both internalises and isolates such notions and their associated actions *within* the client's subjectivity (Spinelli, 2001). In contrast, as I have sought to demonstrate throughout this text, this subjectively centred stance both distorts and obscures the more complex and disquieting implications arising from existential phenomenology's foundational assumption of relatedness. In contrast, as I have sought to express this critical point elsewhere:

> From an existential standpoint, questions of choice, freedom and responsibility cannot be isolated or contained within some separate being (such as 'self' or 'other') . . . Viewed in this way, no choice can be mine or yours alone, no experienced impact of choice can be separated in terms of 'my responsibility' versus 'your responsibility', no sense of personal freedom can truly avoid its interpersonal dimensions. (Spinelli, 2001: 16)

This explicit acknowledgement of an unavoidable and foundational interrelational grounding which is the basis to all subjective experience challenges numerous Western assumptions about what and how it is to exist as a human being. Not surprisingly, these assumptions can be found in the prevalent theories of psychotherapy in both general as well as specific hypotheses regarding the therapeutic relationship.

To my mind, the person who most eloquently addressed these issues within the arena of psychotherapy was the iconoclastic relational psychotherapist, Leslie Farber (1967, 2000; Gordon, 2000). Farber's work as a therapist subverted the exclusivity of the therapeutic relationship and highlighted its possibilities as a unique 'meeting point' between the client's engagement with the therapist and those that he or she undertook in the wider world. Unlike most other therapists, Farber did not attempt to exclude 'the world' either from his consulting room or from the therapeutic enterprise as a whole. Whatever connections the client made as a consequence of therapy needed to find their expression in the wider world and could be seen to have their impact upon it. For Farber, whatever value could be claimed of psychotherapy could not be sequestered within the confines of the therapy world but should rather find its place within the client's ongoing wider world relations.

Farber's attempts sought to highlight the uncertainties and insecurities that arise when conflicts and disturbances are viewed from an inter-relational grounding. Even if an individual manages to adopt a novel stance toward previously debilitating distress and disorders there is no guarantee that this novel stance can exist, much less thrive, in the world beyond the therapy world. Similarly, although that individual may have found the means with which to improve his or her life, that means cannot be removed from its impact upon others in the world. Farber's perspective complicates any notions of therapeutic success, since within his frame-work success can no longer be consigned to notions of individualistic value and benefit. Further, it may irritate the client in so far as it imposes the recognition that no act can be truthfully considered in isolation and instead must be placed within its inter-relational context and that, by so doing, its impact and consequences are rarely straightforward or easily evaluated in terms of 'good or bad', 'positive or negative', 'success or failure'. In my opinion, existential psychotherapists have not paid sufficient attention to concerns such as those being addressed by Farber. I find this somewhat surprising and, more to the point, disturbing. To not do so seems to me to conveniently forget, if not violate, the critical issue of relatedness. One way of addressing this issue within the therapy world is particularly pertinent to Phase Three.

Readers will recall that in the discussion of Phase Two, the topic of the inter-relational realms of encounter was first raised. In that section, the first three realms – the *I-focus,* the *You-focus* and the *We-focus* – were introduced and examples of possible ways of working with these three realms were provided. I now want to address the fourth realm, the *They-focus,* whose relevance to the present discussion should become apparent.

In general, the They-focused realm of encounter concerns itself with the client's experience of how those who make up his or her wider world of 'others' (extend-ing beyond the other who is the existential psychotherapist) experience their own inter-relational realms in response to the client's way of relating to them. They-focused inquiry challenges the client to consider the various facets of relatedness between the client and these others as the client imagines *they* experience and interpret them. Further, They-focused inquiry challenges the client to consider the impact of his or her inter-relational stance toward others in terms of its impact upon the inter-relations between one other or a group of others and a different other or group of others.

As such, the They-focused realm is concerned with:

1. The descriptive exploration and challenge of the impact that a client's dispositional stances may have upon an other's – or various others' – relations to that other's or those others' sense of self. For example: 'Every time my daughter sees me when I am so depressed, I believe that she feels she must blame her self in some way', 'When I am really tough on my colleagues, they realise how lazy they have been', 'If I tell my mother that I will always be there for her, she stops worrying so much about her future', 'My standing up to the CEO made the other members of the Committee feel less assured about them selves than they had previously thought.'

2. The descriptive exploration and challenge of the impact that a client's dispositional stances may have upon an other's – or various others' – way of relatedness to a different other or a group of others. For example: 'Every time my daughter sees me when I am so depressed, she

always ends up having an argument with her brother', 'When I am really tough on my colleagues, some respond by putting the responsibility for the job not getting done on another member of the team whereas others single out a member of the team as not deserving any blame', 'If I tell my mother that I will always be there for her, she gets on better with her neighbours', 'My standing up to the CEO made the other members of the Committee see him as not being quite so powerful as he'd seemed.'

3. The descriptive exploration and challenge of the impact that a client's dispositional stances may have upon an other's – or various others' – relations to the world. For example: 'Every time my daughter sees me when I am so depressed, she loses all of her appetite and is terrified by any unexpected noises', 'When I am really tough on my colleagues, you can be sure that all their conversations for the rest of the day are going to be about what a terrible state the country is in or how the economy is just about to take a major downturn', 'If I tell my mother that I will always be there for her, she pays a lot more attention to the state of her flat', 'My standing up to the CEO made the other members of the Committee feel like there really is some natural justice after all.'

The They-focused realm of encounter serves to acknowledge the presence and inevitable impact of the wider world both within and upon the therapeutic relationship. It is an explicit stance that can be adopted by existential psychotherapists to highlight the inter-relational dimensions of existence and to counter the more common psychotherapeutic tendency to consider the client in isolation, or out of inter-relational context. The exploration of this fourth relational realm is particularly significant when, as a consequence of therapy, the client has reached a point of considering and making choices about newly discerned alternative expressions of relatedness in his or her wider world.

The existential psychotherapist who is attuned to They-focused realm of inquiry, can urge the client to consider the meaning and effect of his or her decision from the standpoint of its impact upon the self-construct of those others in the client's wider world relations who have been singled out as being significant. In addition, the existential psychotherapist can challenge the client to consider the meaning and impact of his or her decision from the standpoint of those others' relations with one another (i.e., the others' other-construct). Finally, the existential psychotherapist can explore with the client the possible meaning and impact of his or her decision from the standpoint of those others' world-construct. The following example should provide a straightforward means to express the impact of the exploration of the They-focus within the therapeutic relationship:

Client: I've finally decided what to do.
Therapist: Oh, yeah? What's that?
Client: I'm going to take the deal on early retirement and invest the bonus on a house in Bavaria.
Therapist: Uhm . . . Sounds like that's what you've been hesitating over for quite some time.
Client: Yeah. But I'm sure about it now.
Therapist: And everyone's happy with the decision?
Client: What do you mean 'everyone'?
Therapist: Well . . . I'm thinking of Dorrie [client's wife], and Karl and Olivia [client's son and daughter], and your mum, and your friends. And, I suppose I'm also thinking of Brutus [client's dog].

Client:	Oh, Brutus is going to love it! All that space and countryside for long walks. He'll be like a puppy again, he will! [**They-focus**].
Therapist:	OK. And the others?
Client:	Uhm.
Therapist:	What's 'uhm' mean?
Client:	It means that we're not all on the same page.
Therapist:	OK.
Client:	Dorrie's fretting about what it's going to be like for her and the kids to have to learn German [**They-focus**]. And Karl's saying he's definitely not going to give up his mates [**They-focus**]. Olivia, I don't know. She hasn't said much [**They-focus**]. And mum's – well, you can imagine.
Therapist:	So not a great deal of cheering going on with regard to your decision.
Client:	You got it. It's just so incredibly dispiriting. They've been going on and on at me for months to do something and get myself out of my depression. And I listened to them, came here week after week to see you, get myself sorted. And now that I know what I want and feel really happy and excited about the new possibilities, they go and ruin it!
Therapist:	And –
Client:	And they're just being selfish! They keep saying that it's for my good that we all really think things over. But I know it's about them and what they want!
Therapist:	OK. Let's look at some of that. So, when Dorrie says to you that it makes sense to look at the decision more carefully, what's that about as far as you're concerned?
Client:	It's about Dorrie needing total security and being scared to try new things, that's what it's about.
Therapist:	OK, so your decision makes Dorrie insecure and brings out her fear of trying new things [**They-focus**]. How do you feel about that?
Client:	I feel bad – I don't want her to feel those things. But she's got to take a risk sometime. Life's too short and –
Therapist:	Will, let me ask you something. Imagine that Dorrie agrees to your plan and she still keeps feeling like she does. So you're all living in Bavaria, and Dorrie's feeling insecure and fearful of all the new things going on –
Client:	Oh god . . . Then the kids and I are going to be eating a lot of meals in the local beer hall!
Therapist:	Why do you say that?
Client:	Because when Dorrie gets like that, she doesn't want to cook [**They-focus**]. And when Dorrie doesn't want to cook, you don't want to eat what she does cook!
Therapist:	And what impact does that have, say, between Dorrie and the kids? [**They-focus query**].
Client:	Oh, Karl just sulks and starts to be a pain with everyone [**They-focus**]. And Olivia gets really angry and says to her mum that she's taking over the cooking just so we don't all have to starve to death and that starts a real battle royal between her and Dorrie [**They-focus**]. And then Karl pipes in that he isn't going to eat anything prepared by his sister and then they start rowing to the point where they'll argue over who has the right to take the damn dog for a walk [**They-focus**] – which usually you have to beg one of them to see to, and . . . Oh, it's just awful.
Therapist:	And all this relates back to the decision you want to make.
Client:	Yeah! But . . . It's not fair! I've dreamed of this for years. And they know that! Why did they let me keep dreaming about it if they knew that they didn't want to be part of it?
Therapist:	And if you can't fulfil your dream without them being part of it?
Client:	You know what? Damn them! I want to fulfil it anyway! I've got a right to have what I want! I slaved for years at that damn job. They should have more concern for me rather than worry about themselves so much! [**client reaction to They-focus**].

Therapist:	Is that what it seems like? Dorrie and the kids and your mum and your friends are more concerned with what they want rather than respect what you want?
Client:	Well . . . I wouldn't say that about my mum.
Therapist:	OK. So what's your mum's view on this?
Client:	Well, on the surface she's being encouraging and telling me to follow my heart.
Therapist:	You said 'on the surface'.
Client:	Yeah . . . I think that deep down – or maybe not so deep down – she thinks that she's being punished by god or something for having had that affair and going ahead and divorcing dad and then things not working out as she'd planned and ending up on her own and now she's going to be even more on her own [**They-focus**]. And it'll be like if she walks down the street or something she'll have the equivalent of the 'Mark of Cain' that the whole bloody world can see and she'll be shunned for the rest of her life [**They-focus**].
Therapist:	And . . . she wants you to follow your heart.
Client:	Yeah.
Therapist:	And does this have any impact on your decision?
Client:	What do you think? But it's still so unfair! And I wish I could just tell them all to let me be so that I can fulfil my dream.
Therapist:	And can you tell them all that?
Client:	I want to.
Therapist:	And *can* you?
Client:	But it's a good dream!
Therapist:	Yeah. It's a good dream. And can you tell them: 'Let me be so I can fulfil my dream'?
Client:	I don't know. I think it's right for me to go to Bavaria. I thought they'd think so too, but they don't. But does that mean they're right? And even if they are, that doesn't mean it's not right for me. Oh god! this is so complicated! Why can't things be simple for once?

What should be clear from the above vignette is that from a therapeutic standpoint that had adopted an non-relational subjective perspective, the client's initial statement that he had decided what he wanted to do and that it felt like the appropriate decision for him to take, the therapy would be seen as having been beneficial. Indeed, from this perspective one could argue that the client is being 'more honest and congruent', more focused upon his 'real self', or more integrated. Equally, even if the subsequent discussion had developed, this non-relational view would adopt a position that assumed that each person was responsible solely for his or her particular experience, that the appropriateness of the choices being considered could be accurately evaluated if considered solely from within the self-structure of each separate person, and that each person's sense of freedom could be understood in terms of their personal congruence with, and allegiance to, their own specific wants and desires.

From the inter-relational perspective adopted by existential psychotherapy, however, it can be seen that the client's decision opens up a great deal to be examined. Via inquiry centred upon the They-focused realm, the challenge to the client is to also consider how he experiences the meaning and effect of his decision from the standpoint of his wife, his children, his mother, the dog, his friends, and so forth. Secondly, from this They-focused perspective, the challenge to the client is also to consider the meaning and impact of his decision upon, for instance, his wife's relations with each of the children, each child's relations to his or her sibling, the client's mother's relations to her world-derived beliefs and values, and so on. What the exploration of the They-focused relational realm makes plain is that there exist so many relations upon which the client's decision impacts that it would be inter-relationally irresponsible not to attend to at least those that the client has highlighted as being significant or meaningful in some way. The acknowledgement of a They-focus as a way of expressing the inter-relational foundation to subjective experiences of choice, freedom and responsibility *embeds* the client's decision within an indissoluble matrix of relations, all of which are affected by, and impact upon, one another in ways both subtle and obvious. They compel the client to acknowledge the existence both of others and of a world *that do not fit his desired experience but which nonetheless exist.*

At the same time, it is important to make clear that the existential psychotherapist's intent behind They-focused inquiry is neither to prevent the client's decision, nor to propose more 'they-friendly' alternative options, nor to impose either the therapist's or the others' own moral stance upon the client's perspective. Nor is it the purpose of They-focused exploration to expose the *actual* views of all of these 'others' in the client's world. Instead, it is simply to acknowledge the inter-relational context that exists for the client and to remind the client that the choices he wishes to make, the freedom they may provide for him and the responsibility that accompanies them cannot be excluded from this context.

My insistence upon this point of view may appear to some readers to be something of an imposition upon the client. Why should the client be forced to accept what is, after all, the existential psychotherapist's stance and which may not be his own? Once again, it is important to make clear that I am not proposing that it is necessary for the client to make only relationally attuned choices. The client has every right to respond to the existential psychotherapist in ways that reject the significance of relatedness. The client could simply state: 'I don't care what others think, I'm still going ahead with my decision.' From an existential-phenomenological perspective, this decision is *still* grounded in relatedness (even if it is that expression of relatedness that seeks to minimise or deny relatedness) and is as inter-relationally valid as any other. In such an instance, the existential psychotherapist would, I hope, acknowledge the client's stance and continue to pursue its clarification in relation to the client's existing worldview. All that is being argued is that the existential psychotherapist cannot avoid raising these inter-relational issues since *the whole of the therapeutic process has been, and continues to be, an investigation of relatedness.* To avoid the implications of relatedness just at the point when the client is reaching, or has reached, change-focused decisions makes no sense within a therapeutic system that claims to be informed by, and expressive of, existential phenomenology. More to the point, this avoidance seems inconsistent with the therapist's claims to represent existential phenomenology in an embodied fashion.

TWO EXERCISES ON THE THEY-FOCUS

EXERCISE 1

1. Working together with a partner, take turns in being therapist and client. Each session should last twenty minutes.
2. As the client, focus on a decision that you have made, or are considering making, about some change in your life that is impacting upon an other or others.
3. As the therapist, assist the client in exploring this decision from a They-focus perspective.
4. When you have both completed the exercise, consider how a They-focused exploration may be of value to the therapeutic process during Phase Three.
5. Discuss your own views on the They-focus and what its place, if any, should be in psychotherapy.

EXERCISE 2

1. Working together with a partner, take turns in exploring your work as a therapist with a client who arrived at a point of making a change-focused decision that had a direct impact upon an other or others in the client's wider world relations.
2. Together, explore the impact of the decision from a They-focused perspective.
3. Consider how the They-focused exploration may have assisted your client, if at all.
4. Consider how the They-focused exploration may have assisted you as a therapist, if at all.

PHASE THREE: BRIDGING THE CLIENT'S THERAPY WORLD AND THE WIDER WORLD

During Phase Three, much of the focus of discussion between existential psychotherapist and client centres upon the client's exploration of the novel and temporary therapy world worldview and how it might now potentially be maintained beyond the confines of the therapy world.

For some therapists, it might be thought that the appropriate outcome of therapy is that in which the divergences and distinctions between the client's therapy world and wider world worldviews are broken down so that the ability to discern one from the other becomes effectively non-existent. My own conclusions on this remain that, however desirable in an ideal sense, this possibility seems altogether too ambitious. For one thing, I believe that important differences between the client's therapy world and the wider world worldviews are bound to remain and, as such, require their acknowledgement. Although I have discussed in an earlier section why I do not believe the therapy world to be artificial or unreal in relation to the client's wider world of relations, nonetheless that should not obfuscate its differences.

For one thing, the therapy world consisting of (usually) only two directly present participants is inter-relationally less complex than the wider world made up of a multitude of participants whose differing views, expectations, demands and behaviours impact upon and 'bombard' the client's worldview in ways that no therapy world relationship could ever fully replicate. Second, it seems to me to be equally apparent that the clarity of the rules and the attempt to respect and follow them set the parameters within which the client's worldview can be explored within the therapy world. These conditions cannot easily, if at all, be maintained in the client's wider world relations simply because, however willing the client might be to address and maintain these inter-relational rules, others' responses to this attempt are far less secure and certain.

As such, what seems to me to be a more reasonable enterprise for existential psychotherapy is the exploration of how *some* novel worldview dispositions derived from the temporary therapy world worldview possibilities might continue to express and translate themselves, whether as a whole or in part, in the client's post-therapeutic wider world worldview.

Because neither the client nor the existential psychotherapist can accurately predict *which* novel therapy world dispositional stances that have impacted upon the client's worldview will lend themselves to extrapolation beyond its confines, Phase Three can be a period for the client to 'test out' various inter-relational possibilities in the wider world and then bring back to the therapy world that which he or she has discovered and concluded about each of these attempts. *In this way, Phase Three can be considered as that phase in existential psychotherapy wherein the client becomes the primary investigator of the worldview as he or she lives, or embodies, it beyond the confines of the therapy world.*

This investigative focus for the client can be both empowering and dispiriting. The client may be pleasantly surprised, if not overjoyed, by the new-found worldview dispositions that can be established, expressed and 'owned' in the wider world. Equally, the client may be forced to confront the limitations of these discoveries and, in turn, face the very real anguish of knowing something of the liberating possibilities of a temporary worldview of which he or she has had direct experience within the confines of the therapy world but which is not able to withstand the relational challenges it experiences in the wider world. *Phase Three, therefore, is also a period of discovery for the client, some of which will allow the establishment of novel wider world worldview dispositional stances that are resonant with those experienced within the therapy world, and some of which will confront the client with the painful awareness of his or her inability to establish or maintain these stances within the wider world worldview.*

How are such investigations to be initiated by the client? Many existential psychotherapists recoil at the thought of providing clients with 'homework' or specified tasks to undertake between sessions. While I freely admit to my sharing their unease, I must also acknowledge that there have been numerous occasions throughout my therapeutic work with clients that I have actively encouraged, and have suggested between-session tasks which the client could report on in subsequent sessions. On reflection, I have concluded that, for my self, my sense of unease with the very notion of homework and the like centres more on what is for me the unacceptable stance of the therapist assigning some task from a position of higher authority. On further reflection, I can recognise that, in many cases, my clients them selves either initiated, or announced their intention to initiate, specified tasks designed to 'test out' possibilities and were either seeking to discuss what had occurred or, alternatively, were attempting to 'check out' my response to and/or encouragement of their proposal. While I retain a (possibly questionable) sense that client-initiated investigatory tasks and assignments may be preferable, I have reconciled myself to the potential value of my offering such assignments so long as it is made clear to the client that the task or assignment being proposed is nothing more than a suggestion that:

- the client is free to refuse to enact;
- the client is free to amend as seems appropriate;
- the client is free to cease at any point.

Together with these, I would expect that some discussion, however brief, regarding the client's experience of the assignment would make up part of our subsequent discussion.

As well as 'between-session' assignments, Phase Three explorations regarding the potential bridging of the client's therapy world and wider world worldviews can include *structured role-play* (with the therapist and client taking turns in representing the imagined wider world response to the client's novel worldview dispositional stances), and *guided imaginary narratives* designed to help the client access and describe his or her expectations, concerns, hopes and fears surrounding the attempt to initiate these with various others or under differing circumstances. Perhaps more controversially (for at least some existential psychotherapists), these explorations might also include the therapist and client together 'testing out' these possibilities beyond the established confines of the therapy world and in the *actuality* of the wider world. In general, all of these Phase Three explorations serve to reveal the extent to which the boundaries between the client's therapy world and wider world worldviews are open to being 'blurred' or even 'broken down', so that they are experienced as being beneficial and desirable to the client.

Just as the therapy world worldview begins to make its impact upon the client's wider world worldview, so, too, do the client's attempts to establish and maintain a novel worldview in the wider world begin to resonate within the therapy world. Some consequences of these attempts may be to make the therapy world seem less special, distinctive and important to the client. Equally, however, some consequences may highlight for the client just how special, distinct and important the therapy world has been, and to some degree still is, in permitting the experience of a worldview that can only be maintained and enacted under particular circumstances, or in a compromised fashion, or not at all in the wider world. Phase Three of existential psychotherapy can therefore be exciting and adventurous for the client, but equally may be tinged with sadness and regret, not merely because of the approaching closing down of the therapy world but also because of the realisation that not all inter-relational possibilities discerned and explored within the temporary therapy world worldview can be expressed in the same way, if at all, in the client's wider world relations.

Indeed, how the client responds to this latter awareness may be a critical indicator of his or her readiness to bring the therapeutic relationship to its ending.

AN EXERCISE ON BRIDGING THE 'THERAPY WORLD' AND THE 'WIDER WORLD' WORLDVIEWS

1. Together with a partner take turns in discussing your attempts as a client to introduce what you had taken and valued from your therapeutic relationship into other wider world relationships. What success, if any, did you have? What failures, if any, did you encounter? How did you experience these instances of success and failure? How did the successes and failures influence your evaluation of the therapy you had undertaken?
2. Discuss your views on structured between-session assignments. As a client, were you ever asked to undertake such? If so, how did you respond? What was it like

    - to attempt them?
    - to complete the assignment or to be unable to complete it?
    - to report back to the therapist?

    As a therapist, or trainee, do you make use of structured assignments and homework? If yes, how do you introduce them to your clients? If no, how do you respond to your clients' requests for such?

PHASE THREE: ENDINGS

Readers who have diligently followed and considered the arguments relating to the structural model under consideration are likely, by now, to register little surprise in reading that, in my view, existential psychotherapy does not recognise one form of ending as being inherently better than, or superior to, any other. When we consider the diversity of endings in our own various non-therapeutic, wider world relationships we realise that endings can, and do, occur in any number of ways and under just about any conceivable set of circumstances. Sometimes endings are planned and prepared and acknowledged through some sort of shared ritual or ceremony. Sometimes they occur without any such planning and at the instigation of one party without the prior knowledge or agreement of the other party or parties. And sometimes endings occur unexpectedly without prior consideration by any party, but simply as a result of unforeseen circumstances or events. Are any of these 'endings' necessarily 'less of an ending' than any other? I doubt it. That the ending before us may not be what either party, or all concerned, would have preferred should not lead us to suppose that an ending has not occurred. So, too, is it the case with endings in psychotherapy. Every model, and every practitioner and client, may have ideas as to what the preferred ending should be like or how it should occur. Sometimes, more often than not I would suggest, the preferred ending *is* the ending that occurs. Sometimes it's not. And it is still an ending.

Like many other therapists from other models and systems, the majority of existential psychotherapists tend to prefer those endings that have been discussed and which follow an agreed plan of action. Most frequently, such plans involve the agreement that the therapist and client will continue to engage in therapy for a specified period of time in order to allow a 'winding down' of the therapeutic relationship. While such a plan of action related to endings may make sense to existential psychotherapist and client alike, and in this sense is desirable, it must still be asked: 'What is it that, from the perspective of existential psychotherapy, requires being "wound down?"' Over the years, I have come to the conclusion that the only sensible answer I can offer to this question reflects, once again, the significance of the Dumbo effect, certainly for the therapist and possibly for therapist and client alike.

Thus, the issue of endings is not so much centred upon endings *per se* but rather has more to do with the degree of openness that exists to whatever form of ending actually occurs. For existential psychotherapists, it seems to me, the critical question for us to ask ourselves is: *'What is it about a particular ending that permits or prevents me from embracing it as appropriate to this particular relationship?'*

In my own experience over the years of practice as an existential psychotherapist, I have worked with endings that followed a pre-arranged plan or which have resulted from a spontaneous decision by the client to end therapy with that session. In one instance of the latter, my willingness to go along with this decision seemed, for the client, to be *the* critical moment of the whole of our therapy together as it brought to life for him the reality that an other could actually accept that he was capable of making sound and appropriate life decisions – and that, as a consequence, *he* could accept his own authority and ability to make appropriate decisions.

Some endings in existential psychotherapy are already included in the contract agreed to at the very start of the therapeutic process. The client and existential psychotherapist may have agreed to a specific number of sessions, or may be limited to a certain number of sessions because of the conditions set by the agency (such as an insurance policy or a National Health Trust) through which the therapist is employed and to whose services the client is entitled. Alternatively, the existential psychotherapist may be meeting the client in a private capacity but for various reasons is prepared to see the client only for a set number of sessions. Equally, the existential psychotherapist may be flexible with regard to the duration of therapy but the client has limited him or her self to a specified number of sessions. In such circumstances, barring the constant possibility of the unexpected event that alters everything, the approach toward an ending is reasonably clear-cut. Indeed, in their text on *Existential Time-limited Therapy*, Freddie and Alison Strasser make a strong case for the value of explicit reminders of the approaching end of therapy throughout the therapeutic relationship and utilise this as a parallel to the 'time-limited' conditions of human existence (Strasser and Strasser, 1997).

The majority of existential psychotherapists who work in a private capacity, however, tend to adopt an 'open-ended' approach to the number of sessions made available to the client. In such instances, the ending of therapy often remains ambiguous and the question of ending only arises when something like 'the idea of ending is "'in the air"' and requires addressing. What factors would indicate that the question of an ending should be broached?

My own sense is that existential psychotherapists are alerted to the possibility of an approaching ending when the client's narratives are increasingly concerned with the impact and effects of 'testing out' the novel therapy world worldview in the wider world. What the client presents of his or her relations with self, others and the world beyond the confines of the therapy world, what his or her behaviours 'out there' suggest, even the clients *way of speaking* about those explorations and their outcomes would usually be reasonably good indicators regarding the introduction of the question of endings. Equally, what the client has to say about his or her relationship to the issues and problems that had initiated the therapy, or, just as importantly, that such are no longer considered either as major areas of discourse or, indeed, have lost (or diminished) their 'problematic' narrational features, would also seem to be reliable indicators of the possibility of an ending. Finally, various noticeable shifts in the client's way of relating directly to the therapist that might, for instance, express the client's increasing focus on the future 'beyond therapy', or which suggest the lessening of the client's reliance upon or 'need for' the therapist (without necessarily also implying a lessening of the client's appreciation towards, or care or respect for, the therapist), would also seem to me to be equally good indicators of an approaching ending. Nonetheless, while such instances often do turn out to be the precursors to an ending, sometimes they are not, and, if anything, act to initiate new investigations that may considerably prolong the therapeutic alliance.

Occasionally, it is the client who first raises the issue of ending. From my own past mistakes, I can alert readers to the fact that while such statements may well be about the desire to end therapy, they can just as likely express concerns by the client that some issue or aspect of the client's worldview is being avoided or missed. Equally, these statements might reveal the client's growing unease and fear that the therapist may be irritated or bored with him or her and, as a consequence, might broach the option of ending even though this is the last thing that the client desires. All these possibilities act to remind the existential psychotherapist never to cease from adopting a stance of un-knowing and not to assume that the client's intended meaning no longer requires descriptive clarification. Equally, the existential psychotherapist's raising of the question of ending may provoke strong reactions of unease, anger, hurt or betrayal in the client. However disturbing or upsetting these may be for therapist and client alike, the therapist who adopts a stance of un-knowing can still respond to such responses as valid and genuine and also as likely indicators of an aspect or aspects of the client's worldview that had been previously missed or which have been prompted by the introduction of the possibility of ending therapy.

Existential psychotherapists might also encounter instances when the client expresses the desire to end therapy, is willing to discuss it non-defensively and consider it in relation to his or her worldview, while at the same time the therapist, acknowledging all of the above, still remains genuinely convinced that there is a great deal more for the client to explore. Although this instance may be one where overt disclosure on the part of the therapist can be helpful, it may also be the case that the most appropriate response is for the therapist to accept the client's conclusion in spite of his or her silent misgivings.

In some extreme instances, clients elect to end therapy simply by no longer attending their scheduled sessions. In some cases, they may inform the therapist before or after the missed meeting. More often, I suspect, they simply cease all communication. Such forms of endings are likely to reflect a prior and unacknowledged critical breakdown in some aspect or aspects of the therapeutic relationship. Perhaps the therapist has shifted too rapidly from Phase One to Phase Two (or from Phase Two to Phase Three) and, by so doing, has provoked an unbearable degree of unease for the client. Just as likely, the therapist may not have challenged the client's worldview sufficiently, or challenged it in ways that generate distrust or a felt sense all too resonant of others' oppressive tendencies for the client. But it may also be the case that this way of ending has been adopted by the client because the therapist has been highly diligent and effective in the way of challenging and its focus and that, in response, the client has decided that it is not what is desired or what he or she is presently able to tolerate. These forms of endings are likely to be the most disturbing for existential psychotherapists, primarily because what has remained unexplained about the client's decision may have come as a genuine surprise or shock. Equally, what may disturb the therapist is the client's covert statement about relatedness, both in general and the specific relatedness established with the therapist, that the therapist finds to be inappropriate or unacceptable to his or her understanding of relatedness.

I suggest that, in such circumstances, it still makes sense for the existential psychotherapist to embrace all of these possibilities as another form of ending. In doing so, he or she is more likely to access that which is disturbing about the client's chosen way of ending and be better able to challenge the assumptions that may be embedded within that sense of disturbance – should the client subsequently change his or her mind at a later point in time. Further, the existential psychotherapist may, for various reasons, contact the client by post, e-mail or text message in order to ascertain the client's intention to return. In such cases, the explicit acknowledgement that this desire to know is primarily for the therapist and is not intended as a covert demand that the client return to therapy seems vital to me. While my own experiences of these instances have often provoked no response from the client, just as frequently they have opened up lines of communication that have clarified the client's decision or have permitted the possibility of the client's initiating therapy once again.

An issue that is often closely related to that of endings is that of *gift-giving*. Occasionally, clients want to mark the end of their therapy with a gift to their therapist. Less common, but by no means unusual, is that therapists may offer a gift to their client on completion of their last session together. This gift may be in the form of a physical present (which has often been carefully considered), an act expressive of affection such as a hug, or both. While some approaches include in their contractual agreement with the client that no gifts can or will be accepted, for existential psychotherapists such decisions rest with each therapist. I, myself, have little hesitation in accepting a gift at the end of therapy and am just as likely to offer one in return usually based upon what I have gleaned over time as an area of particular interest to that client, be it a novel, a non-fiction text, a CD or a DVD. Usually, but not always, gifts are presented by clients with whom I have worked over a substantial period of time. While one can always find good reason to be suspicious of the client's intent, I have, over the years, balanced that with the recognition that whatever hidden motives there may be, it should not eliminate the acknowledgement of the explicit motives that have to do with an appreciation of the work we did together, the desire to mark the ending of our therapy and the wish to commemorate such through the ritual of gift-giving.

The above discussion highlights the conclusion that, at least from the standpoint of existential psychotherapy, there is no one correct way to end, or to know when the indications of an ending have emerged. Equally, the above discussion has attempted to show that every decision made or act undertaken with regard to the question of ending psychotherapy both raises various inter-relational possibilities and prevents others from coming into being.

The conclusion that every acted-upon possibility necessarily eliminates those possibilities that once were but which, in not having been enacted, are no longer, extends beyond the issue of endings and can be seen to be the underlying *motif* throughout the whole of the existential psychotherapeutic encounter. However, if restricted to the issues being considered in this present discussion, it is my belief that if and when the client arrives at that point of embracing both the possibility and regret inherent in all chosen ways of relatedness, then the questions surrounding when and under what circumstances and in which ways therapy should be brought to an end will likely determine their own expression and will find their own process. Following Gadamer on this (Gadamer, 2004), my own conclusion is that if the dialogue is permitted to find and pursue its own direction, it will, equally, address its own way of ending.

AN EXERCISE ON ENDINGS

Working together with a partner, take turns in discussing the following ending-related issues:

- ending therapy as a client
- how you ordinarily work with ending as a therapist or a trainee
- an ending from your own practice that surprised or disturbed you
- what kinds of therapeutic endings you find to be desirable
- what kinds of endings you find to be acceptable
- what kinds of endings you find to be unacceptable.

PHASE THREE: LIFE AFTER THERAPY

What is possible, relationally speaking, for the client and existential psychotherapist after the ending of therapy has occurred? Can they, for example, remain in contact with one another? And, if so, what are appropriate and inappropriate forms of contact? Such questions bedevil existential psychotherapy as much as they might other approaches – perhaps, because of its openness to the uncertain and the possibilities arising from the acceptance of uncertainty, even more so. Further, such questions cannot and should not deny the 'facticity' of professional codes of conduct that may themselves specify what post-therapeutic relations are permissible and which cannot be allowed to occur without their professional consequences.

Unlike some other forms of analytically focused therapy, existential psychotherapy usually leaves open the possibility that a new therapeutic relationship between client and therapist may be established at some future point in time. What is important to understand here, however, is that any eventual relationship cannot be seen to be a continuation of the one that has just ended. Instead, the existential psychotherapist who is willing to establish a therapeutic relationship with a client with whom he or she has worked in the past must attempt to treat the new relationship as he or she would any other that was occurring for the first time. The difficulties of this attempt at bracketing are as plentiful as they are obvious if the therapist persists in imposing the past relationship upon the present one. Nonetheless, the possibility of a new therapeutic relationship with a previous client remains an option. My own limitations in such attempts at bracketing have led me to make it explicit to clients that should they wish to commence therapy with me at some future point, they are welcome to contact me but that they might find it advantageous to leave a substantial gap of time – usually not less than six months – before initiating such contact.

A different, if equally challenging post-therapeutic contact option is that of the client's request to meet up again informally in order to see whether a friendship or some less formal relationship can be established. On this topic, there are often specific guidelines drawn up by professional bodies and I urge readers to ascertain what these may be according to the body that accredits, licenses or charters their professional practice. My own experience, which may or may not be typical, is that very few clients either want or request the possibility of friendship with me. This may say something about the way I present my self or my style of working as a psychotherapist. Equally, however, it may also express the genuine desire to treat the therapeutic relationship, and the often painful honesty exposed therein, as something special and different from other meaningful relationships. Nonetheless, occasionally the possibility of a post-therapeutic development of a friendship does present itself, and while one can interpret the rules set by professional bodies as a means to off-set this challenge, it seems to me also appropriate to consider this dilemma in other ways. My experience as an existential psychotherapist (but I suspect this to be the case with any model of therapy) is that the odds in favour of developing a close friendship with a past client are exceedingly low. My own, admittedly rare, experiences of meeting a former client in a social setting, once an appropriate time since our last professional meeting has elapsed, have tended to be somewhat disastrous in that (a) we found very little to talk about and (b) what we did talk about, and how we talked with one another, more resembled our previous therapy sessions than they did any other sort of dialogue.

Having wondered about this phenomenon over the years, and having heard equivalent accounts from other therapists who attempted something similar, I suspect that what both I and my former clients did not take sufficiently into account was the importance of the very *structural* conditions that defined the therapy world *themselves* playing a pivotal role in permitting a mutual accessing and experience of inter-connection and intimacy. In altering that structure so radically during our social meeting, the deep levels of connectedness and intimacy that we had experienced in the therapy world were not available to us. Indeed, we could only regain something of that closeness when we sought to re-establish the previous frame, even if that was antagonistic to our purpose in meeting. Perhaps, if we had persevered . . . But, again, this has not been the case.

In addition to the above failure, over the years it has also become clearer to me that while the establishment of a friendship with a past client might be possible and desirable to both of us, the price that the client in particular pays for this is the loss of any possibility of a future therapeutic relationship with me. Thus, when requests to explore the possibility of friendship are put to me by clients toward the end of our therapeutic relationship, I present the options. The most common choice by far made by clients when this stark, if honest, choice is put to them is best summarised by the remark made by one of them. 'OK. I'll stick with the possibility that you might be my therapist again at some point in the future. Real friends are tough to find, but finding a good therapist is even tougher.'

Notwithstanding the above, I would be dishonest if I were to claim that the establishment of a close and lasting friendship with an ex-client is simply not possible. As rare as it is, and acknowledging the sacrifice it entails for the former client, much less the existential psychotherapist, it *can* happen and I do have personal experience of it. Interestingly, though we rarely discuss our first relationship as therapist and client, I suspect that this avoidance says as much about what we have lost as it might be a desire to 'let the past lie'. And because I think this, I must also admit to a recurring sense of guilt that however good a friend my ex-client friends may have gained, it may not equal what they have lost.

EXERCISE EXPLORING POST-THERAPEUTIC RELATIONS WITH FORMER CLIENTS

1. Together with a partner, discuss what post-therapeutic social relationship or friendship with your past therapist/s you might have wished to have or would never wish to have. What provokes each of these responses?
2. Discuss your experience, if any, of working with a client with whom you could imagine a social relationship or friendship at an appropriate time following the ending of the therapeutic relationship. What was it about this client that provoked this desire for you? How did you deal with it?
3. Discuss your experience, if any, of working with a client who expressed his or her desire to establish a social relationship or friendship at an appropriate time following the ending of the therapeutic relationship. How did you deal with this request? What other ways, if any, can you consider might be appropriate for you to have dealt with this request?

PHASE THREE: A SUMMARY

Phase Three of the structural model under consideration deals with the various aspects of the therapeutic relationship and focused upon the 'closing down' of the therapy world. Included in Phase Three are those qualities and concerns such as endings, which the existential psychotherapist, like any other therapist, must approach with the client.

In addition, I have suggested that Phase Three of existential psychotherapy plays a pivotal role in the exploration of the potential bridging of the therapy world with that of the client's (and, indeed, the therapist's) wider world relations, as well as those possibilities of post-therapeutic contact with the existential psychotherapist. In this, Phase Three, as I have proposed it, brings to the fore the key existential-phenomenological themes of relatedness, uncertainty and existential anxiety as they may now be acknowledged and expressed by the client in his or her wider world relations. In doing so, Phase Three emphasises that the practice of existential psychotherapy is not only a matter of professional expertise but also a *moral* enterprise grounded in these three critical principles. Personally, I take this to be a matter of substantial significance, not least because that which is explored during Phase Three seeks to address and acknowledge those wider world implications of therapeutic practice which have arisen rather than dismiss or deny them.

The ending of existential psychotherapy can, and often does, provide clients with a sense of elation – both for what has been achieved and for the novel possibilities of living that have been initiated and the genuine sense of choice, freedom and responsibility which accompanies them. At the same time, the ending of existential psychotherapy can also be a period of sober reflection and some regret for the client, in that the uncertainty of a new beginning which does not include the security of a therapy world and the reliability of the therapist's care must also be faced.

A STRUCTURAL MODEL FOR THE PRACTICE OF EXISTENTIAL PSYCHOTHERAPY: A SUMMARY

Part Two of this text has sought to provide a three-phase structural model for practising existential psychotherapy. It has identified various descriptively focused qualities and skills intended to provide interested readers and practitioners with a means by which the key concerns of existential psychotherapy, as far as I currently understand them, can be identified and applied from a practice-based focus.

The structure under consideration has followed a general sequence focused upon the co-creation, exploration and closing down of what I have termed as the therapy world. In doing so, each phase under discussion has raised various associated focal points to be addressed within the boundaries of that world, so that its inter-relational possibilities may be discerned and experienced as fully and openly as its co-inhabitants will permit.

Although the structural model can be seen to be rigorous in its over-riding investigative aim of disclosing the lived world of the client, it is hoped that readers will also have gained some genuine sense of the situated freedom permitted to client and therapist alike within the therapy world that is the setting for such explorations. It was, in part, with this in mind, that I decided to append various exercises following discussion of each of the major points raised. Although they served an instructional purpose in that they sought to offer a means for readers to experiment with these points and to gauge their own responses to them, it is the possibility of their acting as experiential stimuli and catalysts to critical insight that, I believe, makes the engagement with them truly worthwhile.

All forms of therapy entrust their practitioners with an 'awe-ful' responsibility. This responsibility is not merely professional, containing within it ethical codes of conduct and the ability to apply learned skills in an appropriate and respectful manner. More than this, such responsibility lies in a set of moral principles which each therapist seeks to convey in an embodied fashion – that is to say, through his or her very way of being with (and for) the client who is present. Although structural models can only convey a modicum of this moral stance, it remains my hope that something of this has also been communicated throughout Part Two. Beyond skills, beyond rules and regulations, it seems to me that it is *the way* that the therapist responds to the presence of the other who is the client that makes all the difference.

Existential psychotherapy, perhaps more than any other current approach, takes this understanding to the very heart of its enterprise. Whatever its limitations, it remains my hope that the structure just described has honoured that aim.

8

Addenda: Existential Psychotherapy with Couples and Groups

The primary focus of this book has been to examine the practice of existential psychotherapy as would occur in one-to-one therapeutic relationships. While this form of existential psychotherapy remains by far the most common currently practised, this should not lead readers to suppose that it is the only form in this approach. Existential psychotherapists also work under settings and circumstances that involve both therapeutic work with *couples* and with *groups*. While these alternative forms of practice deserve their own extended analysis from an existential-phenomenological perspective, it seems appropriate nonetheless for this text to address and summarise briefly some of the more pertinent features of each.

EXISTENTIAL PSYCHOTHERAPY WITH COUPLES

Although I am personally aware of a good deal of existential psychotherapy undertaken with couples, there appears to be very little that has been written that specifically focuses upon its practice. A recent paper by Digby Tantam and Emmy van Deurzen (2005) provides an interesting, existentially informed commentary on relationships and includes a brief case study focused on a couple, but reveals little of the practical issues and concerns that might arise in undertaking such work. My own chapter on working with couples which appeared in a collection of case accounts from my practice provides my personal views and conclusions regarding existential couple therapy (Spinelli, 1997) but I have, thus far, read no commentary, critique or extension of the ideas contained therein.

It is undoubtedly the case that a great deal of existential psychotherapy with couples parallels work with individuals in terms of its focus and overall aims of descriptive clarification and challenge. A substantial amount of that which has been described throughout this text, for example, would be equally applicable in work with couples. Nonetheless, it remains my view that significant emphases specific to therapy with couples can be noted and articulated. Among these, I believe the most significant to be the following:

1. A couple is seen inadequately if it is perceived only as made up of two people who interact with, and relate to, one another in various ways. As well as acknowledging the worldview of each partner in the couple, what must also be recognised is the existence of the *couple itself* as a structure made up of, but not equivalent to, the separate and combined aspects of the worldviews of each person in the couple. In other words, *the couple as a distinct construct* containing its own worldview requires clarification and challenge.

2. Viewed in this way, the investigatory focus of existential couple therapy is not only upon each individual member of the couple, A and B, but also, and perhaps far more prominently, is attuned to the *couple-construct* which expresses a particular way of relatedness that has been co-constructed by the couple (that is to say, which exists *between* A and B). If the existential psychotherapist does not acknowledge this, he or she falls into the trap not only of *not* meeting with the existing couple, but also, just as likely, of focusing greater attention upon the worldview of one individual to the detriment of the other's.

3. This couple-construct is initially presented and considered by each member of the couple predominantly from the focus of conflict, with its dysfunctional elements being highlighted as its primary defining components. At the same time, however, it is likely that many of the dispositional stances that both underpin and identify the *couple-construct* have *never* been made sufficiently explicit by either member of the couple. The attempt to do so is likely to reveal that (a) each member of the couple has made little if any distinction between his or her own particular worldview and that of the couple-construct, other than with regard to the latter's conflictual stance, and (b) when considered more adequately, the couple-construct is likely to reveal numerous dispositional stances with which both members of the couple are in agreement. This latter point may well serve to provide the *couple-in-conflict* with the insight that they are also, in part, a *couple-in-agreement* and, thereby, permit the awareness and experience of connectedness as well as that of dividedness.

4. The couple-construct's presenting conflict is initially perceived by each partner from his or her own worldview. This viewpoint is typically maintained with little direct communication between the partners. The conflicts threatening the couple-construct are commonly expressed by one or both of the partners in the following ways:

    (i) One partner expresses the view that the other (via his or her behaviour, or perceived alteration in stance, values, attitudes and/or beliefs) threatens the stability of the couple by engaging in, or threatening to engage in, what is perceived to be a dangerous, undesirable or unacceptable activity.

    (ii) One individual expresses the view that he or she has changed, or is changing, with regard to previously held dispositions and that such changes threaten the continuance of the existing relationship.

    (iii) Both individuals express dissatisfaction with some aspect or aspects of the currently existing couple-construct and either may wish to change it but don't know how, or are concerned that any such changes, if accomplished, may themselves threaten the continuance of the relationship.

5. In individual therapy, the primary constructs of the client's worldview are clarified and challenged so that the sedimentations and dissociations that maintain and define them are made

explicit and can be placed alongside the presenting concerns and problems in order to discern potentially significant aspects of relatedness between them. Working with couples extends this enterprise in that the existential psychotherapist engages with both members of the couple in an examination of the sedimentations and dissociations which maintain and define the couple-construct. When the mutually identified sedimentations of the couple-construct are placed alongside the couple's presenting problems it becomes possible to discern potentially significant aspects of relatedness between the construct (and its continued maintenance) and the couple's presenting issues.

6. In listening to the presenting problems brought to therapy by a couple, it is common for each partner to express the view that the stability of the couple-construct is being threatened in some way by the other partner's disturbing, confusing or irrational behaviour. This is often expressed and experienced through the metaphor of the couple-construct's 'illness', the possibility of its 'death', and the fears and concerns surrounding what 'life after the death of the couple-construct' may be like for that member of the couple. The exploration of these concerns with both partners may well facilitate clarification of the couple-construct's limitations, ambiguities and contradictions with respect to each partner's aspirations, needs and desires for him or her self, the other partner, and for them as a couple. It is not unusual for both partners, who might otherwise claim to disagree with one another on practically every other issue, to agree to the 'illness' of the couple-construct. Often, by simply pointing out this shared assumption to them, the existential psychotherapist may increase the possibility of the couple's willingness to address its concerns from a less combative stance.

7. From an existential standpoint, an important, if rarely acknowledged, complexity in couple work emerges: individual therapy can only focus *indirectly* upon the client's other-construct relational encounters with those others in his or her wider world relations, and can explore and challenge these through the client's direct experience of the therapist-as-other. In the case of couple therapy, each member of the couple experiences the direct presence of the therapist-as-other, but also experiences within the therapy world the direct presence of *the other* (i.e., the other member of the couple). In addition, I suggest that through its investigation and clarification as a distinct construct, each member of the couple begins to experience direct access to the *couple-construct-as-other* and, as with therapeutic work with individuals, can begin to clarify and challenge the relatedness of that construct to the self-, other- and world-constructs that make up his or her worldview.

8. Throughout the therapeutic sessions, the existential psychotherapist attempts a predominantly Phase One stance of un-knowing that includes (a) the acceptance of the varied, competing and contradictory views held by each partner in relation to the presenting issues as being initially equally valid to one another; (b) the therapist's willingness to attend not only to the partner who is currently speaking but also to the other who remains silent; (c) the therapist's curiosity in attempting to access as adequately as possible those aspects of the worldview of each partner as that partner experiences them; and (d) through the above points, the therapist's accessing with increasing adequacy the couple-construct that has emerged through the interweaving of both partners' worldviews and whose ambiguities, conflicts and contradictions are the basis to the couple's presenting problems.

9. In an attempt to devise a means whereby the above issues can be explored most effectively, I have proposed a particular sequence for working with couples from the perspective of existential psychotherapy. This sequence follows a repeated five-session pattern made up of the following:

(i) the existential psychotherapists meets with both members of the couple together for sessions one and two;

(ii) the existential psychotherapist meets with each member individually for sessions three and four;

(iii) the existential psychotherapist meets with both members of the couple together for session five.

This sequence is then repeated until such time as couple therapy ends.

The rationale for this sequence is that it maintains its primary focus throughout the whole of the couple therapy upon each partner's particular experiential exploration of the co-created couple-construct. This, in turn, enables each partner to expose, clarify and consider his or her experience of co-habiting the couple-construct. In addition, it permits the clarification of any number of previously unspecified dispositional stances regarding the couple-construct, both as it is perceived to exist, and as it might be desired, by each partner. While the majority of these investigations are conducted in the presence of both partners, sessions three and four allow each partner to engage in such explorations focused upon his or her experience of, and relatedness to, the couple-construct without the presence of the other partner. In part, this stance is taken in recognition that, as a consequence of the conflict each partner experiences with the other, important challenging explorations of the person's self- and other-constructs in particular may be too threatening for that partner to carry out while in the other's presence. At the same time, however, these individual sessions permit the exploration of how each partner imagines the non-present partner's reaction to that which was discussed and expressed during the session had he or she been present. Such considerations often lead to one partner's exploration of what, if anything, of the session, could be conveyed to the other partner either before or during their next session together.

10. If each member of the couple is willing and able to attempt this task, then the couple-construct's inter-relational sedimentations and dissociations can be highlighted. At the same time, this attempt is also likely to expose any number of intra-relational sedimentations and dissociations maintained by one or both partners with regard to the currently existing couple-construct. In general, the descriptive clarification that is such a central enterprise of existential psychotherapy can reveal not only poorly perceived defining aspects of the existing couple-construct, but also those poorly perceived defining aspects that each partner maintains with regard to his or her own self-construct or to the other-construct of his or her partner. In particular, this enterprise can be greatly helped by the existential psychotherapist's focus on the *inter-relational realms of encounter* (as discussed in Chapter 6) to enable the couple's accurate access and clarification of each other's views and statements and for the mutual validation of the accuracy of what has been heard. For instance:

Therapist: Jill, can you repeat to Jack as directly and clearly as possible what it's like for you to hear him question his love for you?

Jill: I feel like I'm being squeezed into a tiny box [**I-focus**]. I can't believe that after all we've worked for over the years, you'd be so easily prepared to give up on us! [**We-focus**]. I can't make any sense of you! [**You-focus**]. And I don't know what you think I've done to you that you would want to hurt me in this way! [**You-focus**].

Jack: But I –

Therapist: Jack, before you give us your response to Jill's statements, could you repeat what you heard Jill just say?

Jack: She basically said she hates me [**You-focus**].

Therapist: You heard Jill say: 'I hate you.'

Jack: Yes.

Therapist: Jill, is what Jack heard what you intended to say to him?

Jill: No! I –

Therapist: [to Jill] Wait. Can you repeat to Jack what you intended to say?

Jill: I don't hate you [**You-focus**]. If I did, I wouldn't be here. I still love you [**I-focus**]. But you've hurt me really badly when you said that you were wondering whether you still loved me [**You-focus**].

Therapist: Jack, what did you hear Jill say now?

Jack: That she doesn't hate me but that I've hurt her a lot [**You-focus**].

Therapist: Jill, is what Jack heard what you intended to say to him?

Jill:	Jill, yes. But not all of it. He missed out that I still love him [**You-focus**].
Therapist:	Jack, did you hear that part of Jill's message, too?
Jack:	Yeah . . .
Therapist:	OK. So is there anything you want to say to Jill?
Jack:	I'm sorry. I didn't want any of this to happen. I don't know what to do [**I-focus**].
Therapist:	Jill, what did you just hear Jack say?
Jill:	That he's sorry and he didn't want this to happen and he doesn't know what to do [**You-focus**].
Therapist:	Jack? Has Jill heard you accurately?
Jack:	Yeah . . .
Therapist:	OK. So, Jill, what's your response to what Jack just said?
Jill:	That I believe him [**You-focus**]. But I don't think that's good enough [**I-focus**]. I think I deserve better than that [**I-focus**]. I think we deserve better than that [**We-focus**].
Jack:	But I don't –
Therapist:	[*to Jack*] Hang on. Can you tell Jill what you just heard her say before you give your response to it?

11. Viewed from the perspective of existential psychotherapy's focus on the descriptive exploration of the couple-construct, the most likely consequences of this investigation are that:

   (i) One partner's worldview is altered in such a way that those dispositional tensions between the couple-construct and relevant aspects of his or her self-construct, other-construct (as focused on the other partner), and the relatedness between these constructs are minimised or alleviated.

   (ii) Both partners' worldviews are altered in such a way that those dispositional tensions between the mutually shared elements of their couple-construct and relevant aspects of each partner's self-construct, other-construct (as focused on the other partner), and the relatedness between these constructs are minimised or alleviated.

   (iii) Significant and shared aspects of the couple-construct are altered so that they more adequately reflect relevant aspects of either or both partners' worldviews.

   (iv) The couple-construct in relation to either or both partners' worldviews cannot be maintained or altered and ceases to exist.

Although this brief exploration of existential psychotherapy with couples reveals numerous similarities with individual therapy, readers will, I hope, have gained an initial sense of the added complexity of clarification and challenge that this approach to couple therapy imposes. Although working with couples from the perspective of existential psychotherapy can be highly stimulating for the therapist, my own experience is that the necessity of maintaining a multi-perspective focus centred upon the worldview of each participant, the make-up and definition of the couple-construct and the inter-relation between these, as well as the immediate inter-relational impact of the therapist's own presence upon any or all of these foci, can be quite exhausting as well. I recommend that existential psychotherapy with couples might be best left to those therapists who have already gained a substantial amount of experience in working on a one-to-one basis with clients.

EXISTENTIAL GROUP PSYCHOTHERAPY

Interestingly, although as far as I am aware existential group psychotherapy remains something of a rarity in practice, literature on the topic is somewhat easier to find than that on couple therapy. In part, I believe that this is due to the happy coincidence that one of the acknowledged modern classics on group therapy is written by a world-renowned author who is also the leading representative of contemporary North American existential psychotherapy.

The fifth edition of Irvin Yalom's *Theory and Practice of Group Psychotherapy* (Yalom and Leszcz, 2005) incorporates numerous viewpoints and ideas that are directly influenced by his understanding of, and approach to, existential psychotherapy. Similarly, Yalom's recent well-received novel, *The Schopenhauer Cure* (2006) contains an accessible exploration of group therapy from a broadly existential perspective. Although I would recommend both books to all readers interested in this topic, I remain in agreement with Hans Cohn's judgement that Yalom's explorations of group therapy provide an excellent focus on the existential issues likely to arise in the course of group therapy, but do not truly discuss a way of working with a group in an explicitly existential manner (Cohn, 1997). Unfortunately, this same critique holds for the great majority of other attempts to discuss this topic. The most recent to be published, by Digby Tantam, though providing a brief case study, conforms to this trend (Tantam, 2005).

Once again, literature on the practice of existential group therapy is scarce. It is, in fact, Cohn's own brief account of it that I believe says more on the topic than anything else I have read (Cohn, 1997).

Cohn begins his discussion by reminding readers that a foundational principle of existential phenomenology is that each individual must always be considered from the perspective of relatedness. From a group therapy standpoint, therefore, each person in the group is always in relatedness to all the other members of the group. From this perspective, each person cannot be considered as a wholly separate entity, since no inter-relational 'gap' truly exists between the members of the group.

For Cohn, the focus of group existential psychotherapy lies in the exploration of the discerned *disturbances of relatedness* as expressed by, and within, the group, rather than in the internalised problems of distinct and separate individuals. It is the group itself, the way of its being and relating, that provides a particular set of circumstances within which disturbances appear, and through which these same disturbances can be observed, clarified and challenged. The group, as well, is its own narrational subject – what occurs within the group and what is brought into the group from outside by its members makes up its narrational focus.

Although the existential psychotherapist has a particular task to perform – which is that of assisting 'in the *process* of clarifying the relational and communicative disturbances and potentialities of the group' (Cohn, 1997: 55) – Cohn insists that it is a distinctive feature of existential group psychotherapy to consider the therapist as a member of the group. From Cohn's perspective, the existential psychotherapist is just one of any number of interpreters rather than its primary one. In addition, the therapist is neither discouraged nor prevented from contributing to group discussion via the expression of his or her own views, thoughts and concerns. In a broad sense, Cohn's account of the existential group therapist is one which acknowledges the therapist's special role in setting up and maintaining the 'structural conditions' within which group therapy can occur. At the same time, Cohn is reluctant to bestow upon the existential group therapist anything that singles him or her out as possessing an authority that is a major determinant of the direction of group discourse. That the therapist presents material that seems worthy of disclosure to him or her should not suggest nonetheless that the therapist can have any idea as to who in the group might 'receive' these disclosures, what reaction they might provoke and who, if any one at all, might benefit from them. Indeed, with regard to the typical role of the existential group therapist, Cohn is adamant that 'the group is the therapist of the group' (Cohn, 1997: 46).

It is my view that Cohn's account of existential group psychotherapy, however brief, provides an initial overview as to its possibilities, as well as indicating how it diverges from other contemporary approaches. Although he does not use the term, I would suggest that Cohn is proposing a primary focus that rests upon what I would call the *group-construct*. In emphasising this focal point, the major tasks of existential group psychotherapy become those of:

(i)   the descriptive investigation of the group-construct as revealed through the interactions between the various group members with each other;

(ii) the descriptive investigation of the group-construct as revealed through the interactions between the various group members in response to what each brings to the group from outside the group;

(iii) the descriptive investigation of those dispositional tensions that arise between the group-construct and relevant aspects of each group member's self-construct, other-construct (as focused on the other group members), and the relatedness between these constructs;

(iv) the descriptive investigation of the impact of those challenges presented to the group-construct by each group member's worldview;

(v)   the descriptive investigation of the impact of those challenges presented to each group member's worldview by the group-construct.

As a final comment on existential group psychotherapy, readers may recall that in an earlier section of this text I discussed why I do not believe the therapy world to be artificial or unreal in relation to the client's wider world of relations, even if the therapy world consisting of (usually) only two directly present participants is inter-relationally less complex than the wider world made up of a multitude of participants whose differing views, expectations, demands and behaviours impact upon and 'bombard' the client's worldview in ways that no therapy world relationship could ever fully replicate. Considering this from the standpoint of existential group psychotherapy, it can be seen that what may be the most significant, as well as most taxing, challenge for both the existential psychotherapist and the clients who, together, make up the membership of the group, is precisely its *inter-relational complexity*. Undoubtedly, it is the multitude of participants whose differing dispositional outlooks, expectations, demands and behaviours impact upon one another that generates this complexity. At the same time, this group-generated complexity arises *within* a structured and distinct therapy world with its explicit and mutually agreed setting, frame and contractual conditions. As such, the therapy world of existential group psychotherapy provides a structure that is both more akin to each group member's wider world relations than any one-to-one form of therapy could ever hope to be. At the same time, however, this same structure is also sufficiently different from each group member's wider world relations so as to be able to provoke the disclosure of and challenge to each group member's currently maintained worldviews.

It is the enterprise of existential group psychotherapy to 'hold the tension' between the therapy world and the wider world. If the experience of the group members is that the group therapy world is too similar to that of their wider world relations, it may be too difficult for the group members to believe in, and relate to, the group therapy world as sufficiently distinct for meaningful explorations and challenges to become possible. Equally, however, if the experience of the group members is that the group therapy world is too different from that of their wider world relations, this over-distinctiveness of the group therapy world is likely to severely restrict the impact of the meaningful explorations and challenges that have occurred within it to be able to extend beyond these confines and into the group members' wider world relations.

9

Conclusion

It has been the aim of this text to provide readers with a descriptive account of existential psychotherapy from a practice-based focus.

Part One presented a necessary overview of what I have argued to be those key underlying principles drawn from existential-phenomenological philosophy which provide existential psychotherapy with its foundational assumptions. This discussion was followed by a brief account of the general implications drawn from these foundational principles that have served to provide existential psychotherapy with its general theoretical rationale for practice.

Part Two provided a descriptively focused structural model for practising existential psychotherapy. Of necessity, this model reflects my own personal interpretations regarding the practice of existential psychotherapy. Having been a practising student and adherent of this approach for close to twenty-five years, I hold no illusion that what I have gleaned, and attempted to communicate in this text, approaches anything resembling a 'final statement', be it personal or in general. Even so, the attempt, as maddeningly frustrating and dispiriting as it often was, did serve to rekindle for me something of my excitement and surprise as an initiate of this approach. I hope that something of that disturbing thrill has been passed on to the reader.

In undertaking to write this text, it was my intent to delineate a structural model that could demonstrate a way of practising psychotherapy from an existential perspective that remains:

- sufficiently open to description;
- structurally coherent;
- consistent with the key principles of existential phenomenology;
- distinguishable from other contemporary models and systems of psychotherapy such that its aims, primary concerns and practices can be compared and contrasted to those of alternative approaches.

Whether or not I have succeeded in this, is for the reader to decide.

Whatever the verdict, however, I am under no delusion that, like *all* structural models, it is limited, if only because it *is* a structure, in its ability to 'capture' and convey the *experience* of practising existential psychotherapy. In this, it reveals the very same possibilities and limitations as those encountered when the process-like experience of worlding is structurally contextualised as the worldview. While the latter can express a truthful attempt to communicate and express that experience, that attempt can only be assessed and evaluated in terms of its relative adequacy rather than hope to achieve, or worse claim, its exact replication.

Within such necessary and inevitable restrictions, it nevertheless remains my hope that readers and practitioners – and not least those who also identify them selves as existential psychotherapists – will have been stimulated and challenged by what has been presented and that, more to the point, they will utilise such stimuli and challenges to identify their own working models and be willing to risk the communication of their conclusions.

I would be not only interested, but grateful, for any comments and critiques and alternative perspectives that readers might wish to offer. I can be contacted at either of the following two email addresses:

spinelle@regents.ac.uk

or

ESA@plexworld.com.

Many years ago now, I chanced upon a poem by e. e. cummings that has remained with me and served as a guiding light (even if I have, nonetheless, all to often blundered into the darkness). Ever since I began to write, I have known that I would someday include it as a means of stating that which I have yet to find my own words to express. As I was finishing the writing of the first draft of this book, I recalled the poem and knew for certain that it would provide the best summary of what this book has sought to express and, as well, its most appropriate ending.

seeker of truth

follow no path
all paths lead where

truth is here

– e.e. cummings –

References

Ablon, J.S. and Jones, E.E. (2002) 'Validity of controlled clinical trials of psychotherapy: findings from the NIMH Treatment of Depression Collaborative Research Program', *American Journal of Psychiatry*, 159: 775–83.

Alexander, R. (1995) *Folie à Deux: an Experience of One-to-one Therapy.* London: Free Association Books.

Alvarez, A. (2006) 'The man who rowed away', *New York Review of Books*, L111 (13): 39–42.

Anderson, H. and Goolishian, H. (1992) 'The client is the expert: a not-knowing approach to therapy', in S. McNamee and K.J. Gergen (eds), *Therapy as Social Construction.* London: Sage.

Bates, Y. (ed.) (2004) *Shouldn't I Be Feeling Better Now? Client Views of Therapy.* London: Palgrave Macmillan.

Becchio, C. and Bertone, C. (2005) 'Beyond Cartesian subjectivism', *Journal of Consciousness Studies*, 12 (7): 20–30.

Berlin, I. (2006) *Political Ideas in the Romantic Age: Their Rise and Influence on Modern Thought.* Princeton, NJ: Princeton University Press.

Binswanger, L. (1963) *Being-in-the-World: Selected Papers of Ludwig Binswanger.* New York: Harper Torchbooks.

Bohm, D. and Hiley, B. (1995) *The Undivided Universe: Ontological Interpretation of Quantum Theory.* London: Routledge.

Boss, M. (1957) *The Analysis of Dreams* (trans. A.J. Pomerans). London: Rider.

—— (1963) *Psychoanalysis and Daseinsanalysis.* New York: Basic Books.

—— (1977) *I Dreamt Last Night . . .* (trans. S. Conway). New York: Wiley.

—— (1979) *Existential Foundations of Medicine and Psychology.* Northvale, NJ: Jason Aronson.

Buber, M. (1970) *I and Thou*, 2nd edn (trans. R.G. Smith). Edinburgh: T. & T. Clark.

Buber, M. (2002) *Between Man and Man* (trans. R.G. Smith). London: Routledge.

Bugenthal, J.F.T. (1981) *The Search for Authenticity: an Existential-Analytic Approach to Psychotherapy.* New York: Irvington.

—— (1987) *The Art of the Psychotherapist.* New York: W.W. Norton.

Burston, D. (2000) *The Crucible of Experience: R.D. Laing and the Crisis of Psychotherapy.* Cambridge, MA: Harvard University Press.

Cannon, B. (1991) *Sartre and Psychoanalysis: an Existentialist Challenge to Clinical Metatheory.* Lawrence, KS: University Press of Kansas.

Cherniss, J. (2006) Introduction to *Political Ideas in the Romantic Age: Their Rise and Influence on Modern Thought* by I. Berlin. Princeton, NJ: Princeton University Press.

Clark, D.A. (1995) 'Perceived limitations of standard cognitive therapy: a consideration of efforts to revise Beck's theory and therapy', *Journal of Cognitive Therapy. An International Quarterly*, 9 (3): 153–72.

Cohn, H.W. (1997) *Existential Thought and Therapeutic Practice: an Introduction to Existential Psychotherapy.* London: Sage.

—— (2002) *Heidegger and the Roots of Existential Therapy.* London: Continuum.

Collins, J. and Selina, H. (2006) *Introducing Heidegger.* London: Icon.

Condrau, G. (1998) *Martin Heidegger's Impact on Psychotherapy.* Vienna: Mosaic.

Cooper, M. (2003) *Existential Therapies.* London: Sage.

Crotty, M. (1996) *Phenomenology and Nursing Research.* Melbourne: Churchill Livingstone.

cummings, e.e. (1965) *A Selection of Poems.* New York: Harvest.

Deurzen, E. van and Arnold-Baker, C. (eds) (2005) *Existential Perspectives on Human Issues: a Handbook for Therapeutic Practice.* Basingstoke: Palgrave Macmillan.

Deurzen-Smith, E. van (1988) *Existential Counselling in Practice.* London: Sage.

Deurzen-Smith, E. van (1994) 'Courting death: mortal ambitions of existential analysis', *Journal of the Society for Existential Analysis,* 5: 2–22.

Deurzen-Smith, E. van (1997) *Everyday Mysteries.* London: Routledge.

Disney, W. (1941) *Dumbo.* Animated motion picture produced by the Walt Disney Studio and directed by B. Sharpsteen.

Ellenberger, H.F. (1970) *The Discovery of the Unconscious: the History and Evolution of Dynamic Psychiatry.* New York: Basic Books.

Evans, R.I. (1981) *Dialogue with R.D. Laing.* New York: Praeger.

Farber, L. (1967) 'Martin Buber and psychotherapy' in *The Philosophy of Martin Buber* (ed. P. A. Schilpp and M. Friedman). LaSalle, IL: Open Court.

—— (2000) *The Ways of the Will: Selected Essays.* New York: Basic Books.

Frankl, V. (1988) *The Will to Meaning: Foundations and Applications to Logotherapy.* London: Meridian.

Freedman, J. and Combs, G. (1996) *Narrative Therapy: the Social Construction of Preferred Realities.* London: W.W. Norton.

Friedman, M. (ed.) (1964) *Worlds of Existentialism: a Critical Reader.* Chicago: University of Chicago Press.

—— (1982) *Martin Buber's Life and Work: the Early Years 1878–1923.* London: Search Press.

Gadamer, H.G. (2004) *Truth and Method.* London: Continuum.

Gallese, V. (2003) 'The roots of empathy: the shared manifold hypothesis and the neural basis of inter-subjectivity', *Psychopathology,* 36: 171–80.

Gay, P. (1988) *Freud: a Life for Our Time.* London: J.M. Dent & Sons.

Gendlin, E. (1988) 'Befindlichkeit: Heidegger and the philosophy of psychology', in *Heidegger and Psychology* (ed. K. Hoeller). Seattle, WA: Humanities Press.

Gillett, G. (1995) 'The philosophical foundations of qualitative psychology', *The Psychologist,* 8 (3): 111–14.

Giovazolias, T. and Davis, P. (2001) 'How common is sexual attraction towards clients? The experiences of sexual attraction of counselling psychologists toward their clients and its impact on the therapeutic process', *Counselling Psychology Quarterly,* 14 (4): 281–6.

Gordon, E.F. (2000) *Mockingbird Years: a Life in and out of Therapy.* New York: Basic Books.

Gray, J. (2006) 'The case for decency', *The New York Review of Books* LIII (12): 20–22.

Havel, V. (2000) 'The first laugh', *New York Review of Books,* XLVI (2): 20.

Heidegger, M. (1962) *Being and Time* (trans. J. Maquarrie and E.H. Freund). New York: Harper & Row.

—— (1976) *What Is Called Thinking?* (trans. F.D. Wieck and J.G. Gray). New York: Harper Perennial.

—— (1977) *The Question Concerning Technology and Other Essays* (trans. W. Lovitt). New York: Harper & Row.

—— (2001) *Zollikon Seminars: Protocols–Conversations–Letters* (trans. F. Mayr and R. Askay). Evanston, IL: Northwestern University Press.

Hodges, H.A. (1952) *The Philosophy of Wilhelm Dilthey.* London: Routledge & Kegan Paul.

Hoeller, K. (1996) 'The tragedy of psychology: Rollo May's Daimonic and Friedrich Nietzsche's Dyonisian', *Journal of the Society for Existential Analysis,* 7 (1): 39–55.

Horney, K. (1991) *Neurosis and Human Growth.* New York: Norton.

Howard, K.I., Orlinsky, D.E. and Lueger, R.J. (1994) 'Clinically relevant outcome research in individual psychotherapy: new models guide the researcher and clinician', *British Journal of Psychiatry,* 165 (1): 4–8.

Howard, K.I., Moras, K., Brill, P.L., Martinovich, Z. and Lutz, W. (1996) 'Evaluation of psychotherapy: efficacy, effectiveness, and patient progress', *American Psychologist,* 51 (10) : 1059–64.

Howe, D. (1993) *On Being a Client: Understanding the Process of Counselling and Psychotherapy.* London: Sage.

Husserl, E. (1931a) *Ideas: General Introduction to Pure Phenomenology*, vol. 1. New York: Macmillan.
—— (1931b) *Cartesian Meditations*. The Hague: Nijhoff.
—— (1965) *Phenomenology and the Crisis of Philosophy*. New York: Harper Torchbooks.
Ihde, D. (1986a) *Experimental Phenomenology: an Introduction*. Albany: State University of New York.
—— (1986b) *Consequences of Phenomenology*. Albany: State University of New York.
I-Hsuan (1993) *The Zen Teachings of Master Lin-Chi* (trans. B. Watson). Chichester, West Sussex: Columbia University Press.
Jaspers, K. (1963) *General Psychopathology*, vol. 1 (trans. J. Hoening and M. W. Hamilton). London: Johns Hopkins University Press.
Kagan, J. (2000) *Three Seductive Ideas*. Cambridge, MA: Harvard University Press.
Karlsson, G. (1993) *Psychological Qualitative Research from a Phenomenological Perspective*. Stockholm: Almqvist and Wiksell International.
Kaye, J. (1995) 'Postfoundationalism and the language of psychotherapy research', in *Therapeutic and Everyday Discourse as Behavior Change* (ed. J. Siegfried). Norwood, NJ: Ablex.
Kierkegaard, S. (1980) *The Concept of Anxiety* (trans. R. Thompte). Princeton, NJ: Princeton University Press.
Kirschenbaum, H. and Henderson, V. L. (1990) *Carl Rogers Dialogues*. London: Constable.
Korzybski, A. (1995) *Science and Sanity: an Introduction to Non-Aristotelian Systems and General Semantics*, 5th edn. Institute of General Semantics.
Kvale, S. (1994) 'Ten standard objections to qualitative research interviews', *Journal of Phenomenological Psychology*, 25 (2): 147–73.
Laing, R.D. (1960) *The Divided Self*. Harmondsworth: Penguin.
—— (1967) *The Politics of Experience and the Bird of Paradise*. Harmondsworth: Penguin.
—— (1982) *The Voice of Experience*. Harmondsworth: Penguin.
Laing, R.D. and Cooper, D.G. (1964) *Reason and Violence: a Decade of Sartre's Philosophy*. Harmondsworth: Penguin.
Laing, R.D. and Esterson, A. (1964) *Sanity, Madness and the Family*. Harmondsworth: Penguin.
Längle, A. (2005) 'The search for meaning in life and the existential fundamental motivations', *Existential Analysis*, 16 (1): 2–14.
Levinas, I. (1987) *Time and the Other* (trans. R.A. Cohen). Pittsburgh, PA: Duquesne University Press.
—— (1999) *Totality and Infinity* (trans. A. Lingis). Pittsburgh, PA: Duquesne University Press.
Luborsky, L., Diguer, L., Seligman, D.A., Rosenthal, R., Krause, E.D., Johnson, S., Halperin, G., Bishop, M., Berman, J.S., and Schweizer, E. (1999) 'The researcher's own therapy allegiance: a "wild card" in comparisons of treatment efficacy', *Clinical Psychology: Science and Practice*, 6: 95–106.
Luborsky, L., Rosenthal, R., Diguer, L., Andrusyna, T.P., Berman, J.S. and Levitt, J.T. (2002) 'The dodo bird verdict is alive and well – mostly', *Clinical Psychology: Science and Practice 2002*: 9: 2–12.
Luca, M. (2004) *The Therapeutic Frame in the Clinical Context: Integrative Perspectives*. London: Brunner-Routledge.
Macfarlane, A. (2006) 'Some reflections on John Ziman's "No man is an island"', *Journal of Consciousness Studies*, 13 (5): 43–52.
Madison, G. (2002) '"Illness" . . . and its human values', *Existential Analysis*, 13 (1): 10–30.
Mahrer, A.R. (2000) 'Philosophy of science and the foundations of psychotherapy', *American Psychologist*, 55 (10): 117–25.
—— (2004) *Theories of Truth, Models of Usefulness*. London: Whurr.
—— (2006) *The Creation of New Ideas: a Guide Book*. Hay-on-Wye: PCCS Books.
Mankell, H. (2002) *The Fifth Woman*. London: Vintage.
Manzotti, R. (2006) 'A process-oriented view of conscious perception', *Journal of Consciousness Studies*, 13 (6): 7–41.
May, R. (1969) *Love and Will*. New York: W.W. Norton.
—— (1981) *Freedom and Destiny*. New York: Dell Books.
—— (1983) *The Discovery of Being*. London: W.W. Norton.
—— (1990) 'An open letter to Carl Rogers', in *Carl Rogers Dialogues* (ed. H. Kirschenbaum and V.L. Henderson). London: Constable.

Mearns, D. and Cooper, M. (2005) *Working at Relational Depth in Counselling and Psychotherapy.* London: Sage.

Merleau-Ponty, M. (1962) *The Phenomenology of Perception* (trans. C. Smith). London: Routledge & Kegan Paul.

—— (1964a) *The Primacy of Perception* (trans. C.W. Cobb). Evanston, IL: Northwestern University Press.

—— (1964b) *Sense and Non-Sense* (trans. H. Dreyfus and P. Dreyfus). Evanston, IL: Northwestern University Press.

Messer, S.B. and Wampold, B.E. (2002) 'Common factors are more potent than specific therapy ingredients', *Clinical Psychology: Science and Practice*, 6: 21–5.

Midgley, D. (2006) 'Intersubjectivity and collective consciousness', *Journal of Consciousness Studies*, 13 (5): 99–109.

Misiak, H. and Sexton, V.S. (1973) *Phenomenological, Existential, and Humanistic Psychologies: a Historical Survey.* New York: Grune and Stratton.

Nishida, K. (1990) *An Enquiry into the Good* (trans: W. Kaufman and R.J. Hollingdale). New York: Random House.

Norcross, J.C. (ed.) (2002) *Psychotherapy Relationships that Work: Therapist Contributions and Responsiveness to Patients.* Oxford: Oxford University Press.

Nowotny, H. (2006) 'An act of cognitive subjectivity', *Journal of Consciousness Studies*, 13 (5): 64–70.

Orlinski, H.K. and Lueger, R. (1994) 'Clinically relevant outcome research in individual therapy', *British Journal of Psychiatry*, 165: 4–8.

Parks, T. (2006) *Rapids.* London: Vintage.

Pilgrim, D. (2000) 'Psychiatric diagnosis: more questions than answers', *The Psychologist*, 13 (6): 302–5.

Piper, W.E. (2004) 'Implications of psychotherapy research for psychotherapy training', *Canadian Journal of Psychiatry*, 49: 221–9.

Pope, K.S. (1990) 'Therapist–client sexual involvement: a review of the research', *Clinical Psychology Review*, 10: 477–90.

Pope, K.S., Tabachnick, B.G. and Kiethe-Spiege, P. (1986) 'The human therapist and the (sometimes) inhuman training system', *American Psychologist*, 41 (2): 147–58.

Pope, K.S., Sonne, J. and Holroyd, J. (1993) *Sexual Feelings in Psychotherapy: Explorations for Therapists and Therapists-in-Training.* American Psychological Association.

Rasmussen, S. (2004) 'The imperfection of perfection', *The Psychologist*, 17 (7): 398–400.

Rennie, S. (2006) 'The end . . . or is it?' *Existential Analysis*, 17 (2): 330–42.

Røine, E. (1997) *Group Psychotherapy as Experimental Theatre.* London: Jessica Kingsley.

Rowan, J. and Jacobs, M. (2002) *The Therapist's Use of Self.* Maidenhead: Open University Press.

Salkovskis, P.M. (2002) 'Empirically grounded clinical interventions: cognitive-behavioural therapy progresses through a multi-dimensional approach to clinical science', *Behavioural and Cognitive Psychotherapy*, 30 (1): 3–11.

Sands, A. (2000) *Falling for Therapy: Psychotherapy from a Client's Point of View.* London: Macmillan.

Sartre, J.P. (1973) *Existentialism and Humanism* (trans. P. Mairet). London: Methuen.

—— (1985) *Existentialism and Human Emotions* (trans. B. Frechtman). London: Citadel Press.

—— (1991) *Being and Nothingness: an Essay on Phenomenological Ontology* (trans. H. Barnes). London: Routledge.

Sherwood, P. (2001) 'The client experience of psychotherapy: what heals and what harms?' *Indo-Pacific Journal of Phenomenology*, 1 (2): 24pp. Retrieved August 2002 from http:www.ipjp.org.

Siderits, M. (2003) *Empty Persons: Personal Identity and Buddhist Philosophy.* Burlington, VT: Ashgate Publishing.

Smith, D.L. (1991) *Hidden Conversations: an Introduction to Communicative Psychoanalysis.* London: Routledge.

Spiegel, D. (ed.) (1999) *Efficacy and Cost-Effectiveness of Psychotherapy.* American Psychiatric Publishing.

Spinelli, E. (1994) *Demystifying Therapy.* London: Constable.

—— (1995) Afterword, in R. Alexander, *Folie à Deux: an Experience of One-to-one Therapy.* London: Free Association Books.

—— (1997) *Tales of Un-Knowing: Therapeutic Encounters from an Existential Perspective.* London: Duckworth.

—— (2001) *The Mirror and the Hammer: Challenges to Therapeutic Orthodoxy.* London: Sage.

—— (2005) *The Interpreted World: an Introduction to Phenomenological Psychology,* 2nd edn. London: Sage.

—— (2006) 'The value of relatedness in existential psychotherapy and phenomenological enquiry' *Indo-Pacific Journal of Phenomenology,* 6, August, Special Edition on Methodology, 15pp. Retrieved 20 November 2006 from http://www.ipjp.org

Stadlen, N. and Stadlen, A. (2005) 'Families', in *Existential Perspectives on Human Issues: a Handbook for Therapeutic Practice* (ed. E. van Deurzen and C. Arnold-Baker). Basingstoke: Palgrave MacMillan.

Stern, D.N. (2004) *The Present Moment in Psychotherapy and Everyday Life.* New York: W.W. Norton.

Strasser, F. and Strasser, A. (1997) *Existential Time-Limited Therapy: the Wheel of Existence.* Chichester: Wiley.

Tantam, D. (2005) 'Groups', in *Existential Perspectives on Human Issues: a Handbook for Therapeutic Practice* (ed. E. van Deurzen and C. Arnold-Baker). Basingstoke: Palgrave Macmillan.

Tantam, D. and van Deurzen, E. (2005) 'Relationships', in *Existential Perspectives on Human Issues: a Handbook for Therapeutic Practice* (ed. E. van Deurzen and C. Arnold-Baker). Basingstoke: Palgrave Macmillan.

Tillich, P. (1980) *The Courage to Be* (2nd edn). New Haven, CT: Yale University Press.

Valle, R.S. and King, M. (1978) *Existential-Phenomenological Alternatives for Psychology.* Oxford: Oxford University Press.

Wahl, B. (2003) 'Working with "existence tension" as a basis for therapeutic practice, *Existential Analysis,* 14 (2): 265–78.

Wittgenstein, L. (2001) *Tractatus Logico-philosophicus.* London: Routledge.

Yalom, I. (1980) *Existential Psychotherapy.* New York: Basic Books.

—— (1989) *Love's Executioner and Other Tales of Psychotherapy.* Harmondsworth: Penguin.

—— (2001) *The Gift of Therapy.* New York: HarperCollins.

—— (2006) *The Schopenhauer Cure.* London: Harper Perennial.

Yalom, I. and Leszcz, M. (2005) *Theory and Practice of Group Psychotherapy,* 5th edn. New York: Basic Books.

Ziman, J. (2006) 'No man is an island', *Journal of Consciousness Studies,* 13 (5): 17–42.

Index